Volkswagen T3
Transporter, Caravelle, Camper and Vanagon 1979–1992

Volkswagen T3

Transporter, Caravelle, Camper and Vanagon 1979–1992

Richard Copping

The Crowood Press

First published in 2011 by
The Crowood Press Ltd
Ramsbury, Marlborough
Wiltshire SN8 2HR

www.crowood.com

British Library Cataloguing-in-Publication Data
A catalogue record for this book is available from the British Library.

ISBN 978 1 84797 239 2

Acknowledgements
For once there are just three acknowledgements to make!

The first is to Crowood, who suggested the title in the first instance and set me the challenge of writing the first English-language version of a book dedicated entirely to the T3. Without the benefit of the works of other authors with which to compare notes, more research was required and a greater degree of time had to be spent delving into the sales brochures and technical specifications than would normally have been the case. But in doing that, more enjoyment was achieved in writing the book; the historian in me found the task both entertaining and rewarding, while attempting a topic which I hadn't covered in detail previously hopefully confirmed that my academic training of some 35 years and more ago hadn't gone entirely to waste!

The second is to Brian Screaton, a particularly knowledgeable enthusiast in his own right, who diligently set about trawling his own archive and the collections of others to bring me a whole host of material, particularly in the form of previously elusive Vanagon information, dealer educational material supplied by Volkswagen, and a wealth of contemporary press imagery. Without this collection at my fingertips it would have been impossible to portray the third-generation Transporter in anywhere near so an exhilarating way.

The third is to Peter Cain, whose T3 graces a number of pages, including the cover and frontispiece. We first met at a Volkswagen enthusiasts' event, his first and somewhere approaching my 200th! As the first and only owner of this remarkably pristine and totally original vehicle he should be immensely proud and I am extremely grateful to Peter for agreeing to have his vehicle photographed. The day after the photo shoot the Holdsworth Villa conversion was set to journey to France, proving it was not some mollycoddled pet, and during that holiday it celebrated its twentieth birthday – truly amazing.

Thank you to each of you.

Typeset by Jean Cussons Typesetting, Diss, Norfolk

Printed and bound in India by Replika Press Pvt Ltd

contents

introduction

T3 – UNLOVED BOX TO CULT FIGURE

Who would have thought it only a few short years ago? A book dedicated to the third-generation Transporter and not to its illustrious predecessors would have been unthinkable. There was a stigma associated with ownership of a vehicle that was no longer available from Volkswagen's showrooms and was merely an old bus with a propensity to premature seam rusting. Camera clickers wouldn't waste a single exposure, never mind a roll of film! For the hardened VW enthusiasts of the eighties and nineties to whom the words water and Volkswagen were as incompatible as longevity and Ford, the third-generation Transporter was the devil incarnate; at least after 1983, when its engines were no longer windswept and interesting. Here was a vehicle destined to join the ranks of the VWK70, the VW Santana, the VW Derby, the VW Jetta in Mk1 guise and possibly even the VW411 and 412 as long since discarded and disowned models in Wolfsburg's index of options.

Frail, elderly members of the Volkswagen enthusiast fraternity may recall the days when all Transporters played second fiddle to the mighty Beetle and the delectable Karmann Ghia. Even the rarest of the rare couldn't command a serious book price. But that was when the T3 was a current model and camper conversion firms were falling like flies as interest in the great outdoors linked to glorified tents had taken a serious nose dive. Who in the materialistic 1980s seriously wanted to paddle across some damp and dingy field to a communal loo of questionable standards?

But of course lifestyles change, trends mould our sheep-like aspirations, and even flares make the occasional comeback! Hippies of the sixties and seventies who had grown into respectable 2.4-children parents with the weight of a mortgage around their necks were watching their fledglings fly as the decades turned and hankerings after 'get away from it all', 'back to basics' weekends clouded judgements centred on luxury leather, air conditioning, 6-CD interchangers and alloys. Smart young executives found it cool

to head off into the wild blue yonder and rough it in the back of an old van. In Volkswagen terms the Beetle lost its vice-like grip as respect, even worship, of the first-generation Transporter pushed prices ever higher. Soon many a first-generation Transporter was out of the price range of everyday folk, a situation more recently exacerbated by a fascination with retaining or even creating patina, warts and all, making rust, faded paint and homely patches saleable commodities. What was (and is) also deemed entirely acceptable was to rip out the decidedly underpowered but distinctly characteristic motor and squeeze as much beef as possible into the space. With upgraded brakes and suspension, the Transporter had a reasonable chance of getting to its destination in good time without creating in its wake a queue of vehicles reminiscent of those beloved by owners of farm implements.

Inevitably, while the dedicated first-generation bus owner spent a fortune on restoring the barn find he'd already paid over the odds for, prices for worthy examples of the second-generation Transporter started to march steadily upwards until they too were desirable in any state of repair. While such models lacked a little in terms of true nostalgia, they were sufficiently venerable to qualify for retro adoration, and eminently more practical in terms of capabilities and specification than their predecessor. This naturally encouraged would-be buyers of a first-generation example to compromise and turn to the second-generation model. A growing number found that if they wished to join the craze, the only option remaining to them was to turn their collective attention to the unloved and unworthy holder of the Transporter name between 1979 and 1990.

Nowadays, there isn't a generation of Transporter on the road that doesn't have a trail of admirers, and third-generation examples have attracted both a hefty rise in market value and enthusiast following. While not yet in the same league as the first-generation Transporter but considerably more affordable than out-of-the-showroom camper conversions (both official and

unofficial), third-generation Transporters are present in force at enthusiast shows, often attracting an extravaganza of digital camera clicks. Journey to a campervan mecca such as the Cornish coast and suddenly the T3 is likely to eclipse all others. Desirable yet still reasonably affordable as the second decade of the new millennium unfurls, the third-generation Transporter is inevitably maturing, in the best of single highland malt traditions, into a practical classic – with all that entails.

THIRD-GENERATION NAMES DEFINED

Those conversant with the launch of the first 'van' will be aware that while each model was granted a title, a generic name wasn't initially forthcoming. However, by 1951 at least one brochure covering all Volkswagen's available models, while still referring to the Beetle as nothing more than 'Die Export Limousine' and 'Das Cabriolet', designated the 'van' as 'Der Transporter', while subcategorizing the windowed options as 'Der Kleinbus'.

Behind the scenes, inevitably the Transporter had official 'Type' or 'Model' designations. As the Beetle was the first vehicle to have been introduced, it was predictably the Type One, and, as might be anticipated, the second vehicle, the Transporter, was the Type Two. As the range developed, so the straightforward Delivery Van became the Type 21, the people-carrying Microbus the Type 22, the versatile Kombi the Type 23 and so on.

Both labels – type number and model name, the word brand being as yet a little over the top – are relevant to the naming of the generation which forms the subject of this volume, as is the emergence of descriptive terms favoured by Volkswagen in America. The Microbuses became 'Station Wagons' in the USA, while the commercial end of the Transporter range was collectively referred to as 'Trucks' or simply 'Vans'. To European eyes, the bulky Transporter was somewhat large to be given the Station Wagon title, such vehicles normally being defined as saloons with a combination of additional windows and extra luggage capacity at the rear and widely referred to as estate cars or variants.

The arrival of a second-generation of Transporters in the summer of 1967 had little effect on the names by which the vehicles were known, both in sales brochures and in the showrooms. Similarly, behind the scenes, the Transporter was still the Type Two, while individual models retained the two-digit designations from their previous incarnation. However, people inevitably began to refer to the first-generation Transporter as the T1 and the new model as the T2. (The older model of Transporter could not be referred to as the Type 1, as this term was already allocated to the Beetle.) In America public face usage of the term 'Station Wagon' continued, but increasingly literature also made reference to the people-carrying options as 'Buses'. In Britain, as an example of European practice, the term 'VW Commercial' was increasingly used, so that by the end of second-generation production sales literature might well bear a title such as 'The VW Commercials – Van, Pick Up and Microbus.'

The naming of the third-generation Transporter on its debut in August 1979 would have been fairly straightforward if the pattern established over the previous thirty years had been followed. However, nothing in life is ever quite so simple. In Germany and other European countries the progression from T2 to T3 was clear, but in Britain the misnomer T25 was adopted. Various suggestions have been made as to why this occurred, including the adage that as old school air-cooled engines were fitted to the new Transporter it was little more than a stopgap vehicle and therefore warranted a halfway stage designation of T2 and a half, T2.5, or T25. Whatever the truth of the matter the name stuck for many years and only relatively recently has the T3 designation become widely recognized in the UK.

Similarly, the all-embracing nature of the 'Transporter' designation was challenged, at least in the UK. Although all third-generation models continued to be referred to as VW Commercials, the Delivery Vans and Pick Ups became Transporters and the people-carriers were referred to as Buses. Later in the production run of the T3 the Commercial tag was dropped and full-range literature would carry the dual headings of VW Transporter and VW Caravelle,

this new term replacing use of the word 'Bus'. A variation on this theme was the occasional use of the self-explanatory VW Passenger Range label, but at least behind this opening statement the Caravelle, in varying levels of trim, remained. Further subdivisions in the model line-up such as Der Multivan and the Caravelle Carat, and the 'syncro' name proffered to promote third-generation Transporter developments with permanent four-wheel drive, will be covered later in this book.

In America, however, the third-generation Transporter was endowed with a completely new name. Out went the terms 'Station Wagon' and 'Bus' and in came a name that might be despised on this side of the Atlantic as an unacceptable conglomeration of words but at least remained uniform and told all who saw it what exactly was in the can. A short extract from an early third-generation Transporter brochure produced for the American market defines the new name:

Vanagon. What does it mean? … 'Vanagon' is a new name. You probably haven't seen it before. It's actually a combination of 'van' and 'station wagon'. Vanagon. Not only a fresh new name – a totally new kind of vehicle from Volkswagen.

Of significance is Volkswagen of America's decision to brand the fourth-generation Transporter as the Volkswagen Eurovan when it was introduced at the Boston Auto Show in late 1991 and to dealers almost a year later. Thus the Vanagon handle is synonymous with the third-generation Transporter, and might even have been an appropriate designation for use here, if it hadn't been for its decidedly contrived and possibly even unpalatable nature to British tongues!

Finally, in this saga of deciphering the ploys of Volkswagen's branding departments, it is appropriate to turn to those names that were never endorsed officially but which are widely used amongst enthusiasts. Ask what a Splitty is and few enthusiasts wouldn't be able to identify this as a first-generation Transporter; similarly, the second-generation Transporter is widely known as a Bay, thanks to its panoramic windscreen, at least when compared to the

split panes of its predecessor. Enter third-generation Transporter territory, though, and nicknames are not as widely used, possibly because those chosen aren't really terms of endearment. Some have been known to refer to the T3 as the Brick, no doubt due to its largely slab-sided, rectangular appearance. Others designate it as the Wedge, presumably due to its more raked windscreen. Of the two the latter name is more prevalent, but perhaps the lack of any form of enthusiast's name for the T4, the Transporter that replaced the third-generation model in the high summer of 1990 and a vehicle that is increasingly gathering its own band of dedicated followers, serves to explain the somewhat lukewarm endorsement of third-generation Transporter nicknames.

PRODUCTION STATISTICS

Year-on-year production figures for the third-generation Transporter appear to suggest that either retention of air-cooled capabilities at the vehicle's launch was a costly mistake or conversely that the decision to abandon Volkswagen's traditional means of engine cooling in 1983 for conventional radiators and oodles of water caused legions of loyal buyers to turn traitor once and for all. Neither assumption is correct.

Production of the original first-generation Transporter grew each year, culminating in an all-time high of 187,947 such vehicles being built in 1964, the year when the second-generation Transporter became something more than merely a figment of more adventurous imaginations. From its debut, the second-generation Transporter outshone its predecessor in terms of volume as it immediately broke the 200,000 unit barrier by a considerable margin at 228,290 vehicles manufactured in the twelve-month period encompassing 1968. By 1972, this number had risen to a commanding 259,101 Transporters emerging from Hanover and Emden factories alone. When production came to an end in Germany in the latter months of 1979, a total of 2,465,000 second-generation models had been built in Germany, or just a little short of three million units if production at satellite factories is taken into account – a figure that totally eclipsed the once remarkable number of 1,833,000 vehicles of the original type built over seventeen and a half years. That such a figure had been achieved in just twelve years added grist to the newer model's mill.

In 1980, the first full year of third-generation production, 217,876 Transporters were built worldwide, although of course this figure included a percentage of vehicles which were based on the second-generation model. In 1981 production fell to 187,327 units and a virtually identical number followed in 1982 at 188,681 Transporters. The following year bore witness to a further decline, with only 155,500 vehicles being built. The remaining years of third-generation Transporter production saw a succession of similar numbers, with 157,596 in 1984, 155,423 in 1985, 161,712 in 1986, 145,380 in 1987, 150,999 in 1980 and 147,539 in 1989, the last full year of dedicated manufacture. The crossover year of 1990 saw production tumble to no more than 130,370 units in total. Such a desultory record appears to suggest that one-time buyers turned away from the third-generation Transporter in their droves.

However, what these figures don't reveal is that in fact second-generation Transporter figures took a big tumble partway through the production, a drop that saw the record 259,101 units manufactured at Hanover and Emden in 1972 fall to 174,121 vehicles produced in Hanover alone just two years later. Recessionary times made production at Emden surplus to requirements.

Such is the importance of the mid-1970s to the story of the emergence of the third-generation Transporter that a considerable section of this book is dedicated to those tumultuous few years. For the moment it is best to summarize, with the statement that all motor manufacturers suffered considerable trauma and that in Volkswagen's case no model in the range to date has outshone some of the production figures of the first years of that decade.

Volkswagen frequently declares that the Golf is the most popular car of all time, but even setting aside the somewhat dubious amalgamation of various generations to achieve this claim, the model with the most vehicles of a single type to be produced in a twelve-month period remains the Beetle, and this is unlikely to change in the foreseeable future. In 1971, just a year away from the Transporter's zenith year, 1,291,612 Beetles were manufactured. To date, the Golf appears to have peaked in 1992 at 927,286 cars. A contributory factor here has to be America's long-standing love affair with the Beetle and its equally lengthy rejection of the Golf as a worthy successor. Suffice to say Volkswagen became something of a lost brand in America following the demise of the Beetle, with sales eventually falling to an all-time low of just 49,533 of all types in 1993, a couple of years after the Vanagon had disappeared from the dealers' stock of new vehicles. Export figures specific to the Vanagon are singular by their absence, but clearly Volkswagen's larger people carrier and workhorse also suffered from the general lack of faith in the brand generated by the Golf, while this deficiency in valuable export volume contributed to the drop in overall production numbers at the Hanover factory.

Similarly, just as the Beetle had been forced to face increasing competition from home and abroad, so too did the Transporter. Leaner, meaner times drove other manufacturers to either develop new models or to enter the market once dominated by the Transporter. In a situation where the size of the cake shrank due to economic circumstances beyond the control of Volkswagen, more manufacturers – particularly in the Far East – wanted to claim a slice, and did so by building to specifications that quality-led Volkswagen were unable to match on cost grounds. Shrinkage was inevitable.

A MOST UNUSUAL BIRTH

Finally in this necessary but reasonably lengthy introduction, a word or too has to be said about the third-generation Transporter at its launch, even though the subject will be covered in far greater depth later.

Following Volkswagen's wholesale abandonment of the concept of rear-wheel drive vehicles propelled by air-cooled, flat-four engines, the dismissal of the Beetle in favour of the Golf and the Polo, the replacement of the VW 1600 saloon and its larger brother, the short-lived VW 411 and 412, with the Passat, motoring experts and news hacks almost to a man were expecting that the new Transporter would follow suit with a conventional cab over engine design. Water-cooling was heavily anticipated, and most, if not all, professional reporters were amazed by what they saw in sneak previews and at the official press unveiling. Similarly, the buying public, depending on whether they preferred traditional Volkswagen or conventional practice, were either mightily relieved or decidedly disappointed. Few, if any, were aware of the reasons that led to the emergence of the third-generation Transporter in the guise it took at its launch and nobody

Transport to an enthusiasts' gathering in Hampshire.

took sufficient trouble to investigate the circumstances – by this time Volkswagen certainly wouldn't have encouraged such investigations. This lack of analysis led professionals and public alike to be largely critical of the new model's old technology and to lay the foundations for a misconception that was to persist for many years to come.

This book affords the most comprehensive account of the third-generation Transporter to be written to date in the English language. While inevitably descriptive for a good proportion of the time, a primary aim is to set the record straight both for current and future generations. Hopefully, it will prove to be both revelatory and provocative in nature. If so, it accomplishes what the author set out to achieve.

The incredible popularity of the first two generations of Transporter has resulted in droves of enthusiasts turning to the T3 as a more affordable option. Wherever you go in the summer, to Volkswagen gatherings, on holiday, or simply out and about, it won't be long before a T3 appears. Often bruised and battered, their collective charm is nevertheless irresistible.

TOP RIGHT: A glorified beach hut in Cornwall.

BOTTOM LEFT: Camping in Nottinghamshire.

BOTTOM RIGHT: Spending the weekend at a VW event in the Scottish Borders.

Volkswagen's press department have been fond of producing imagery depicting various generations of Transporter side-by-side. This photograph mirrors the content of this chapter, with the first generation Transporter shown to the left, its successor in the middle and the T3 to the right. The picture also gives a foretaste of the size of the third-generation model compared to its predecessors.

1 *before the third-generation Transporter, 1949–79*

SETTING THE SCENE

The origins of Volkswagen's legendary and highly successful Transporter lie variously in 1947, 1948 and 1949. That is an important opening statement to make as it dismisses any assumption that if Ferdinand Porsche created the Beetle, then he must by extension have been responsible for the concept of a load-carrying vehicle that could double as a people-carrier. Porsche was working for Hitler and the Nazis; that was the price he paid to achieve his long-term ambition of successfully launching a car suitable for the German people. Hitler wanted to motorize the German nation. A large percentage of the population had no realistic chance of ever owning a car on the simple ground of cost, so the mass production of a very cheap vehicle would satisfy the Führer's wishes and the people's needs. Self-interested resistance on the part of the German motor industry resulted in the Beetle becoming a Nazi

party-owned product. Hitler could gain no propaganda value out of a load carrier, however, so, while one or two Beetles did emerge that featured strange shed-like structures balanced precariously over the engine and other rearward parts, that is where it ended. The enormous factory we know as Wolfsburg and in the Nazi era was the KdF-Wagen works, or Strength-through-Joy plant, was constructed for the sole purpose of building Beetles.

That the Beetle factory was owned by the Nazis is also important. Hitler's suicide and Germany's unconditional surrender brought the war in Europe to a welcome end and resulted in, amongst many other actions, the abolition of the Nazi party by Allied decree. This left the factory ownerless. It is not appropriate here to narrate how Wolfsburg became vital in the process of providing much-needed transport for military personnel, but this does help to explain why it wasn't summarily demolished and why, with its future

apparently secure, it was necessary to appoint a professional native manager rather than leave it in the hands of a well-intentioned but inexperienced alien amateur. Heinz Nordhoff – the candidate selected – was most recently the director of the country's largest truck-making facility at Opel. Undoubtedly he would have appreciated the potential of a whimsical notion for a small commercial vehicle drawn up by the entrepreneurial and hugely extrovert Dutchman Ben Pon and duly presented to Wolfsburg's British management. The idea was subsequently squashed by the higher echelons of military government on the grounds of over-stretching; the Beetle remained the all-consuming priority.

Ownership, or the lack of it, continued to be an important issue. In September 1949 the British military government handed over the Wolfsburg works to the state of Lower Saxony with the proviso that they were to take control on behalf of, and under the

Pictured on the occasion of the Beetle becoming the most manufactured car in history, third Director General Rudolph Leiding's real claim to fame was his decision to develop the Golf and its siblings at the expense of the Beetle and other air-cooled models.

supervision of, the federal government in Bonn. True ownership remained unclear and this, coupled to the somewhat vague and rambling structure of control predictably associated with state bureaucracy, allowed a skilled manager like Nordhoff the manoeuvrability and authority more normally associated with a private family business. How to progress the Beetle and, more importantly in this instance, the development of the Transporter was more or less Nordhoff's decision alone.

Nevertheless, partial government ownership did play an important part in the later management of Volkswagen. The foundation of an advisory council in May 1951 (replaced by a supervisory board in August two years later) established the pattern whereby Nordhoff met with this group and summarized his activities over the years. The act passed in the German parliament in August 1960 allowing for the creation of Volkswagenwerk Aktienge-

sellschaft, or Volkswagen Joint Stock Company, demanded that 60 per cent of the company's capital be sold as 'people's shares', while the remaining 40 per cent be divided equally between the government in Bonn and the state of Lower Saxony. This had the effect of clarifying ownership and the state's influence – increasing, by inference if nothing else, the authority of the supervisory board.

Nordhoff reached the customary retirement age on 6 January 1964 but made it abundantly clear that he intended to continue as Director General for some years to come. It was in this era that the second-generation Transporter was both conceived and launched, which not only confirms its identity but also clarifies its pedigree. The year 1966 saw the first real recession in post-war Germany: a deep, biting downturn that affected all levels of society and every aspect of industry, motor manufacturing included. Ford

and Opel, the other two giants in the business, both laid men off in droves. Nordhoff battened down the hatches, instigated a shorter working week and launched an economy version of the Beetle, which, while it didn't make a great deal of money for Volkswagen, helped to keep the workforce at least partially gainfully employed. However, he also took the Bonn government to task for their lack of support for this vital industry. Nordhoff openly criticized the resolve to raise petrol taxes, the laxity with which automobile insurance rates were allowed to spiral upwards and the decision to slash in half the tax concession German workers received if they drove their cars to and from work. The backlash of such statements was near instantaneous, with the bumptious finance minister, Franz Josef Strauss, leading the attack. Volkswagen had produced too many cars, they had been asleep, the Beetle was uncomfortable and it was too old a design to bear the flag for the company. What had Nordhoff been doing all these years: he had to be replaced as quickly as possible!

Strauss's tentacles stretched far and wide in typical politician fashion and included one Josef Rust – an industrialist, a former aide, and now crucially chairman of Volkswagen's supervisory board. Nordhoff had spoken of retiring a few days before his seventieth birthday and had been carefully grooming, amongst others, the former head of Volkswagen in America, Carl Hahn, to succeed him; Rust and his associates made sure that this didn't happen. Instead Kurt Lotz was appointed as Nordhoff's deputy, a man with no relevant experience but one supreme qualification – and that was to toe the party line to the full. To make matters worse, during this process, Nordhoff's health began to fail. A prolonged period away from his desk in 1967 was followed by an apparent revival and a determination to continue as would a man of half his age. But Nordhoff exerted himself once too often in March 1968: he collapsed on the way back from making a speech and died in Wolfsburg hospital the following month.

Lotz's four-year period at the helm of Volkswagen was an unmitigated disaster. He openly criticized Nordhoff and the way he had run the business and made it abundantly clear that his main aim was to rid the company of the Beetle, but only succeeded in turning the once hugely profitable giant into one bordering on making its first loss in its history. His one model introduction, the NSU-developed K70 was distinguished by its indifferent design, unreliable nature, high cost to manufacture and remarkable tendency towards premature rusting. His one achievement had been to convince sufficient people of influence that a change of direction for Volkswagen was essential with or without his presence at the helm.

Lotz's successor was Rudolph Leiding, a hard-working, decidedly blunt executive from within the Volkswagen group, a man who had a proven track record of success wherever he had been sent by Nordhoff. Leiding knew his challenges and ruthlessly set about the task of replacing every model in the range with a new generation of water-cooled, front-wheel drive vehicles. In

priority terms the biggest money earner for the company had to come first: the Beetle had to be displaced by the car that would be christened the Golf as soon as it was ready. The larger air-cooled saloon, fastback and estate, the VW 1600, would be chopped out in favour of the Passat. On the peripheries, the classic Karmann Ghia would go in favour of the Scirocco – just as much a Golf in disguise as the so-called sports car of the range had been a Beetle – while circumstances would dictate that the sister company's Audi 50, a pocket handkerchief hatchback due for launch at roughly the same time as the Golf, would be built at Wolfsburg and given a VW Polo badge. This left the second-generation Transporter, a reasonably recent introduction of the old school dating from August 1967, as the lowest priority on Leiding's lengthy list.

However, time and circumstances were not on Leiding's side. Just when he needed every note and coin he could muster to pay for the most extensive range development of any motor manufacturing company, and at a time when he had been forced to up the cost of a Beetle in increments amounting to 20 per cent for that very purpose, the world collapsed around him. Externally, the Deutschmark's rise in relation to the dollar caused the Beetle and its contemporaries to rise in price by as much as 40 per cent one year and 20 per cent the following one. In the spring of 1974 Leiding even went so far as to say that 'our cars can't get any more expensive', knowing what such hyper-inflation would mean for Volkswagen. Successive oil crises and spiralling fuel prices at the pumps made any vehicles that were less than totally fuel efficient a liability, roaring inflation across Europe and in the United States saw car prices bounce up in leaps and bounds, while wages and salary increases were either marginal or non-existent for many and the ranks of the unemployed broke their banks in the biggest flood for many a year. Enforced price increases, which occurred twice in the spring of 1974 and on a third occasion in August of the same year, although essential, did little to boost sales. Volkswagen's showrooms were more or less deserted, volume tumbled just as it did for other manufacturers and the inevitable happened. From

slender but growing profits in his early days, Leiding's record became one of mounting losses. In 1973, when the economy began to turn really sour Leiding had spent 755 million DM and made a profit of 109 million DM, a year later he'd committed to 1,187 million DM worth of investments and recorded a massive 555 million DM loss. Political commentators were only too eager to shout that Volkswagen was losing its place in the world, pointing out that where once it had been first amongst industrial giants it had now slipped to seventh place.

Whether or not Leiding was pushed or retired from his post is of only peripheral interest to a book about the third-generation Transporter, but the background against which it originated most certainly is not, if for no other reason than that the form it took becomes almost self-explanatory. Most have credited Leiding's successor, ex-Ford man Toni Schmücker with its inception, but for the moment remember the name Rudolph Leiding while attention is turned to the two earlier generations of Transporter.

THE IDEA OF A TRANSPORTER

The Pon family, based in Amersfoot in Holland, were one-time Opel dealers who became involved with Volkswagen because they felt unable to trade with General Motors when the American giant acquired its new German satellite. Becoming a stop-gap agency for American Federal Trucks was rightly perceived as offering much less in the way of potential income, and leading brother Ben Pon instead fast-tracked himself into the path of Ferdinand Porsche – and some say the Nazis themselves – in search of Beetles with which to line his family's pockets. War stopped Pon in his tracks but, once liberated, the irrepressible trader was in action once more. Various stories are in circulation of how Pon made his entry to Wolfsburg in the days of British control, but the most intriguing has him gaining a temporary commission as a full colonel in the Dutch army with the necessary impressive uniform, acquiring an elderly Mercedes from an appropriate staff car park complete with a suitably servile chauffeur, and triumphantly arriving at Wolfsburg's gate puffing on a large cigar and waving regally to curious passers-by.

The result of Pon's endeavours was the establishment of a congenial relationship with officer in charge Ivan Hirst, and a trickle of Beetles flowing from Germany to Holland in what was undeniably the first export deal between supplier and – with effect from 8 August 1947 – the Netherlands' official importer. Pon became a frequent visitor to Wolfsburg and so saw at first hand one of Ivan Hirst's finest acts of improvisation – an answer to the desperate need for means to transport materials from one part of the factory to another. This was the so-called *Plattenwagen*, or flat car, essentially a *Kübelwagen*, the military version of the Beetle chassis with a bolt-on driver's cab balanced precariously over the trusty 1134 25PS engine. The trader in Pon immediately saw an opportunity to market this simple but practical vehicle in Holland, where the only alternative was a three-wheeler of dubious capabilities with little more than pedal power to move it on its way. Sadly for Pon, he was thwarted in this enterprise by the Dutch Transport Authority, who decreed the *Plattenwagen* entirely inappropriate, as the driver sat at the rear rather than the front of the vehicle.

Never one to take such a blow as final, Pon bounced back to Wolfsburg with a new variation on the theme. Few who know anything about Volkswagen's first Transporter can be unaware of the famous sketch quickly scribbled on a leaf from the equivalent of a modern Filofax. Probably taking less than a minute to execute, the rudimentary sketch depicted a box-like vehicle with its engine over the rear wheels, the driver perched ahead of the front wheels with no more than a single sheet of metal between him and the vehicle in front, and able to carry some 750kg (1,650lb) of goods in the centre section. Buoyed over with Pon's enthusiasm, not to mention the prospect of becoming a genuine car manufacturer in his own right, Ivan Hirst hot-footed it to Minden to gain approval to proceed from his boss, Colonel Radclyffe. Sadly, it was not to be. Radclyffe was concerned that not only was basic Beetle production lagging, but also Wolfsburg's structure, which had more gaping holes than the average castle ruin,

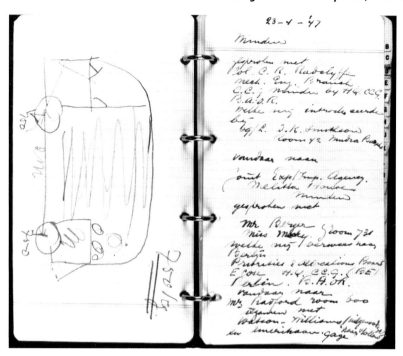

Ben Pon's crude sketch from 1947 – long claimed to herald the birth of the Transporter.

and that both areas took precedence. Manpower wasn't easy to come by and, if truth be known, British supervision at Wolfsburg was intended to be no more than a caretaking exercise. It seemed as though the plan to evolve a Transporter was over before it even started.

THE REALITY OF A TRANSPORTER

Heinz Nordhoff's views on both the Beetle and Wolfsburg when he first arrived at Volkswagen are well known. That he appreciated the enormity of the task that lay before him can be seen by the way he spent his first six months at the factory working seven days a week and sleeping in a single bed in a room adjacent to his office. Nevertheless, his training, background and management skills suggested to him that he would be missing a golden opportunity if he didn't invest in a second vehicle for the factory to build.

Most of Nordhoff's working life had been spent at Opel, where he had risen to the rank of member of the board of management by 1936. From a posting to Berlin in 1939 to direct the office there, he moved to Brandenburg in 1942, then home to the largest truck-making factory in Europe. As Director General at this sprawling Opel plant he was responsible for producing 4,000 vehicles per month, despite the deprivations of war. With such a background

there was no better individual to promote a commercial vehicle as Volkswagen's second product after the Beetle.

Progress to production of the Transporter was rapid and undeniably fraught with problems. Nordhoff set incredibly tight schedules and was far from sympathetic to pleas for more time even when setbacks occurred. A detailed study of the progress from initial prototype to press launch is not warranted here, other than to make reference to the financial constraints that resulted in a first attempt utilizing the Beetle's chassis buckling under its own weight on its inaugural outing and to note Nordhoff's unending determination to produce a dynamic vehicle, as close to perfection as humanly possible. Wind tunnel tests demanded that initial front-end plans were modified to make use of a wooden mock-up, which was determined to be 'highly streamlined', prototypes covered some 12,000km (7,500 miles) of tests, including some of the roughest roads Lower Saxony had to offer, to iron out any teething problems, and the Transporter's roof design was amended at the last minute to improve the vehicle's rigidity. Cost restraints prevented the development of a larger and more powerful engine than that afforded to Volkswagen's saloon, but the dividend came in the fitting of the wartime *Kübelwagen*'s reduction hubs to produce lower gearing, while an adjustment in the height of the Beetle's borrowed front suspension increased ground clearance.

Crucially, Nordhoff was adamant that for the press launch in November 1949, more than just a delivery van should be presented. His vision was to produce a whole range of vehicles all emanating from the same basic design, including a pick-up, an eight-seater minibus, an ambulance and a vehicle for the *Bundespost*, the German post office. Although the Delivery Van would always be a best seller, without the other options the emerging story wouldn't have been anywhere near so rosy. Indeed, one of the additional vehicles presented in the run-up to Christmas 1949 triggered an idea which, after a slow start, but certainly within ten years, generated a great deal of additional business for Volkswagen and a phenomenon that has assisted production numbers for all subsequent versions of the Transporter, including the T3.

DEFINITION OF A TRANSPORTER

The speech Nordhoff delivered to the press when he launched the Transporter gives a fascinating insight into the management capabilities of Volkswagen's leader, but for the purposes of this book it is only necessary to establish what set the Transporter apart, and why the concept was so successful that it warranted long-term production and, Beetle fashion, a programme of continuous improvement.

Nordhoff divulged that, despite the Pon sketch, work had started from scratch with careful market research.

We arrived at the conclusion that it was not the typical half-tonner on a car chassis that was required, but a 50 per cent bigger three-quarter-tonner with as large as possible load space; an enclosed van which can be used in many different ways …

The Director General then revealed that what he was unveiling was a vehicle exhibiting unique characteristics, one that would take the world of the small commercial vehicle by storm.

We didn't begin from an existing chassis, as this would have badly hindered

Heinz Nordhoff – Director General of Volkswagen 1948–68 – steered the Transporter from concept to production.

the logical solution we wanted, but instead we started from the load area – actually much more obvious and original. This load area carries the driver's seat at the front, and at the rear both the engine and the gearbox – that is the patent idea, free of compromise for our van, and that is how it is built.

Nordhoff's description of the make-up of the first-generation Transporter applies almost as much to the T3 (with the proviso of differing capacities and minor adjustments), and this narrative will become a matter of interest as the vehicle's story unfurls.

The van comprises a main area of three square metres of floor space plus, over the engine, an additional square metre, and 4.5 cubic metres of volume. At the front there is a three-seat passenger

and driver's area with very easy access and an unbeatable view of the road. At the back … there is the engine, fuel tank, battery and spare wheel. In short, neither the load area nor the driver's area is restricted by these items. All this is produced as a complete self-supporting steel superstructure, with a low and unobstructed loading area … This vehicle weighs 875kg in road-going condition and carries 850kg, thus representing a best-ever performance for a van of this size, with a weight to load ratio of 1:1 …

Nordhoff explained to his audience what to us might appear blatantly obvious but at the time was groundbreaking.

With this vehicle the load area lies exactly between the axles. The driver at the front and the engine at the rear match each other extremely well in terms of weight. The axle load is always equal, whether the vehicle is empty or laden …

What might have been seen as a bar to true versatility was swept away with consummate ease. Restricted rear access was a feature of the first-generation Transporter, its successor and the T3, but this had no effect on sales. For that reason, if no other, Nordhoff was proven to be much more than a smooth-talking salesman.

With a standard van you are in the predicament that it has to have its loading doors at the rear; our quandary is that we cannot do this. However, if I weigh the two scenarios against each

Courtesy of Volkswagen's archive, this unique image portrays a special edition T3 Double Cab Pick-up towing a prototype first-generation Transporter. Nearly forty years separate the two vehicles.

other, then I am glad to be in our shoes because the loading and access from the side is natural and normal – who would think of getting into a limousine from the back? Our van doesn't need any clear space behind when it parks to unload, and the next vehicle can be close behind it. With regard to the sill height of the loading area, this is close to the kerb height – it is incomparably easy to load and unload.

The Transporter was a truly revolutionary vehicle, and the Director General's press launch speech makes it abundantly clear what set the Volkswagen van apart from its contemporaries, such as they were, and why it was at the forefront of technology.

The famous 'cab over engine' arrangement gives such terrible load distribution ratios in an empty van that it was never an option. You can tell from the state of the roadside trees in the entire British Zone how the lorries of the English Army, which have been built according to this principle, handle when they are unladen.

Those defining words of Heinz Nordhoff made in 1949 to launch the genre are equally applicable to the second-generation on its debut nearly two decades later and to the T3, the inception of which he played no part in, a further ten years after that.

ONE VEHICLE – DIVERSE OPTIONS

Nordhoff's demand for a range of options based on a single chassis with the same basic body shell came into place with remarkable alacrity. Production of the basic Delivery Van began with an earnest trickle in February 1950. In April a prototype Microbus was delivered to a valued customer for evaluation and on 22 May production began.

The Microbus was variously described as the VW Kleinbus or the VW Achtsitzer, the 'small bus' or the 'eight-seater'. Here was the first definitive people carrier, with a trim level to match many a saloon of the era. From its full headlining to vinyl clad fibreboard trim panels, the Microbus could never be described as a load-lugging de luxe option, even its seats were firmly bolt-

Two very early Transporters depicted in 1950. In the foreground is a Microbus, while in the background a Delivery Van is being loaded.

Nordhoff envisaged a full range of vehicles all using the same basic body. The Delivery Van led the field in workhorse models, while the Microbus might be described as the first ever people-carrier.

ed to its rubber clad floor. But its role was diverse nevertheless, one minute it was a school bus, the next a taxi, and from there a family vehicle and much more.

However useful the Microbus, it was with the Kombi – the name reveals its personality – that Volkswagen struck gold. Times were still hard for many in 1950. It was inconceivable that a small business – such as a grocer, tobacconist, baker or butcher – would be able to afford one vehicle for work and a second one for weekend use as a passenger carrier. In the Kombi, Volkswagen had the answer. Here was a basic, and as a consequence, practical, vehicle. From Monday to Friday the seats came out and the vehicle was a delivery vehicle

with side windows. There was little in the way of floor covering, the absence of a headlining was hardly noteworthy, and the practicality behind bare metal side-panels was unquestionable. However, a few spins of a set of wing nuts later, and to all intents and purposes you had a people-carrier with the same weekend capabilities as a Microbus.

The Kombi also held the key to a development that only its practical nature allowed. This wasn't part of Nordhoff's master plan, but in the long term was set to pay Volkswagen enormous dividends. If the Kombi could accommodate seats one moment and space the next, surely the same could be done with the rudiments of camping equipment. In 1950 such a notion was a little way off; by the mid-fifties it was openly promoted, albeit the sales response was a trickle rather than a raging torrent. By the early sixties, however, demand had grown to previously unimaginable proportions and nowhere more so than in the USA. There Volkswagen of America had little option but to ask local firms to produce camping interiors similar in style and finish to those of the German firm of Westfalia, founding father in the field and Volkswagen's official partner in such matters. The evolution of the Camper is covered in more detail later in the chapter.

Theoretically the next pea out of the pod for Volkswagen should have been something like an ambulance, a post office van or a pick-up. In practice it was none of these. The first two had somewhat limited potential in terms of vast returns, while the last mentioned wasn't a straightforward package that could be developed at little extra cost. Wishing to plough as much back into the operation as possible, Nordhoff decreed that as the demand was there for a De Luxe version of the Microbus that option should be the next requirement to be met. The new model went into production in June 1951 and could be distinguished from its more lowly brethren by an abundance of chrome trim, a greenhouse-like number of windows – including Plexiglas roof lights and wraparound 'glass' bored into the upper rear quarter panels – in most instances a full-length roll-back sunroof, a special dashboard unique to this specification level, and deep pile interior trim. Although this model didn't prove the most popular in the range, it was nevertheless a worthwhile addition and an asset that was perpetuated into succeeding generations, finally becoming more important than ever in the T3 years.

Despite the break in the proposed sequence of launches, the original promise of a factory-built ambulance proved not to be an idle one, as this was the next model to leave Wolfsburg, making its debut at the end of 1951. This was the first member of the range to have a rear-opening door, but more relevant to the story of the T3 is its promotion alongside the mainstream models. Nordhoff cannot possibly have imagined that he was going to make

Volkswagen rich out of niche market ambulance sales, yet not only did he go ahead with his original intention of producing such a model in the range, but even went to the lengths of including it in promotional material, despite its minuscule sales. The most likely explanation is that he saw it as a way of advertising the versatility of the Volkswagen Transporter.

In the not-too-distant future it would be possible to order just about every quirky special model conceivable. Many of these decidedly oddball variants weren't stitched together at Wolfsburg but were built by specialist workshops on the back of a vehicle supplied from the factory. Special literature was prepared for dealers to hand out to interested parties, ranging from full-blown catalogues to little more than double-sided sheets limited to one unusual model. In theory at least each such special model was given its own unique code, although such arrangements weren't formalized until 1957. A few examples illustrate the diversity of the options. Would-be owners could specify a mobile shop, or a mobile shop with a high roof. They could opt for a refrigerated vehicle with 140mm insulating board, a hydraulic tipper truck, an exhibition or display bus, or perhaps a mobile library. A sales brochure entitled 'VW commercials equipped for many purposes' even included imagery of mobile milking parlours, a dough-nut-making van, and a workshop for demonstrating the attributes of the latest models of Singer sewing machines. Such apparently obscure options were carried forward onto the second-generation Transporter and therefore by implication to the T3. However, to generate a reasonable percentage of the more weird and wonderful options Volkswagen had to spend a little more money and launch the promised pick-up.

The Pick-up arrived on Volkswagen's books towards the end of August 1952. The reason for the delay of some sixteen months between the Microbus De Luxe and this latest model was simple; the Pick-up was a costly exercise to develop and a bit of money back in the bank was required first. Consider the unique elements of the vehicle's make-up, which included a new and much smaller roof panel: relocation of both

the spare wheel and more importantly the petrol tank to accommodate the Pick-up's hallmark low platform; and redesigned and incredibly important cooling vents.

Two more models were sufficiently mainstream to warrant status over and above that of the special models. The first was the Double Cab Pick-up, a particularly versatile vehicle and a forerunner to the numerous pick-up models used and abused by owners in Britain keen to emphasize load-carrying abilities and play down people-transporting duties and the tax implications thereof. Another model that would be carried forward as far as the T3 was the versatile (and lucrative) four-wheel drive syncro, released as a mouth-watering taster in 1958. Finally, in September 1961 along came the High Roofed Delivery Van, a vehicle particularly suited to the clothing trade or similar businesses. Sales brochures might divert into Pick-ups with extended platforms and suchlike, but in reality the core range was complete by the end of the second year of the new decade.

SALES SUCCESS

In 1950 Volkswagen produced 8,059 Transporters. Two years later, with most of the range in place, that figure had risen to 21,665. By 1955, when the decision was made to create a separate factory specifically for the Transporter, the annual total had bumped up to 49,907. By 1960, when Nordhoff announced to the world that he had finally managed to balance the demand for Beetles with what he was able to supply, the Hanover factory was churning out 139,919 Transporters over the twelve-month period. Production of the first-generation Transporter peaked in 1964 at a highly respectable 187,947 units, two and half years before a new model was launched.

During the course of 1955, the split in terms of production between different models was, in order of volume: Delivery Van 17,577; Kombi 11,346; Pick-up 10,138; Microbus 7,959; Microbus De Luxe 2,195; and Ambulance 694. Nearly a decade later in 1964 the running order had changed a little to: Delivery Van 48,481, thus retaining its pole position in the line up as might be expected; Kombi 44,659, once more a worthy runner-up; Microbus 40,115, leaping ahead of the Pick-up, despite the addition of the Double Cab version to boost that model's appeal; Pick-up 39,832; Microbus De Luxe 14,031; and trailing way behind the others, the Ambulance at 829 vehicles. The decision to go forward to a second-generation Transporter and a model available in all guises was taken in 1964 so in some ways total production numbers of a given variant are academic, at least as far as Volkswagen's policy-making progress is concerned. However, for the combined enthusiast and would-be scholar of the Transporter, the total of first-generation Delivery Van and Kombi over the production years (with the exception of 1967, when models changed in August) proves informative. Of the grand total of 1,833,000 Transporters built at Wolfsburg and Hanover between 1950 and 1967, 403,069 were Kombis and 518,829 Delivery Vans. The combined figure for these two models accounts for over 50 per cent of total production.

With both its own factory (Hanover opened in 1956) and such profitable production numbers the Transporter's future was undoubtedly secure. Volkswagen had successfully created the product, added so many elements to its composition and remained so far ahead of would-be competitors that both a second- and third-generation Transporter was guaranteed.

THE ALL-NEW SECOND-GENERATION TRANSPORTER

In true Nordhoff style the last of the first-generation Transporters had moved on considerably from the specification of the earliest models, though details of the changes made over the years are irrelevant here. Nordhoff, who was later to be condemned for not having brought out a model to replace the Beetle, was not a head-in-the-sand conservative incapable of developing new product, but this becomes more significant in the context of events in the mid-1970s, a matter for discussion in the next chapter.

That the second-generation Transporter was all-new when it made its debut is important. Concurrent with its debut was the launch of a Beetle

Like all Volkswagens of the Nordhoff era, the Transporter evolved. This Microbus De Luxe dates from the mid-1960s.

From 1955 to the end of first-generation Transporter production, the interior looked similar, if not identical, to that shown here.

Introduced in August 1967, the second-generation Transporter's most notable feature was its panoramic windscreen, the size of which earned the vehicle the nickname of the Bay.

sufficiently altered in its appearance for the marketing wing at Volkswagen to brand it as *der neue Käfer* (the new Beetle), but everyone knew that the changes were essentially cosmetic. However, while Volkswagen's and, more particularly, Nordhoff's critics (and around this time there were more than a handful) could have pointed fingers of condemnation at the rehashed saloon, they would have been hard-pressed to do so with the Transporter.

The second-generation Transporter dispensed with its predecessor's antiquated split-pane windscreen and was graced with a panoramic affair equating to 27 per cent more glass and such a contemporary appearance that it quickly became known as the Bay. Gone was the combination of small side windows and blank metal on the sides of the passenger-carrying vehicles, which had been characteristic of all earlier versions except the Microbus De Luxe. Instead three dominant panes of glass sold a bold message of modernity, just as did the less complicated, less elaborate swage lines. Who in 1967 could have countenanced introducing a new vehicle with the first generation's frontal 'V' as an intrinsic part of its design? Likewise, there was no longer any need to complicate manufacture with a subtle screen overhang to conceal ventilation meshes that were a desperate attempt to avoid steaming-up when the weather was poor, and stickiness when it proved to be anything more than simply fair. Ventilation

was now more than adequately catered for by an ample and appearance-enhancing grille below the windscreen outside and improved channels to circulate air inside the vehicle.

Thanks to a combination of those much larger windows and the fact that the Bay had an overall length of 4,420mm compared to its predecessor's 4,280mm, a width of 1,765mm, 15mm wider than that of the first-generation model, and an increase in height from 1,925mm first time around to 1,956mm now, the inside both was and felt much roomier and airier. The new dashboard, while still showing Volkswagen's preference for conservatism, despite the near-revolutionary appearance for the first time of an element of protective and non-reflecting vinyl padding, was nevertheless a big advance on the all-metal, painted affair of old. Improved upholsteries and carefully redrafted trim panels had a similar effect.

Then, despite the inevitable increase in body weight – up from 1,070kg unladen in the case of the first-generation Transporter in Delivery Van guise to 1,175kg for the new model in the same specification – brought about by the new Transporter's enlarged size, the vehicle had more power, better through-the-gears acceleration, more chance of overtaking in safety, and greater capabilities in heavy urban traffic, where the first-generation model had been so hampered by its sloth-like capabilities. For the new Transporter

had a new engine, a 1584cc unit with a bore and stroke of 85.5mm × 69mm, a compression ratio of 7.5:1 and a maximum of 47PS achieved at 4,000rpm. On paper that didn't appear a great increase in any respect to the outgoing 1500cc unit – after all, what does a 3PS improvement amount to amongst friends – but nevertheless the upgrade was more than sufficient for the purpose in 1967.

On a similar if somewhat greasy and oily tack, antiquated reduction gears disappeared overnight, as did the occasionally wayward swing axle, replaced in the latter instance by the genuine upgrade to a double-jointed rear axle. When coupled to an increase in track, this gave the new Transporter something bordering on car-like handling capabilities. However, where there was no need to make improvements Nordhoff's engineers didn't introduce change for change's sake. The delightfully smooth gearbox action of days gone by was retained, as was Professor Porsche's independent torsion bar suspension.

Perhaps the most significant glory of the second-generation Transporter was that all the model variations, from Delivery Van to Kombi to Clipper and Clipper L (the new if somewhat briefly held names for the Microbus and Microbus De Luxe), were instantly available at launch. Together with the wealth of improvements already listed, this gave the Bay a more than fair opportunity to overwhelm any potential challengers from the fledgling group of small commercials under development by rival manufacturers, particularly those emerging from Japan.

Sales and More Sales

The second-generation Transporter's sales progress is of great significance to the tale of the emergence of its successor. For the moment all that is necessary is to record the success story.

First-year production totals are somewhat complicated by the inclusion of the last of the first-generation models. The first-generation production peak set in 1964 of 187,947 Transporters was overtaken time and time again in the early years of its successor. In 1968 Hanover churned out 228,290 Bay window models. In 1969 that total

An extraordinary level of Westfalia Camper sales in the United States added to ever-growing demand for the second-generation Transporter.

Second-generation Transporters converted to Campers by a variety of firms generated a great deal of business for Volkswagen.

jumped up to 244,945 Transporters, a figure eclipsed in 1970 by 257,873 vehicles. Then in 1971, output dropped to a still respectable 250,802 examples, only for production to bounce back the following year to 259,101 and a production peak that has never been equalled since. From this high, second-generation Transporter production ebbed and flowed for reasons that will become apparent in the next chapter.

Looking at the figures in more depth, we can see that the once top-of-the-tree Delivery Van instantly lost its pole position to the Kombi, and was also eclipsed by the Microbus. In 1968, 50,880 Delivery Vans left Hanover compared to 68,597 Kombis and 64,411 Microbuses. The best overall year on record, 1972, also saw Kombis peak, on this occasion at a startling 90,712 vehicles, while the Microbus's best year was 1971, when 74,850 vehicles left the factory. The Delivery Van's top rating again came in 1972, with 56,119 vehicles. No model in the range slipped to such an extent that it would be considered inappropriate to build it in the days of the T3.

As a preview to T3 production levels, its first full year on the scene was its best in terms of volume, with 217,876 examples leaving Hanover; 41,225 fewer vehicles than in the Bay's peak year and a percentage drop of close to 16 per cent. Does such a figure imply that the second-generation Transporter was a better vehicle than its successor? Avid readers will have to wait and see!

The story of the latter years of German second-generation Transporter manufacture lies firmly in the camp of the emergence of the T3. For the moment, suffice to say the Bay went through a revamp in the summer of 1972, and as the years went by was also offered with increasingly larger engines.

DIVERSIONS INTO CAMPING

To imply, as might have been the case earlier in the chapter, that all Campers originated from the Westfalia fold or were copies thereof would confuse. In Britain, for example, a whole raft of soon-to-be-famous names were galvanized into action towards the end of the 1950s, some of them producing the most exquisite craftsmanship for what was essentially a glorified tent. Sidmouth-based JP White, builders turned cabinet makers, traded under the Devon brand, evolving models such as the all-singing, all-dancing sixties-style Caravette, and the more basic economy model, the Torvette. Peter Pitt's products, later to be engulfed into the Canterbury Pitt brand, were at one stage of equal significance, while a name virtually everyone had heard of then, Dormobile, jumped on to the bandwagon when they saw others raking in the cash. A latecomer to the game, if 1965 can be considered thus, has to be Danbury, whose appeal lay in the simplicity of their designs and definitely not in their marketing literature, which started out as little more than a series of typed and no doubt partially corrected sheets.

With the advent of the second-generation Transporter the camping or camper business really began to boom. Westfalia were hard at work in Germany, notching up their 30,000th conversion in March 1968, their 50,000th just one year and two months later and bounding ahead to the 100,000th Camper by 1971. Of these, in 1968 an astonishing 75 per cent were bound for North America, while by 1971 a further surge had occurred, lifting the total to 84 per cent. For Westfalia the simplicity of the former two-model range had gone, with as many as six variations being offered, each one being granted the name of a city. In the USA, despite such a general approach being applicable, Westfalia's products were generally referred to by the grammatically abhorrent name of Campmobile,

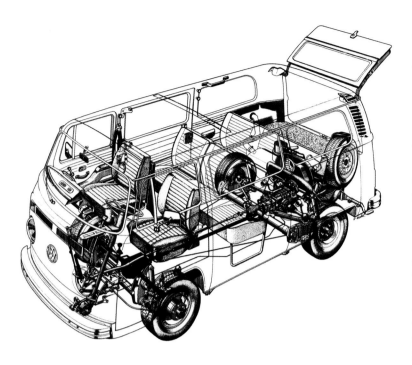

The notion of a four-wheel drive second-generation Transporter emerged towards the end of German production of the model. Volkswagen's carefully drawn cutaway image illustrates the technicalities as well as giving a general overview of the Bay.

such terminology only being eclipsed in the days of the third generation Transporter.

GENERATIONAL OVERLAP

First-generation Transporter production didn't come to a total end when Hanover switched to the new Bay model in the summer of 1967. Satellite operations such as Brazil, Australia, Mexico and South Africa had either progressed to full-scale manufacture in their own right over the years, or had assembled CKD (Completely Knocked Down) kits supplied by Hanover. Of these, the Brazilian operation at São Paulo was not only the most prolific but also the most independently minded. Succinctly, a Brazilian-manufactured Beetle of 1967 vintage carried various characteristics of earlier years and would continue to do so until production ceased nearly two decades later. So it won't come as a great surprise to hear that Brazil continued to produce their version of the first-generation Transporter until October 1975. To complicate matters, they also supplied Volkswagen of South Africa with CKD kits, which the Uitenhage plant assembled and sold alongside the new second-generation Transporter, marketing the product of Brazilian origins as the Fleetline and selling it at a price that undercut the 'new' Transporter by a considerable margin.

Unsurprisingly, when Hanover turned from the second-generation Transporter, the South American satellites didn't follow suit, and on this occasion it wasn't a matter of a few years before they opted to catch up. Today Brazil still produces an instantly recognizable version of the second-generation Transporter, albeit that under its skin it is powered by a 1.4-litre water-cooled engine, has a modified roof line compared to the German models and various other less prominent changes. Similarly, the factory at Puebla in Mexico continued to produce the second-generation Transporter until 1988, complete with 1.6-litre air-cooled engine. After that, they squeezed in a 1.8 in-line engine borrowed from the Golf, glued a radiator on to the front of the vehicle, in the process destroying its archaic charms, and raised the roof line on all options, which included 'La Combi' and 'La Panel' from days gone by and 'La Caravelle', a luxury alternative for the well-heeled. During 1996 production ceased, to be replaced by imports from Brazil, a state of affairs that is still in place at the time of writing.

In South Africa, Brazilian second-generation Transporter kits replaced the Fleetline models in 1976 and were imported until January 1979. However, while Brazil and Mexico would never gravitate towards the T3 or any of its successors, the South African factory adopted the third-generation model virtually at the same time that the design was launched from Hanover. Curiously, though, they decided to cling on to this model for a further twelve years after general production ceased in Germany in 1990. In that respect the T3 shared the stage with the Mk1 Golf, which, branded as the Citi Golf, remained on the books until the early days of 2010, a final edition of 1,000 cars being announced on 2 November 2009. The South African T3 will reappear later in the book, but for the moment it is worth noting that Volkswagen's empire is global and, while it is useful on occasion to refer to the quirks of satellite production, generally the narrative pertains solely to production of the T3 at Hanover.

This attractive image is claimed to be of a prototype T3 in Wolfsburg's wind tunnel chamber. According to Volkswagen's accompanying information, 'turning vanes in the wind tunnel redirect the wind flow through a nozzle that accelerates the stream to 112mph'. The majority of the images in this chapter take the form of archive pictures designed to illustrate the care taken to develop as near a perfect vehicle as possible.

2 from design concept to production, 1973–79

FOUR WASTED YEARS

Nordhoff's death at the age of sixty-nine in the spring of 1968 was set to change Volkswagen for ever. Had he stayed at the helm for a further ten years, which was unlikely, a very different third-generation Transporter might have emerged, and at a different time. Nordhoff's disagreement with the coalition government at the time of the first post-war recession in 1966 had the effect of putting someone in place to step into his shoes that was not of the Director General's choice. That person, Kurt Lotz, wilfully and deliberately tried to undo the work of the last twenty years once he was sat in the hot seat. During his mercifully brief period in office, even the most ardent detractor of the Nordhoff era wouldn't have wished it be extended, as Lotz fumbled with a dream of replacing the Beetle, damaged the launch of Nordhoff's last model, the VW 411, and slung a hefty weight around Wolfsburg's neck with his insistence that the thoroughly flawed K70 saloon inherited from NSU should spearhead the path to a front-wheel drive, water-cooled world for Volkswagen. While the second-generation Transporter prospered, spurred on in part by the newness of its design and to some extent by the burgeoning Camper revolution, Volkswagen's profits tumbled.

RUDOLPH LEIDING AND VOLKSWAGEN'S NEW STRATEGY

When Lotz was ousted in the autumn of 1971, he was replaced by Rudolph Leiding, an old hand in the Volkswagen group. Taking stock of what he had to offer, would-be buyers across the world and the potential impact of the changing times on each Volkswagen model, the ruthless but highly effective new Director General inevitably targeted the Beetle as his first port of call. If the Beetle fell, there was grave danger that Volkswagen would follow. While demand for the car showed no signs of abating, a combination of its elderly design, somewhat sluggish performance in comparison to much newer rivals and the fact that Lotz had hit it as hard as he could for four years, made Leiding's strategy unavoidable. The Beetle would be replaced by a front-wheel drive small family car, designed by external resources and powered by a now conventional water-cooled engine of sufficient power to ensure it was equal to, or preferably ahead of, the competition.

Leiding's second priority was a replacement for the aging VW 1600 and, almost more by implication than definite decree, the Lotz-wounded and scarred VW 411 and the disastrous K70. The VW 1600 had been introduced in the autumn of 1961 as a vehicle that Beetle owners with growing families might aspire to and at a time when Wolfsburg could realistically cope with the addition of an extra model to its production schedules. Known for several years as the VW 1500 because of its engine size, the vehicle was available as both a saloon and an estate, or variant and for some markets as a van. In August 1965 a fastback was added and sales grew steadily, if not on a scale comparable to the Beetle. By 1964 production stood at 262,000 units; two years later this had grown to 311,701 vehicles, but after that it petered out in the face of the recession. While the Beetle bounced back, the VW 1600 took a massive hit and only climbed part way back, peaking in its second phase at 272,031 cars in 1970. The 1971 production figure Leiding inherited was down to 234,224, which still appeared reasonably good compared to the following year's total of 157,543.

Nor could Leiding satisfy himself that the 411 was soaking up potential purchasers of a larger Volkswagen saloon. Launched in the dying months of 1968 against a background of Lotz helpfully saying it was 'no metal Adonis', production appeared healthy at 22,922 units. However, the car simply didn't take off and production had only grown to 42,587 cars in 1970, although it did bounce up a little the following year to 79,270 cars. Leiding was entirely right to decree that a new water-cooled larger family car would replace both models and that as soon as humanly possible both cars would be axed, together with the misnomer of the K70.

Although the much-loved and enduringly attractive Karmann Ghia, a vehicle whose origins could be traced back to August 1955, was peripheral to Volkswagen's profitability and survival it too faced Leiding's axe. It was to be replaced by a vehicle with a similar sporty appearance, which, like its predecessor would be built at the Karmann works in Osnabrück.

Of Nordhoff's line up of 1968, that left the Transporter, the youngest design by far and a vehicle that was performing well. We have already seen that the second-generation model had consistently eclipsed its predecessor's totals – remember that 1972 peak of 259,101 vehicles. As Leiding took stock of what he had inherited and the challenges that lay before him, unquestionably the Transporter was the least of his concerns. Nevertheless, it lay in his sights as the odd man out in the planned water-cooled world. It would be last definitely, but assuming a two- to three-year development period, it could slot in during 1976 or 1977 with ease.

Quick Change

The VW Passat, the first of the water-cooled models and the successor to the VW 1600 and VW 412, went into production in May 1973. Leiding had been able to cut some corners, in that he borrowed more than just the technology behind the Audi 80, but the deed was done. The start of production of the Giugiaro-designed Golf followed in January 1974, but to test the waters, the Scirocco, a vehicle that was essentially the same in terms of platform and mechanics but sported a startlingly attractive coupé body, was launched first. The addition of the VW Polo, a rebadged clone of the Audi 50, came in March 1975, but by this time Leiding was gone.

VOLKSWAGEN'S CRISIS-TORN WORLD

The advent of the less costly VW Polo and the crediting of Leiding's successor Toni Schmücker with the success story that grew out of Volkswagen's new range are two of the consequences of turmoil stretching far beyond Wolfsburg's portals. This same set of circumstances prevented the evolution of a third-generation Transporter to Leiding's chosen schedule and led to Schmücker's widely acknowledged status as the architect of the third-generation Transporter.

Volkswagen's mounting losses towards the end of Leiding's tenure of office were touched upon in the previous chapter. Volkswagen's own historian, Markus Lupa, closely supervised and edited by Dr Manfred Grieger, head of the group's corporate history department, traced Volkswagen's wider ills back to May 1971 and the final months of the Lotz era, when the German government moved to flexible exchange rates.

> Lower demand and the high valuation of the German Mark made Volkswagen's products more expensive abroad and the imports of foreign competitors cheaper on the German market. Volkswagen reacted to the exchange rate policies … by raising prices because higher production costs and lower yields left no other course of action. The prices relative to other manufacturers and the company's competitive position on important foreign markets worsened.

Using the pivotal American market to illustrate the consequences, we can see that not only was there the problem of the exchange rate, and the growing realization that Germany as a whole and Volkswagen particularly were becoming prohibitively expensive in terms of wages, but America was also feeling the effects of the economic gloom. As a result, President Nixon's government took action to protect its own industries. This took the form of a transitory tax on imports equating to some 6 per cent of the total price of every car and every Transporter, with the net result that sales to the American market took a serious tumble. Analysts reckoned that the US action cost Wolfsburg 25 million DM in 1974 with more to follow.

Coupled to the exhaustive investment programme necessary to transform the range of models offered, a sum that was set to total 2.5 billion DM between 1972 and Leiding's intended completion date of 1976, losses were virtually inevitable. While the new cars helped Volkswagen on the domestic market, where generally demand had fallen to an all-time low and some manufacturers were recording drops in demand of up to 40 per cent, the same could not really be said of exports to other European countries or to the USA and Canada. By 1974 jobs were in jeopardy, with Leiding forced to threaten mass redundancies. Production at Wolfsburg, Emden and other plants dropped to no more than 61 per cent of potential output, creating an unprecedented surplus capacity. To make matters worse for the factory workers, they had been granted an 11 per cent pay rise in 1973, making a Wolfsburg employee more costly than the crème de la crème of the American workforce. Under these circumstances, hard-headed Leiding had little option but to turn to the satellite plants for help, and both Brazil and Germany created and shipped numerous parts to Germany to save money. Nothing, it appeared, could save the German workforce, and in the ten months following Leiding's own departure a further 32,000 employees left Volkswagen for good.

In Volkswagen's unusually illustrious history, the year 1974 stands apart from the crowd as one of the few to show a loss, and certainly by far the most substantial. Coupled to what appeared to be a realistic prediction of further troubles ahead, it was inevitable that what had been planned for a third-generation Transporter had to be curtailed. Perhaps it is amazing that Leiding had even contemplated pushing ahead with a new model at all when the company was under such pressure. But make no mistake about it: although the third Transporter wouldn't be launched until four and a half long years had elapsed after his departure from Volkswagen and the form it took surprised all but Wolfsburg's innermost circle, it was Leiding's brainchild and not that of Toni Schmücker, contrary to what has been written in many a history book.

T3 PLANNING

Minutes of planning meetings relating to the third-generation Transporter are all neatly on file in Wolfsburg's archive. Even the most cursory of scans through this comprehensive documentation reveals that during the course of 1974 not only had detailed plans been drawn up that depict a vehicle remarkably similar in appearance to the T3 as it was launched in the high summer of 1979, but also that at some stage in September a first prototype had emerged from the boffins' workshops.

Leiding had announced his intentions at a board meeting held on 4 December 1973 by stating that the third-generation Transporter would be 'front steered with rear engine, rear gearbox with four gears and auto gearbox.' Why he decided on such a course remains something of a mystery, for while there were already signs that distinctly troubled times for the world in general and Volkswagen in particular lay ahead – so conceivably cost constraints might have been lurking in the depths of his mind – Leiding's model strategy to that point had been far from conservative in all respects. Further, considering that work on a new breed of larger commercial vehicle was already well advanced and that this range of models would emerge less than two years later with engines at the front mounted under a box in the

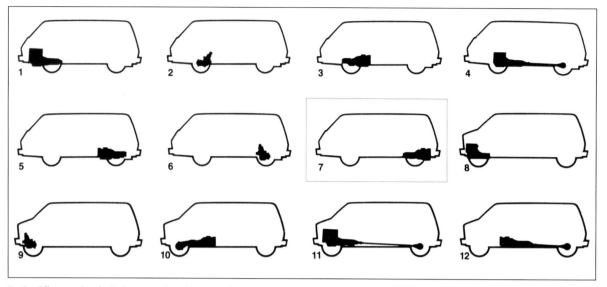

Twelve different styles of vehicle were evaluated before Leiding gave the go-ahead to the seemingly traditional and out-of-place T3.

driver's cabin, Leiding's approach to the evolution of the Transporter appeared at best unusual. Broadening Volkswagen's range of commercial vehicles, on the other hand, went hand in glove with Wolfsburg's relatively recently found ability to utilize technology, designs and even engines developed by its subsidiary, Auto Union GmbH. The visual similarity of the larger commercial, which was known as the LT, of April 1975 vintage to the T3 Transporter only serves to muddy the waters further. Why did Leiding discount the LT's design of an engine mounted under a box in the driver and front seat passenger cabin even before the first draftsman had put pen to paper?

For the record, the LT proved to be a great success and within a short time of its launch had captured 40 per cent of the home market for vehicles in its class. It was initially available in three nominal payload categories, LT28 (2.8 litres or 1.45 tons), LT31 (3.1 litres or 1.63 tons) and LT35, (3.5 litres or 1.8 tons) and offered with a choice of either a 2.0-litre OHC water-cooled petrol engine, a 75PS development of the Audi 100 engine, or a 2.7-litre, 65PS diesel engine, which had been developed for Volkswagen by the British company,

According to near-contemporary reports the T3's designers and engineers were set the task of evaluating twelve basic vehicle concepts, including front engine/front-wheel drive, front engine/rear-wheel drive, rear engine/rear-wheel drive and a variety of engine locations in between. Each possibility was ranked according to a register of fifty-two separate criteria – a list that ranged from metered performance and utilization of space, to comfort, economy and versatility.

Possibly to Leiding's surprise, particularly as the same conclusion had not been reached when evaluating the options for the LT, the verdict was not to opt for front engine/front-wheel drive. The projection for a rear-wheel drive/ rear engine Transporter was that 68 per cent of the road surface occupied by the vehicle transferred into visible interior space, compared to only 56 per cent with a short-hooded, front engine/ rear-wheel drive layout appears to have determined the matter, despite such a decision apparently going against Volkswagen's general direction of the time.

Although compared to the Golf, Passat and even the LT, the proposed specification of the T3 appeared remarkably conservative, there was one element of Leiding's decree that would have gone a long way to completing the circle of new designs if it had come to fruition. He demanded of his engineers and designers that they provide a purpose-built, water-cooled diesel engine with which Volkswagen could not only stay ahead of the competition in terms of performance but also counter the biggest drawback of the second-generation Transporter in times of spiralling fuel costs: namely its thirst.

From left to right: Mock-ups were tested in Volkswagen's climatic wind tunnel at Wolfsburg. Thousands of heat lamps heated the air to simulate desert conditions. The stylists' task was to refine the design to make it as attractive as possible to customers.

Second-Generation Larger Engines

As has already been noted, the second-generation Transporter was launched with a more than adequate 1584cc 47PS engine. Few, if any, journalists had anything other than praise for the Bay at its launch, but within a few short years all had changed. In 1970, the 1600 engine had been the subject of a makeover with modified cylinder heads offering twin rather than single inlet ports. Output lurched up to 50PS as the engine could breathe more easily. For the 1972 model year, the 1600 engine was supplemented by a 1700 unit, which, although new to the Transporter, was in reality the property of the large saloon, the VW 411. This 1679cc engine developed 66PS at 4,800rpm. Still challenged by would-be rivals, just two years later and after the second-generation had undergone a safety-enhancing, more contemporary styling exercise, an 1800 engine replaced the 'seventeen'. Again borrowed from the VW 411, which by this time had been rebadged as the VW 412, the overall increase in power amounted to no more than 2PS and a total of 68PS, while the vehicle's top speed of 82mph (132km/h) was allegedly only 4mph (6.5km/h) faster than that of its predecessor. The value of the latest engine came in the substantial increase in torque, up from the 1700's 81lb at 3,200rpm to 92.4lb at 3,000rpm. One more hike in the size of the second-generation Transporter's engine would occur, but only after Leiding had left office. The 2.0-litre offering that displaced the 1800 in August 1975 would be borrowed from the VW Porsche 914. It offered more of the same, and like all the other larger air-cooled engines was far from fuel-efficient. This was Leiding's primary concern: an average of no more than 22mpg (12.9ltr/100km) if a driver was light-footed and realistically often less than that was not good news in difficult times.

A Pressing Need for a New Model

Even though the Transporter was justifiably the least of Leiding's concerns, there were nevertheless good reasons over and above the hefty fuel bills for owners why Volkswagen should press

Stylists worked on both full-size and scale model mock-ups as they strove to create the ideal design for the second-generation Transporter's successor.

Dimensions were carefully checked and assessed using a full-scale model.

ahead with a third-generation Transporter despite the mounting tide of potential loss. Essentially there was nowhere to go with the second-generation model without spending seemingly extortionate amounts of money on a design that had been on the road for over seven years.

Such a scenario of rapid model change would have been inconceivable during the Nordhoff era, but Volkswagen under Leiding had changed direction into a more mainstream way

of thinking. From the days when the Director General ridiculed the industry level 'of hysterical stylists trying to sell people something they really do not want to have', Leiding had turned the company on its head. Leiding's strategy was to drive Volkswagen down a different road, a much more conventional carriageway of replacing vehicles as frequently as finances would permit. While advertising agency DDB had once been able to make great capital out of Volkswagen's very lack of change, this was not an image Leiding had any desire to promote. He spurned the notion of an advert with a large blank area where a picture would normally go and a heading, 'No point showing the '62 Volkswagen. It still looks the same,' and he must have been both frustrated and disappointed after his departure to find the admen promoting the second-generation Transporter in a similar way in 1976. 'The VW Commercial has nothing new to offer,' they proclaimed, adding a less than entirely convincing, 'which is precisely why it is so remarkable'. In an emerging world of Golfs, Passats and Polos, the new face of Volkswagen, the Transporter was rapidly becoming the odd man out and an older-generation embarrassment.

THE END OF THE LEIDING ERA

As was evidently standard practice, Leiding was in the chair for the latest gathering of minds of the EA389 progress committee, this particular meeting taking place in November 1974. (EA389, or *Entwicklungsauftrag* (development order) 389, was the project number initially allocated to the creation of a third-generation Transporter.) Beleaguered by harbingers of financial doom in the form of grey-suited, grey-faced accountants, besieged and constrained by the constant nag of depressed sales, the last thing Leiding wanted to hear at the meeting was that a serious and potentially costly hitch had occurred in the progress towards a new Transporter. Minutes of the meeting, however, record that this is exactly what occurred, as the shame-faced

boffins and gloomy upper echelons of Volkswagen's management advised their leader that:

> The engine space available and the increase in costs which is expected, rule out a water-cooled diesel engine for EA389. As a priority, however, we will check whether an air-cooled diesel engine, based on the Type 4 engine, or a water-cooled diesel engine, based on the Passat engine, are technically possible to meet the competition.

This near literal transcript of the minutes might at first sight appear contradictory but it seems clear that Leiding was being advised that a purpose-built engine for the Transporter was no longer practical despite the projected investment of 305 million DM, a figure which was confirmed at the same meeting. Whatever Leiding was thinking inwardly he nevertheless decreed that the third-generation Delivery Van would go into production in August 1977, to be followed by the Kombi and other more luxurious passenger-carrying models the following month, with versions destined for the American market and the inevitably slightly differently panelled Pick-up variations following in October. To ensure such targets were met – and incidentally theoretically accomplishing the replacement of every model in Volkswagen's range within the remarkably short period of just over three years – Leiding committed to still further spending by sanctioning finance to allow the research department to build twenty-nine prototypes with diesel engines.

Virtually concurrent with this meeting, the supervisory board of Volkswagenwerk AG acquired a new chairman and little more than a month later, on 10 January 1975, Rudolph Leiding resigned his role as Director General, allegedly 'for reasons of health'. To this day Volkswagen's historians are careful to repeat the story as regurgitated in this brief extract from *Kleine Chronik – The History of the Volkswagen Factory*: '1975 – 10-01 Rudolph Leiding resigns from the Chairmanship of VW AG's Board of Management at his own request.'

More realistically, most are aware that Leiding was forced out of office, target of a bitter battle with the unions, who inevitably tried to protect as many jobs as possible despite the circumstances; victim of politically motivated members of a supervisory board who felt unable to support him in his battles to keep Volkswagen afloat if the human consequences might endanger them; and casualty of the result of his predecessor's inaction at a crucial time. His downfall came in part too from his seemingly unquenchable thirst for cash to save Volkswagen and his ostensibly cold-hearted ruthlessness, which the supervisory board came to interpret as a lack of charm, or even deferential politeness, towards them.

Leiding's strivings saved Volkswagen and brought it back to full efficiency at a speed that even the most optimistic financial forecaster would have been loath to commit to. From that horrendously gloomy loss of 555 million DM in 1974, there was a dramatic, new model-related upturn resulting in a much reduced deficit in 1975 of 145 million

The effectiveness of the T3's sound-deadening insulation was tested in the acoustic chamber at Wolfsburg's research and development facility.

The T3 prototypes were thoroughly tested at Ehra-Lessien – Volkswagen's massive all-weather proving ground.

DM, which in turn was replaced a year later by a highly gratifying profit of 784 million DM, to be followed by two years of respectable figures of 332 and 368 million DM respectively. Taking into account further heavy investment for the future, few, if any, could have been dissatisfied. There was, however, one potential victim of Leiding's exit and this was the third-generation Transporter, the only model still under development at the time the axe fell. The new man at the helm could do what Leiding had done to Lotz's model plan, if there had been one. He might not have coffers of money available but his background and outlook might have led him to think that what Leiding had determined on was wrong for a new Transporter.

Wolfsburg's archive indicates how sudden the change at the top was. One minute Leiding's name was written in large letters as chair of a Transporter development meeting, the next it was hastily scored out and replaced in little more than pencil by that of a new man, ex-Ford boss, Toni Schmücker. Although concerned about Leiding's seeming ability to squander Volkswagen's hard-earned cash, and intrinsically hostile to him thanks to his lack of diplomacy, at least the supervisory board had learned its lesson. Volkswagen's new Director General was no Lotz; he had the relevant manufacturing expertise to appreciate what was required for Volkswagen.

TONI SCHMÜCKER

Toni Schmücker took over what some of the wittier members of the press chose to refer to as the 'Wolfsburg ejection seat' on 10 February 1975 with the unanimous backing of all twenty-one members of Volkswagen's supervisory board. His background was impeccable. His formative working days had been spent at Ford, where he unravelled the art of sales as a trainee. Inevitably the war years broke his continuity of service, but after hostilities ended Schmücker returned to Ford in Cologne, initially back in sales, before embracing first finance and then export. His progress to purchasing manager in 1956 was a further step on his journey to being invited to join the management board in 1961. Following his appointment as sales manager in 1967, Ford's request the following year that he should move to England in one of their customary musical chairs management cycles resulted in Schmücker's departure to take a highly challenging role with the Rhinestahl group, an ailing steel and iron giant, with a diversity of plants and ineffective operations. Although Schmücker had to perform a series of seemingly ruthless tasks, which included sacking one director for incompetence and disposing of those parts of the organization that looked as though profitability would always elude them, his reputation as a diplomat and skilful negotiator were further enhanced when he took the remaining workforce into the jaws of rival manufacturers Thyssen by selling the original steel-producing base to them. Although his own future was secured too, Schmücker felt his main task had been accomplished and welcomed the call from Volkswagen to take up another challenge.

Schmücker's personal charm and his proven experience stood him in good stead not only to placate a traditional and once wholly loyal and now somewhat recalcitrant workforce in the inevitable process of job rationalization when they had the full backing of Volkswagen's politically driven masters, but also to reap the benefits of all Leiding's crucial model development work. Unlike both Leiding and Lotz, Schmücker would eventually leave Volkswagen at the end of 1981 more or less of his own choice, after a heart attack the year before. The progress of the third-generation Transporter to production was less frenzied than if Leiding had still been at the helm, though whether the vehicle's apparent transitional nature would have been quite so evident can only be a matter for speculation.

THE T3'S ROAD TO LAUNCH

Less than four months after taking control at Volkswagen, Schmücker announced in May 1975 that the next generation of Transporters would remain rear-engine vehicles. As the inner workings of Volkswagen, like any other manufacturer's, were then, and are now, strictly out of bounds, contemporary journalists inevitably assumed that Schmücker's announcement was the first move towards the replacement of the second-generation Transporter with a new model. As Volkswagen's archives are the subject of a thirty-year rule, later commentators and authors have accepted such a hypothesis without question. For example German author Randolf Unrah came to the conclusion that Schmücker 'considered the Transporter to have no direct competition due to its particular design and mechanics' and acted accordingly!

Despite the setback of late 1974, it appears from minutes of later meetings that all hope of launching the third-generation Transporter with a water-cooled engine had not been entirely abandoned, although the board clearly recognized that the traditional air-cooled engines might have to act as a stopgap, as this extract from minutes taken in August 1976 indicate:

The space for the engine is designed in such a way that apart from the air-cooled flat-four motor, a water-cooled 4-cylinder, and if necessary, a water-cooled 5-cylinder diesel engine (at a 50-degree angle), can be offered.

Amongst those voicing an opinion at this particular meeting was future Director General Ferdinand Piëch and the minutes record that this was not the first occasion when he had taken the floor:

Herr Piëch repeated his thoughts expressed during the course of previous meetings. He advised that although the design of the Transporter included a lowered floor over the engine bay, installation of water-cooled engines at an angle was not an insoluble technical problem. However, initially this would cause an increase in development costs, as practically every water-cooled engine produced by the company would have to be planned with the Transporter in mind. This would also result in making the production programme more complicated.

The meeting concluded that there was little option under current financial constraints but to launch the third-generation with an air-cooled engine or engines. One member present requested general agreement 'to the planned higher engine capacity of 2.0 litres for the air-cooled engine', while production of the new model was set to commence in January 1979 in the case of the Delivery Van and two months later for all other options. Clearly the intention was the same as it had been when the second-generation Transporter made

DEVELOPMENTAL NUMBERS FOR T3 MODELS	
EA162	Van, Kombi, Bus, Pick-up, Double Cab
EA357	Camping Vehicle
EA162/10	1.6L (Type 1 based)/ 2.0L (Type 4 based) engines with fuel injection or a single carburettor
EA162/02	Diesel Engine (1.5L) 1.6L (EA827 based)

The T3's near 50/50 axle load provided consistent, predictable handling when tested at Ehra-Lessien.

its debut: there must be continuity in availability and the full range of options were to be launched more or less simultaneously.

Confirmation of the decision came in a footnote indicating a range of developmental numbers, which covered each model in the third-generation Transporter's portfolio.

Such was the extent of future planning at this meeting that a further note indicated that the 1.6 diesel engine would be introduced 'at the time of the model change in 1981; that is two years after the start of series production.'

The die was cast, and with the exception of a few months' slippage of the launch, one meeting had confirmed what to date had taken over thirty months to progress. May 1979 saw the press launch, the following month production began in earnest, and in August 1979, at the start of the 1980 model year, the third-generation made its debut. Chris Barber of *Beetling* magazine, now many moons later reborn as *VW Driver*, was one of many journalists 'privileged' to attend the unveiling, and he duly reported the story of the third-generation's birth in the manner that Volkswagen had chosen to present the work of the last six years.

In order to be competitive throughout the eighties, VW had to produce a new Transporter in the 1 ton class. The drawing board was bare: the designers could have front wheel drive, front engine with rear wheel drive (as on the LTs), or rear engine. There were various combinations of engine/drive considered, and compared with all the known competitors from Europe and Japan. The points of comparison were many and varied: space, performance, road behaviour, comfort, reliability etc. Each of the comparisons received a weighting factor, and the result was … rear engined, flat four engine behind the gearbox! But let it be said: that is just about all that is taken over from the old Transporter!

The wider track and longer wheelbase of the T3, together with its well-positioned centre of gravity, gave it cornering characteristics not that far removed from those of a car. This was the big claim made after many hours of testing at Ehra-Lessien.

3

the third-generation
Transporter

Although the most noteworthy element of the third-generation Transporter at launch was undoubtedly the choice of two traditional air-cooled engines, now that the background to its overdue appearance has been fully disclosed, their stopgap nature is clear. Motoring journalists of the day devoted many a column inch to Volkswagen's seemingly unusual decision, while aficionados of air-cooled engines, who had seen the passenger range decimated in the last few years, breathed a sigh of relief, little realizing

what was coming in the none too distant future.

The anomaly – or even anachronism – of air-cooling seems sadly out of place in an analysis of Volkswagen's Transporter for the 1980s. Hence, in the concluding section of this chapter, where the dusty words of long since retired pressmen are aired and were in a large part devoted to engines, air cooling has been strictly edited and only receives no more than a passing mention, as it does in the introduction to the T3 that follows below. The story

of the T3's engines is saved for the ensuing chapter.

Similarly, before launching into the story, it might be useful to illustrate the wide variation in cost between the most basic of the new third-generation Transporters and the top of the range model, and in passing to demonstrate just how many options were available. Below is a UK price list from the early days. The differential between these prices and the prices of Volkswagen's passenger car range was very similar to what it is today.

UK Transporter Prices at Launch		
Model	**Engine capacity**	**Price (sterling)**
Delivery Van	1600	£4,807.00
Delivery Van	2000	£5,218.70
High Roof Delivery Van	1600	£5,347.50
High Roof Delivery Van	2000	£5,759.20
Pick-up	1600	£4,835.75
Pick-up	2000	£5,247.45
Extended Platform Pick-up	1600	£5,106.00
Extended Platform Pick-up	2000	£5,517.70
Double Cab Pick-up (with rear seats and side windows)	1600	£5,575.11
Double Cab Pick-up (with rear seats and side windows)	2000	£6,021.11
Bus Range		
8 seater	1600	£5,874.11
8 seater	2000	£6,320.11
9 seater	1600	£6,117.05
9 seater	2000	£6,563.05
8 seater L	1600	£6,318.87
8 seater L	2000	£6,764.88
9 seater L	1600	£6,561.81
9 seater L	2000	£7,007.81

The Delivery Van as it was launched in 1979, courtesy of more recent Volkswagen archive imagery.

LAUNCH OF THE T3

To set the scene for a detailed study of the attributes, good or bad, of the third-generation Transporter as it was launched, there follows a series of extracts from *Safer Volkswagen Motor-* *ing's* article of May 1980 written by Chris Burlace and entitled 'New (still air-cooled) Type 2 VW is a winner'. Note should be taken that although production of the T3 began in May 1979 models like the Delivery Van and Pick-up didn't go on sale in Britain until Novem- ber, while official and other motor car-avan conversions didn't emerge until shortly before the article penned by Chris was published.

The new generation of Volkswagen Transporters was launched in May last year, and devotees of the air-cooled VW were pleased to find that the broad black grill spanning the front did not conceal a radiator. The new Type 2 remains true to tradition, with an air-cooled flat-four engine in its tail. Despite the most sweeping changes ever made, at a stroke, to any VW model, the Transporter has not lost the characteristics which have endeared it to owners and users for 30 years….

It is easy to spot the ancestry of the new Type 2 … It bears much resemblance to its predecessor but with a strong hint, particularly in the steeply raked screen, of its big brother, the LT….

Inside, the striking feature is the reduction in the height of the engine deck at the rear … and resultant load height at the rear and better rearward visibility … The reduction in engine deck height … has been made possible by adopting the Type 4 engine configuration, with the fan driven directly from the end of the crankshaft, for both the 1.6 and 2-litre engines …

Basically the VW air-cooled engines are unchanged in the new model … It is in the suspension and steering departments of the new van, however, that the most sweeping changes have been made. Gone at last, after 30 years, are the torsion bars which have carried Volkswagens successfully over the roughest roads ad terrain in the world. Coil springs are now the order of the day … Complementing the all-new suspension, is a rack and pinion steering system … Collapsible elements in the system ensure a very high degree of safety in the event of a front end collision. … The large turning circle of the old Type 2, just over 40', was one of its drawbacks and a welcome benefit of the revised suspension and steering set-up is a reduction to 34½'….

The disappearance of the torsion bars makes way for another welcome change, the relocation of the spare wheel, which is now carried on a cradle beneath the front of the van. At last a solution to the problem which has plagued VW motor caravan designers for so many years! …

The weight of the new model is about 100lb more than that of the old, partly due to the increase in size but partly to modifications to the front and rear sections of the 'chassis' and to the doors to give increased protection to the occupants of the vehicle in the event of a crash.…

The new van meets not only current crash safety regulations but also those proposed for well into the 1980s. The overall result of the changes is to distribute the weight of the van almost equally between the front and rear wheels …

The Launch Story of August 1979

Volkswagen's press releases and promotional material placed a seemingly disproportionate emphasis on the new model's heritage. Success, they insisted, was guaranteed when measured against a backdrop of 4.8 million individually victorious ancestors, each of which had undergone rigorous scrutiny to ensure continued technical improvement.

Similarly, the story was that the new Transporter couldn't fail when a proven basic drive concept had been retained while every other aspect of the vehicle was the subject of major or minor improvement. Of most significance both then and in future years was the bold, bordering on blunt, utterance that 'the engine remains where an engine ought to be in a vehicle of this calibre'. While diehards were delighted at this apparent bolstering of the recently rapidly crumbling fortress of rear-wheel drive/rear engine supremacy, sceptics would laugh out loud when the fourth-generation Transporter made its debut in 1990, and others would point out the seeming contradiction in thought processes between the Transporter and the larger and recently introduced LT. Moderates, with no other axe to grind than to believe that products offered by Volkswagen

This contemporary image of the T3 Delivery Van dates from 1981, when black plastic grilles were added to the engine air intake vents in the upper rear quarter panels.

While the new T3 Double Cab Pick-up dominates this press image, the single cab Pick-up and the Kombi are also shown to the exclusion of the Delivery Van, the most important element of the VW Transporter workhorse range.

were invariably more robust than those of the manufacturer's competitors, were consoled in the knowledge that the presentation of the rear-mounted engine had been amended. Volkswagen's press office banner headlined the story that the engines were sited both lower in the skeleton of the vehicle and were flatter in their nature – in true suitcase style. Like many a body before and after them charged with the task of developing sales, the press department adapted the facts to build more of a story, so the previous developments of the suitcase 1700, then the 1800 and most notably the 2.0-litre engines introduced in the second-generation Transporter were conveniently overlooked. The truth of the matter was that the compressed nature of the engines fitted to the T3 was only new in the context of the 1600.

The big story to sell was of the height of the loading floor above the engine being much lower than that of the previous generation, offering a distinct advantage to more than simply the punier members of Volkswagen's buying fraternity. The pummelling of the engine headline laid the road clear to

proclaim the merits of a larger tailgate – which owners could shelter under when necessary – and, crucially, ensured near waist-level loading.

From such a platform facts and figures flowed with consummate ease. An improvement in space availability in the Delivery Van was trumpeted – an

additional 24cu ft (0.7cu m) gained through the twofold measures of increasing the width of the vehicle generally and lowering the main loading area floor. Quick as a flash to head off any potential criticism of bloating or bulk, it was added that the T3 was as 'easy to park as ever it was', while a

Volkswagen's UK press department added the following caption to this image of the new T3 Pick-up. 'The Volkswagen one ton single cab Pick-up, available with a 1.6 and a 2 litre engine, has a load space of 50.6 sq ft and a payload of 2,360 lbs on the 1.6 version'.

multi-storey car park was no obstacle and a domestic garage no hindrance, because the overall height of the T3 remained the same. The turning circle was tighter as a direct result of an infallible combination of a wider track and longer wheelbase. Road-holding was effectively dismissed in one simple, but incredibly effective sentence. Once again referencing wider track as a pivotal factor in the production of both neutral steering and good camber, the selling crux balanced on a 'rear engine, rear wheel drive low centre of gravity and perfectly balanced axle weight, ensur[ing] a firm grip and safety on any type of road – laden, partly laden or empty'. Such was the thoroughness of the press and public relations work that even the relative triviality of a wider sliding door affording easier access for both passengers and loading bay was given due prominence.

The smoothly flowing cascade of reasons for buying the new Transporter ended with the assertion that the interior had been transformed. The ingredients of a thoroughly modern dashboard, an alleged plethora of instrumentation and better all-round visibility each contributed to a recipe

for a 'family saloon' rather than a glorified commercial vehicle.

SPECIFICATION AT LAUNCH

Just as had been the case for many years, when the time came to launch the T3 Volkswagen at home and abroad issued its dealers and sales force with detailed guides to the attributes and particular features of each model in the range. Yearly updates were readily available, so the advent of a new model led to a particularly healthy crop of reading matter for all involved with its promotion. Would-be purchasers of a T3 were presented with a glossy brochure, carefully written by skilled copywriters with a handle on the craft of marketing, backed up by specialist photographers who knew how to present the least glamorous of models in a favourable light, while Volkswagen's sales force had much more at their fingertips. Fortunately, examples of both types of literature remain reasonably readily available and it is with the aid of both and Volkswagen's releases to the press of the day that the T3's specification is compiled here.

The quotations that follow – except

the one referring to weight – are taken from launch or early brochures and have been chosen as testament to the skills of the copywriters employed to promote the third-generation Transporter. What will emerge is that the T3 presented a combination of the innovative and classic VW technology.

Size

Parked next to its look-alike larger brother, the LT, the T3 inevitably looked compact, although definitely not bijou. Here was state-of-the-art design for a new decade; crisp and angled rather than smoothed and curved, slab-sided in preference to the rounded contours of yesteryear, the similarity in frontal appearance between the two commercials even extended to what air-cooled advocates feared might be a grille to conceal a radiator, but in reality was nothing more than a decorative trim.

Placed next to the second-generation Transporter, the new model appeared to dwarf its predecessor in all respects, although, according to figures released by Volkswagen at the time, the disparity in height between the Bay

Although technically of little value, there's an intrinsic fascination in a cutaway drawing of any vehicle. In the case of the T3 the image provided confirmation for all to see of a vehicle with its engine at the rear, which is what all the journalists writing about the new model were keen to illustrate to their readers.

and the Wedge amounted to just 6mm in favour of the older model (1,956mm height second-generation, 1,950mm height third-generation). Without doubt though the T3 was a bigger vehicle; in length it had grown 60mm to 4,570mm, while in turn the wheelbase was extended by 60mm to a total of 2,460mm. This was a clever move, as the overhang at both the front and the rear of the new model was virtually as before, even though budding salesmen were advised to sell the increase in extravagant manner.

> This long wheelbase offers the benefit of comfort and convenience through the greater interior roominess and extra cargo carrying capacity it allows.

Similarly, the wider track, which now stood at 1,570mm at both front and rear, compared to the second-generation model's vital statistics of 1,384mm and 1,425mm respectively, armed showroom personnel with a catalogue of advantageous selling points for the latest Transporter. The US version of their training manual proclaimed that:

> The Vanagon's wide tracks helps lessen body lean when turning and also pro-

vides resistance to cross winds. The benefits here are improved handling and manoeuvrability. The wide track also helps create a more spacious interior, which ultimately benefits the occupants with increased comfort.

A further benefit of the slightly larger wheelbase and wider track was a turning circle of only 35ft (10.7m). This was a distinct improvement on that of the smaller second-generation Transporter, which took over 40ft (12m) to perform the same job. This was particularly useful in America, where comparison with the ill-fated but much smaller VW Rabbit, whose turning circle was practically identical, made the Vanagon feel less like a station wagon and more of a 'large sedan'.

Of most significance in straight dimensional terms was the third-generation Transporter's expansion in width – up by 125mm compared to the old model - an increase which took the T3 up to a palatable, rather than bloated, 1,845mm. Acknowledging this noteworthy increase, Volkswagen pointed towards the demands placed upon them by dealers from Scandinavia and the Benelux countries who had faced repeated requests for more

cab room to accommodate three people up front with ease.

So far, all figures quoted have been general across the whole range, and show the differences between the third-generation Transporter and its predecessor. Model-specific dimensions of the basic range of T3 models are shown in the dimensions chart below.

Weight

As might have been anticipated with a vehicle that was longer and wider than its predecessor, the third-generation Transporter was heavier than the second-generation model, the average increase across the model range being in the region of 50kg (110lb). However, while increased size, particularly width, did play a part, most of the increase could be attributed to the new front and rear sections of the chassis and to improvements to the doors that now gave increased protection to occupants in the event of an accident. Not surprisingly, the marketing gurus had nothing specific to say on the subject of weight. However, and much more importantly, they did refer to the third-generation Transporter's even more careful distribution of weight than had

Transporter Dimensions							
	Delivery Van	High Roof Delivery	Kombi	Pick-up	Pick-up with enlarged platform	Double Cab Pick-up	Bus (passenger-carrying vehicles)
Overall dimensions							
Length (mm)	4,570	4,570	4,570	4,570	4,636	4,570	4,600
Width (mm)	1,845	1,845	1,845	1,870	2,000	1,870	1,845
Height (mm)	1,965	2,365	1,960	1,930	1,930	1,925	1,950
Wheelbase (mm)	2,460	2,460	2,460	2,460	2,460	2,460	2,460
Track, front and rear (mm)	1,570	1,570	1,570	1,570	1,570	1,570	1,570
Interior dimensions							
Length (mm)	2,780	2,780	2,780	2,730	2,820	1,880	2,780
Width (mm)	1,590	1,590	1,590	1,735	1,895	1,735	1,590
Height (mm)	1,465	1,880	1,465	365	405	365	1,465
Load space	5.7cu m (201.3cu ft)	7.6cu m (268.4cu ft)	5.7cu m (201.3 cu ft)				
Load area	4.36sq m (46.9sq ft)	4.36sq m (46.9sq ft)	4.36sq m (46.9sq ft)	4.73sq m (50.0sq ft)	5.34sq m (57.5sq ft)	3.24sq m (34.9sq ft)	
Under platform compartment dimensions							
Length (mm)				1,500	1,500	650	
Width (mm)				1,650	1,650	1,650	
Height (mm)				390	390	390	

This VW UK publicity shot of the T3 Bus was accompanied by the following caption, which suggested a reluctance to lose business through glib acceptance of the latest model terminology handed down from Germany. 'The Volkswagen 8-seater microbus [sic] is based on the world's most successful commercial vehicle. It is available with a 1.6 or 2 litre engine and has a luggage compartment of 49.4 cu ft.'

been achieved previously, creating a greater degree of stability in the process.

The emphasis was on road-holding and how this was achieved thanks to the drive concept. While it was obvious that the driver's weight was at the front – a skin of metal being the only defence between him or her and the open road – what was nowhere near as clear was that the comparative lightness of even the most portly of front-seat occupants was balanced by the relocation of both the spare wheel and the fuel tank to the front to balance the axle loadings. The concept of a load area in the middle of the vehicle remained important for Volkswagen, with the added benefit that the content of a load was irrelevant; the vehicle had balanced handling with or without packages, passengers or paraphernalia.

From the start and Leiding's internal announcement that the T3 would have its engine at the rear, the stability of the latest Transporter was given priority status. The eventual 50kg overall increase in weight between the second and third-generation models was laudable considering the latter model's size. The desire to push weight to the front of the vehicle to counterbalance the bulk of the engine at the rear resulted in just about the ideal 50/50 situation with the front axle taking the same

degree of load as the rear. The German magazine *Motor und Sport* gave extra support to the claims of increased stability through its references to the vehicle's increased track.

> The handling of the VW Bus when cornering is helped not only by the modified axles but also by the wider track and improved axle load distribution, with 51 per cent on the front axle and 49 per cent on the rear. This helps to reduce body roll and a tendency to over-steer. Handling has improved and is much closer to that of a passenger car.

Similarly, the American magazine *Road and Track* told a scintillating tale of the handling that the powers at Wolfsburg and Hanover would have loved to hear:

> To whittle down the side wind problem, the designers increased the wheelbase 2.4 inches, which in combination with the new body shape enabled them to move the centre of gravity to a point just ahead of the van-bus body's centre of pressure in the side view. Although such slab sides necessarily mean a lot of push from a crosswind, at least the change centres that push behind the centre of gravity instead of ahead of it. The result: Wind force tends to steer the vehicle back into the wind, rather than

in the wind direction. To a degree, then, the vehicle tends to self correct, reducing the wind's effort.

With the additional upgrade to generally beefier tyres, there was a general feeling amongst those who took the trouble to try out the third-generation Transporter that its road-holding was exceptional and that throwing it into a typical bumpy, bendy rural road at speeds higher than would normally be appropriate in such circumstances wouldn't lead to any problems as far as stability was concerned. Handling was now more or less neutral; the traditional over-steer of older Volkswagens, commercial and passenger cars alike, was now a thing of the past.

As for the salesman's manual, reference to weight was very specific, albeit with a totally different angle and emphasis, and for good promotional reasons too.

> Special lightweight steel is used in the manufacture of the Vanagon. This contributes to a light overall body weight. The Vanagon's kerb weight is 3075 pounds, about 1000lbs lighter than some competitors. Low weight, of course, ultimately means a saving in fuel, since it requires less energy to move a lightweight car than a heavy one.

LIFE ON THE T3 PRODUCTION LINE

ABOVE: The computer programmed robotic T3 assembly line at Hanover.

RIGHT: Volkswagen was clearly proud of their modern technology as they also provided the press with a close-up of the robot assembly line.

ABOVE: Robots worked at break-neck speeds to complete hundreds of spot welds in no more than a matter of seconds.

BELOW RIGHT: This archive colour shot of hand welding and brazing is suitably dramatic if less obvious.

BELOW LEFT: Inspectors rigorously checked the finish of the body shell before it headed off to the paint workshops.

ABOVE: State-of-the-art swivel frames held the partially completed bodies in a position where hand welding could be accomplished without the operator having to stoop down.

Transporter Weights *source: Volkswagen*	Delivery Van	High Roof Delivery Van	Pick-up	Pick-up with enlarged platform	Double Cab Pick-up	Bus (passenger carrying vehicles)
Gross vehicle weight	2,361kg (5,194lb)	2,361kg (5,194lb)	2,361kg (5,194lb)	2,361kg (5,194lb)	2,361kg (5,194lb)	2,310kg (5,082lb)
Maximum permissible load						
Front Axle	1,100kg (2,420lb)	1,100kg (2,420lb)	1,100kg (2,420lb)	1,100kg (2,420lb)	1,100kg (2,420lb)	1,100kg (2,420lb)
Rear Axle	1,300kg (2,860lb)	1,300kg (2,860lb)	1,300kg (2,860lb)	1,300kg (2,860lb)	1,300kg (2,860lb)	1,300kg (2,860lb)
1.6-litre engine						
Kerb weight	1,290kg (2,838lb)	1,340kg (2,948lb)	1,290kg (2,838lb)	1,385kg (3,047lb)	1,375kg (3,025lb)	1,410kg (3,102lb)
Payload (includes driver)	1,070kg (2,354lb)	1,020kg (2,244lb)	1,070kg (2,354lb)	975kg (2,145kg)	955kg (2,101kg)	900kg (1,980lb)
2.0-litre engine						
Kerb weight	1,320kg (2,904lb)	1,370kg (3,014lb)	1,320kg (2,904lb)	1,415kg (3,113lb)	1,405kg (3,091lb)	1,440kg (3,168lb)
Payload (includes driver)	1,041kg (2,290lb)	990kg (2,178lb)	1,041kg (2,290lb)	945kg (2,079lb)	955kg (2,101lb)	870kg (1,914lb)

The weight chart above summarizes the various weights attributed to, or permissible for, the third-generation Transporter.

'Giving Greater Visibility'

The biggest story when the second-generation Transporter had been launched some twelve years earlier had unquestionably been the considerable increase in the size of its windscreen. The antiquated split screens of the first-generation Transporter had been replaced by a panoramically proportioned single sheet of glass that was to epitomize the new model and earn it the nickname of the Bay. Now, with the debut of the third-generation Transporter, the increase in glass sizes extended to each and every window.

Although this time round the size of the window glass in general played second fiddle to other features, of the windows, the windscreen naturally received the greatest coverage once again. Not only was it 21 per cent larger than it had been previously, but it also extended further into the roof space, and the Transporter's generally less curvaceous, or perhaps more aptly, its deliberately angled, rearward-sloping, profile was more advantageous than that of the preceding model in terms of aerodynamics, allowing smoother airflow over both the sides and the top of the bodywork.

To put the increased size of the windscreen into perspective, the previous increase had amounted to 27 per cent, of which a reasonable amount could be attributed to the fact that there was no longer a central rib of metal, which necessarily ate into the visibility offered to both the driver and front seat passengers. However, the all-encompassing T3's salesman's bible even went as far as to suggest that the third-generation's frontal profile contributed to lower fuel costs.

The … sharply angled windshield helps give … a distinctive and functional profile. The angled windshield was developed to meet definite aerodynamic specifications dictated by rigid wind-tunnel testing. As a result, the Vanagon offers a lowered resistance to headwinds. Its drag coefficient, which measures wind resistance, is a low 0.44. A tangible benefit of the … aerodynamic design is good fuel economy …

A particularly eager press release even went so far as to advise journalists that although the width of the third-generation Transporter was up by some 7 per cent on its predecessor, the wind resistance was more or less the same, which meant that the specific resistance (Cw) had been reduced by an equivalent amount.

With a 24 per cent increase in the cab side windows and a more modest 10 per cent boost to the dimensions of the remaining glasswork, excluding that in the substantial rear tailgate, the brochure writers could write of 'large windows' providing 'superb visibility all round', which in turn made for 'a bright and pleasant atmosphere'.

Mention should also be made here of the knock-on effects of a slightly larger wheelbase, as just with the second-generation Transporter compared to its predecessor, the sliding door and cab doors were bigger, making loading and driver and passenger access easier.

The North American version of the T3 was known as the Vanagon. This black and white US press image shows the top-of-the-range Vanagon Bus L with the extra-cost addition of alloy wheels.

'The Floor Height in the Rear has Been Significantly Reduced'

All other increases in glass sizes, however, paled into insignificance compared to the massive 92 per cent jump in the overall glass coverage in the third-generation Transporter's unprecedentedly large tailgate. Yet the near doubling of the glass size wasn't a headline grabber; that fate was reserved for the tailgate itself and not all news stories were entirely complimentary towards the latest design.

To the amusement of more cynical enthusiasts and others with good knowledge of the earliest of Transporters, Volkswagen's latest offering in some ways bore a remarkable resemblance at its rear end to the very earliest of the first-generation models, the so-called 'barn-door' Transporters built before March 1955; these vehicles had a colossal engine compartment lid that gave the easiest possible access to the tiny and extremely easy-to-work-on 25PS air-cooled engine. Of course, having such an unwieldy engine lid denied admittance to the main load area of the

van, and access had to be through the side doors instead. In direct contrast, the T3's still traditionally top hinged, but now thankfully easier-to-manage tailgate (due to the presence of two gas-filled struts), opened up the rear of the vehicle in a way that no previous Transporter had done, a feature that should have been generally applauded if it wasn't for one near inexcusable downside to the design: with a tailgate measuring 980mm tall by 1,540mm at its widest point there was little or no room left for an engine lid cover. (By way of comparison, the second-generation Transporter's tailgate was 730mm tall by 1,230mm wide.)

Volkswagen's designers had gone full circle – from massive engine lid and no load access to generously proportioned tailgate comparable to those offered by front-engined rivals, and no engine lid. Bluntly, Volkswagen had compromised on access to the engine to stave off the competition when it came to ease of load access. Admittedly, oil levels could be checked by means of a small flap under the rear licence plate, which, when pulled open, revealed the dip-

stick. Volkswagen even made sure that the filler neck would slide up to make the sometimes messy job of topping up the oil from a can easier.

Nevertheless, routine servicing and certainly more major work demanded the tailgate should be open to the elements and that whatever covered the platform above the engine – rubber or carpet – be removed so that a trapdoor-style arrangement could be revealed; which, when somewhat laboriously unfastened, finally gave access to the engine in its full glory. Woe betide the hapless owner if a mechanical defect occurred when the vehicle was fully laden. Undoubtedly under such circumstances the Pick-up was the best model to work on.

In reality the drawback of more restricted access to the engine compartment, in itself only made possible by the compressed style of the engines, was more than compensated for by the increased ease of loading goods. The platform above the engine – in effect the main loading area of the passenger-carrying versions of the Transporter – was now 145mm (5.7in) lower

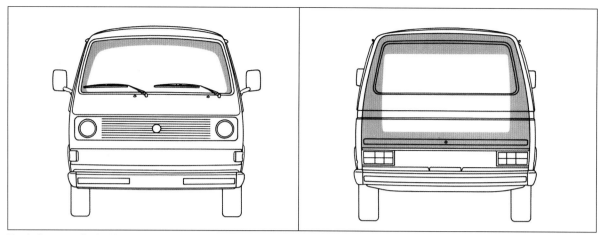

Total glass area in the Vanagon is 22% larger than in the old VW Bus. The spacious rear hatch opening is 75% larger.

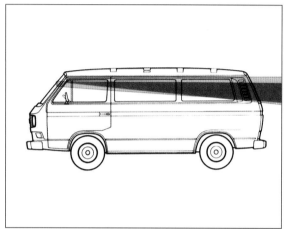

The 50% larger rear window provides a full view of the road behind.

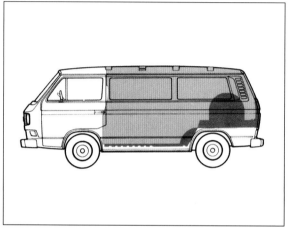

By lowering the floor and engine compartment, interior capacity has been increased by 40%.

ABOVE: *Volkswagen's PR department prepared outline drawings and captions to illustrate the improvements achieved through the design of the T3.*

BELOW: *Sales material for the Vanagon was decidedly more inspired than that produced for European markets. Here is the Vanagon GL as depicted on the back and front cover of a 1983 model year brochure.*

than on the second-generation model, while the volume over the engine available for stowage was increased by 40 per cent. Paul Harris, writing in *Beetling*, pointed out when test driving the T3 that it was 'possible to store suitcases upright without obscuring visibility from the rear window. There is … space enough in the rear for eight good size cases … plus room for many bits and pieces.'

Volkswagen of America went one stage further, illustrating how a box measuring 45in wide by 34in high by 25in deep (1,143mm by 864mm by 635mm) would fit easily behind the third seat. A different way of looking at carrying capacity was simply to measure the cubic area over the engine, which Volkswagen of America duly did, producing a figure of 1.4cu m (49.7cu ft), or with the rear bench down, an 'unbelievable' 2.6cu m (92.9cu ft). Finally, never missing a possible marketing angle, Volkswagen noted that the size of the tailgate offered 'protection from the elements' when loading, thus making piling in the luggage in the rain altogether a less frustrating experience.

The main load or passenger floor was also lower than it had been previously and to the substantial tune of 100mm (4in). The most important benefit of this was that it meant loading volume could be increased without having to resort to raising the roofline. Furthermore, the lower floor line made access much easier for passengers, while less effort was required to heave bulky or heavy objects into the Delivery Van or partially stripped-out Bus models. One or two commentators even mentioned the advantage of a reduction in the height of the floor level in terms of the consequent lowering of the centre of gravity, but this was a more minor consideration.

Technical Details

Most agree that despite Volkswagen's decision to retain a traditional position for a classic flat-four engine, by placing it at the rear of the vehicle over the driving wheels and behind the gearbox that, with one other exception, is more or less where continuity ended. That other exception was the body/chassis unit, which, as with the two previous

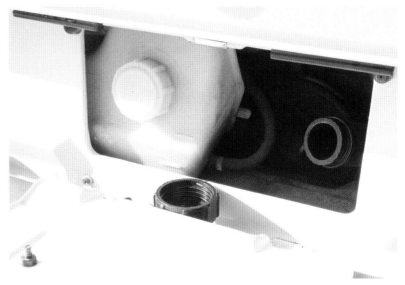

Volkswagen's ingenious flap under the rear licence plate ensured that oil levels could be checked without taking luggage off the shelf above the engine.

This somewhat suspect press image of the T3's luggage compartment was taken to illustrate the extra space gained by lowering the height of the engine compartment.

generations, was of unitary construction, with the body shell being welded directly to the frame that formed the basics of a chassis. This in turn retained the long-established principle of twin box-section longitudinal members, supplemented by cross-members and outriggers which were welded to the floor panels, their job being to both support and strengthen the construction. In line with advances made during the lifetime of the second-generation Transporter, the new model was generally well in advance of safety regulations, with crash zones both at the front and rear, but this is a subject to return to.

Sadly, although time and money had been spent on the aerodynamics of the vehicle generally, no consideration had been given to the all-important underside of the vehicle. In fairness to Volkswagen, few if any other manufacturers had extended their own design techniques to this area of the vehicle either.

Also retained was the style of the construction of most of the body panels. In a nutshell, most consisted of a single skin of metal which clung limpet-like to an inner framework. A glance at the interior of a Delivery Van, inevitably bereft of much of the trimming associated with passenger-carrying vehicles in the range, reveals this to perfection. Similarly, the floor of the load or passenger-carrying area, the cab and the panel over the engine bay, were single-skinned, but the metal was corrugated to add necessary strength. As something of a relevant aside, the practice of fitting the Pick-up's steel platform with wooden battens was also continued, partly for the protection such items afforded, but also for ease of loading.

Suspension and Steering
Radically different was the third-generation's suspension arrangements. It was inevitable that the famous torsion bar springing, patented by Ferdinand Porsche as long ago as 1931 and used by him in his design for the Beetle and adopted by Nordhoff for the first-generation Transporter, should go. Despite their tough and eminently durable nature, plus the excellent ride comfort they afforded, torsion bars were expensive to manufacture and, as they were housed in hefty steel tubes, took up too much space for a thoroughly modern design. With the introduction of the Passat, Golf and Polo, Volkswagen's passenger range had abandoned torsion bar technology in favour of coil springs. The Transporter simply followed suit.

While a salesman worth his salt would wish to be completely au fait with the technicalities of the T3's suspension, Volkswagen appear to have assumed that the buying public were satisfied with a few simple technical phrases, an assurance that the costs involved in updating the traditional specification were well worth it, and reference to the T3's time at its state-of-the art testing ground at Ehra-Lessien. This seems rather patronizing, so what follows has a two-fold purpose. First and foremost, following the new model's move away from the Volkswagen enthusiast's comfort zone of torsion bar suspension, the new arrangements are explained comprehensively. Secondly, this knowledge is revealed through the words specifically written to train Volkswagen of America's salesmen, thus affording a rare opportunity to enter territory normally kept under strict lock and key by Volkswagen and any other manufacturer.

The training manual prose at first sight appears quite laboured, but a re-read proves it to be informative and, at best, inspirational, at least with regard to the T3's rear suspension. With reference to the front, the text is less convincing. Nevertheless, few could claim not to understand T3 suspension technology after such intensive 'training'.

The [Vanagons] … offer a smooth, comfortable, 'passenger-car' ride. The ride is an improvement both over that offered by other van-type wagons and over that previously offered by the … [Volkswagen]. A great deal of thought and engineering expertise have gone into the design of the suspension system which makes such a ride possible.

The use of fully independent suspension in the Vanagon is the prime source of the smooth ride. All four wheels are suspended independently. The movement in one wheel – as it hits a bump or pothole for example – will not directly affect the other wheels. Passengers ride in greater comfort, due to the smooth ride. The system also offers the driver better control over the vehicle. It is ordinarily offered only on more expensive, performance-orientated automobiles, such as Porsche, BMW, or Mercedes Benz.

A double jointed axle is the most prominent feature in the rear suspension. It allows for fully independent suspension of the (rear) drive wheels. The final drive is connected by constant velocity joints to half-axles, through which power is delivered to the drive wheels. Semi-trailing arms help locate the rear wheels in relation to the vehicle's body. When the Vanagon hits a bump, the wheel is quickly returned to the road, for a more even ride and better tracking. Progressively wound coil springs also serve to absorb the impact of bumps. Spring vibrations are dampened by telescopic shock absorbers. All this engineering results in the benefits of comfort, manoeuvrability and performance.

The technology can be summarized thus: at the rear of the T3 semi-trailing arms in combination with progressive coil springs and double-acting shock absorbers were the effective and essentially sophisticated components of the vehicle's suspension system.

The front suspension uses two 'A' arms, upper and lower control arms, to suspend each front wheel independently. Again, coil springs are used to absorb impact; telescopic shock absorbers dampen spring vibrations.

Due to its abbreviated nature, the explanation in the salesman's manual relating to the front suspension is less clear. Equally succinct, it is perhaps clearer to mention the combination of unequal length control arms, progressive coil springs, telescopic shock absorbers and an anti-roll bar. The

The T3's front suspension and steering illustrated in suitably cute diagrammatic form.

associated selling points of the T3's all-new suspension follow.

> The suspension system works together with other design elements to offer specific Vanagon advantages. For example, because it is space efficient, the suspension system makes more interior room available for use. With the weight of the engine over the rear drive wheels, and the wide track found on both front and rear, the Vanagon offers superb traction on all road surfaces. And the rear suspension design results in low unsprung weight, for better road-holding and longer shock absorber life.

One advantage of the new suspension system has already been implied, while a second has already been outlined. To reiterate the latter, it would have been impossible to relocate the spare wheel to its new position if torsion bars had been a part of the third-generation Transporter's make-up, while the new and more compact form of suspension, epitomized by the use of short 'Miniblock' units at the rear so as not to intrude too far into the available load space, contributed to a general feeling of roominess, brought about principally by the vehicle's increased width and lower floor levels.

To complement the new suspension set-up, Volkswagen turned to rack and pinion steering, a system that the salesman's manual described as 'the most direct steering system available.' Just in case a dealership lacked the technical know-how to describe the beneficial aspects of such a system a technical copywriter was drafted to reveal all.

> The system's operation is quite simple: as the steering column is turned, a circular pinion gear at the base of the steering column engages a horizontal rack to turn the vehicle's wheels. Because the gears mesh directly, the driver has quick, precise control of the steering. Such control offers performance benefits and some safety advantages, since the driver can react quickly to avoid a pedestrian or pothole.

An added benefit of the combination of the innovative suspension system and the rack and pinion steering sys-

The rear suspension of the T3 is comprehensively illustrated in these two images.

tem (new to the Transporter, but already in widespread use across other models in the Volkswagen range of the late 1970s) was the reduction in the turning circle. Whereas the second-generation Transporter was criticized for the 12m+ (40ft+) or so required, the turning circle for the new model was reduced to no more than 10.5m (35ft).

That the two-spoke steering wheel was more upright, in what might be termed 'car' rather than 'commercial vehicle' fashion, is not very relevant here, but its connection to the rack and pinion arrangement is. From the wheel, a steering rod led back to the rack and pinion arrangement via a two-section column to a bevel box. Collapsible elements throughout guaranteed a notable safety level in the unfortunate event of a front-end collision.

Brakes

In keeping with the practice established during the second-generation Transporter's reasonably lengthy run, the latest generation featured disc brakes at the front and drums on the rear wheels. As may have been anticipated, given that it was a heavier vehicle, an upgrade had taken place and the dual-circuit hydraulics featured

278mm discs, with either Girling or Teves double-piston fixed callipers and 252mm diameter single leading shoe drums. A servo was added to the package when the vehicle was endowed with the 2.0 litre engine, but not for versions with a 1600 engine. As with the second-generation models, the dual-circuit arrangement wasn't diagonal from face to rear but rather front and back, with the emphasis being placed firmly on the front circuit, the rear one playing a secondary role. Thanks to the inclusion of a pressure regulator dependent on retardation on the rear circuit, there was considerably less chance that the wheels would lock when hard braking occurred.

Wheels and Tyres

Linking neatly to wheels and tyres from brakes, the third-generation Transporter simply inherited its predecessor's five bolt $5\frac{1}{2}$J × 14 perforated wheels. Likewise there wasn't a great deal of change when it came to tyres, for as yet Volkswagen hadn't rid itself completely of cross-ply tyres. Reserving judgement on the 1.6-litre engine for another time, it is sufficient to note here that all but the Bus L fitted with such a

A special team checked the wheel alignment of each T3 as it approached completion.

power unit had wheels shod with 7.00 × 14 8PR cross-ply tyres. The final years of second-generation Transporter production had seen use made of the same cross-ply tyres on all 1600 models except the Microbus L and the 1.2 Ton Delivery Van, which were allocated 185R 14C radials. All third-generation Transporters endowed with the meatier 2.0-litre engine benefited from radials. For the record, these were rated in the brochures as 185SR 14 reinforced. The only previous generation model with a 2.0-litre engine to have been offered with tyres of this

specification was the top-of-the range Micro Bus L, the rest being allocated the less robust 185R 14C radials.

Gearbox and Clutch

Divorced from its engine, which will be covered in the next chapter, the gearbox somehow appears to be stranded in splendid isolation. There is little to say about its make-up, insofar as its ribbed alloy casing was to Volkswagen's tradition design; but despite the gearbox's longevity, devotees of the marque were disappointed

and rival manufacturers delighted because the new Transporter lacked a fifth gear, an overdrive option, and, as a result, fuel consumption suffered. Most, if not quite all, of Volkswagen's rivals were offering five-speed boxes as standard. An average fuel consumption of 20mpg was not particularly good news as the eighties dawned, and just possibly the more cost-conscious, long-term buyers of Volkswagen's Transporter models might have been tempted elsewhere – that is, of course, if they could find comparable build quality.

A single dry-plate clutch was fitted in all manual models; although in the case of the 1600 engine Transporter it measured 215mm in diameter and was operated via a cable, while the 228mm diameter version used in conjunction with the 2.0-litre engine was hydraulically operated.

Gear ratios for the manual boxes are best expressed in a convenient chart, which also includes a column for the automatic box (which could only be specified, at extra cost, in conjunction with the 2.0-litre engine).

While the American market lapped up the three-speed automatic Vanagon, despite the somewhat primitive nature of Volkswagen's torque converter technology in comparison to the offerings coming forth from Detroit, European owners largely steered clear of the slightly clunky and even thirstier auto box. And the Vanagon handbook reference to 'the driver of an automatic transmission Vanagon' being able to 'retain the sporty feel of a manual transmission' does seem open to claims of exaggeration at best and downright deception at worst.

Safety

With the exception of the US market, where the activities of one Ralph Nader, succinctly described by a former vice president of corporate relations for VW of America, Arthur Railton, as a self-styled 'knight in armour … batt[ling] against what he perceived to be the indifference of the industry to highway safety', had brought restrictive state legislation into play with a vengeance, in 1979 the world hadn't gone health and safety mad. For Volkswagen it would be the start of the 1990s before reams of brochure space were allocated to safety considerations as key selling points for each latest model. Perhaps, then, it was with an eye to the US market that the third-generation passengers and driver were cocooned in a vehicle somewhat ahead of its time. At the third-generation Transporter's launch Volkswagen chose to highlight its crash zones by showing a film where a T3 and a middleweight car were deliberately driven into each other. As viewer Chris Barber reported at the time: 'the bus looked remarkably good afterwards, and yet the crunch zone had done its job most

Gear ratios	1.6-litre engine	2.0-litre engine	Automatic
First gear	3.78:1	3.78:1	2.65:1
Second gear	2.06:1	2.06:1	1.59:1
Third gear	1.26:1	1.26:1	1.00:1
Fourth gear	0.82:1	0.88:1	–
Reverse gear	3.78:1	3.28:1	1.80:1
Final drive	5.43:1	4.57:1	4.36:1

Gear Ratios for Different Engine Sizes

effectively … All the regulations well into the 1980s are fulfilled.'

Particularly during the era of the Mk3 Golf, or the first years of the 1990s, a great deal of emphasis was placed on the numerous steps taken to enhance each Volkswagen model's safety, partly as a result of state or community interference – or beneficial intervention, dependent on the prevailing point of view at the time – and seemingly to continue the trend first established with the arrival of the T3 more than a decade earlier.

For evidence of this, you need only look at the inordinate amount of space afforded to the enduring good health and accident-proof safety of its occupants in just about every piece of promotional literature produced, at least for the European market. Accordingly, the chassis or frame was described as sophisticated, while dual-circuit brakes deserved passing comment, with roadholding meriting serious evaluation. However, the nub of the third-generation Transporter's safety advantages were deemed to have been born out of rigorously extensive crash testing. The

T3 was so designed that the impact of a collision was initially absorbed by the front bumper, but if the impact was severe, this transmitted to a deformation element that ran the full width of the vehicle. This element was in turn mounted on a forked frame that included pre-programmed deformation points on the torsionally rigid floor assembly. These were the mainstays of the T3's safety programme, but cutaway sectional diagrams of the Transporter also referred to the safety steering column with a detachable coupling and two flexible struts, collapsible struts under the dashboard and door reinforcements. The overall message was one of a 'safety cell' enveloping and protecting the driver and all passengers alike.

Salesmen in the dealerships were inevitably presented with a similarly groundbreaking package but they were also offered a slightly different tale. Their selling points included an element of technological jargon no doubt intended to convince a potential purchaser of even more significant advances than reality allowed.

Extra Safety All Round

This cutaway drawing is intended to illustrate the torsional rigidity of the floor pan, how the bumpers withstand impact energy, and the progressive full-width deformation element.

All … Vanagons feature a bifurcated frame design to provide safety in the event of an accident or collision. Bifurcated means branched or fork-like. The frame is divided into branches, or arms, which bear against a deformation element which supports the front bumper. This deformation element helps absorb energy during an impact. It is made from pressed and spot welded steel.

The sales material goes on to explain how practically every feature of the Transporter contributes to its enhanced safety. (These selling tips were prepared for US salesmen, and so the specification of UK models, even home-market T3s, might vary a little.)

Unitized body construction … the passenger compartment is surrounded by a framework of reinforcements, welding strengthens body. Dual brake circuits … if one brake circuit fails, another is designed to stop the car. Huge glass area … permits 'all-around visibility'. Abundant padding. Electric rear window defroster. Inertia reel seatbelts … lock in event of a crash. Large marker lights … allow vehicle to be seen from all angles. Left and right outside rear-view mirrors. Inside day/night rear view mirror. Self adjusting front wheel disc brakes. Radial tyres … maximum contact with road surface helps driver maintain control while turning. Hatch pneumatic supports … hatchback won't fall. Halogen headlights … provide 60 per cent more illumination than conventional cars; greater night-time visibility. Rear brake pressure regulator … equal front and rear braking power is designed to prevent over-braking and premature locking of wheels. Electric rear window defogger/defroster … keeps windshields clear and un-fogged. Electric windshield wiper/washer system … keeps windshield clean for visibility. 'Ergonomic' dashboard layout and instrumentation arrangement … easy to see and easy to operate, keep's driver's eyes on road. Large back-up lights. Transaxle design … weight over driven wheels; better traction on slippery roads. No front hood … greatly increases visibility directly in front. Headlight with large dispersion pattern … increases night-time visibility.

Part way through the production run of the T3, the West German Allianz Centre for Technology GmbH, a quasi-official body that was dedicated to research involving the economics and techniques of accident repair for insurance reasons, crash tested seven vehicles in the one-ton, forward-control van category and produced results that were exceptionally flattering to Volkswagen. It was the only roadworthy survivor, the others all being insurance write-offs. It is worth noting that each of the other models was of Japanese origins, a definite challenge to VW supremacy, and a contributory factor in the lower production numbers of T3s compared to the second-generation Transporter. The group consisted of: Isuzu Cargo Van, Mitsubishi L300, Nissan Vanette, Nissan Urvan, Toyota Liteace, Toyota Hiace and the third-generation Transporter.

To eradicate any potential unfairness, all the participants were in as-new condition and therefore without any traces of corrosion, or defects caused by inadequate maintenance over a period of two or three years. Amassed records of head-on collisions indicated that half of the total number of accidents involved overlapping by as much as 50 per cent at the drivers' side, so it was decided that each vehicle to be tested would be driven into a rigid steel barrier which would cover 40 per cent of each van's frontal width. It was also determined that the crash would occur at 35–38km/h (22–23mph). A dummy was positioned in the driver's seat of each vehicle and held in place by the three-point seat belts fitted to each van as part of the standard equipment. The measured

A late model T3's grille insignia: smaller than those fixed to the vehicle's predecessors and in some instances significantly so.

results of the programme centred on the likely injuries a driver would have received in such circumstances and the degree by which the vehicle was damaged, or more specifically, structurally deformed.

The VW not only came out of this exercise as the only commercial vehicle that could have been repaired at a realistic price, it triumphed in all other aspects too. As a starting point, the only vehicle where the doors remained easily openable after impact was the Transporter; in the case of the Toyota Liteace the lock was torn from its mountings and the door flew open as the crash occurred, while the other vehicles' doors jammed, which meant that the only way to get an occupant out would have been to use a crowbar. The T3 illustrated the least dynamic deformation at 360mm, while the Liteace was the worst, with 650mm. Only with the Toyota Hiace and the T3 was the dummy not trapped by at least one leg, but with the former there was a distinct possibility of head injuries, indeed the highest risk of all entrants, while deformation on this vehicle extended right to the rear of its frame. In summary:

In all the Japanese vehicles, the driver incurred a high risk of injury, especially to the legs. The Nissan Urvan proved to be particularly bad … In contrast to the Japanese models … the VW Transporter … has excellent safety characteristics for those inside. The VW … is the only test vehicle where one can certify that the safety of those inside is equal to that of people in a private car.

Volkswagen must have been delighted that their product was superior, in terms of safety, to any potential Japanese threat. The general public, however, tempted as they were by a proliferation of gadgetry and advantageous price points, both hallmarks of products from the Far East and Japan particularly, seemed to take little notice, as the comparatively gentle sales performance of the T3 shows.

'That Touch of Distinction to a Classic Design'

Without question the most noticeable

A row of early Vanagons ready for despatch; as many journalists of the era commented, the plastic grille, assumed incorrectly by many to mask a radiator air intake, was the vehicle's most striking feature.

feature on the front of the third-generation Transporter was the large plastic grille running virtually all the way from the left to the right of the vehicle, which incorporated the vehicle's headlamps and their surrounds as part of the design. Similar in appearance to the grille concealing the radiator on the larger LT model, air-cooled aficionados subjected to a sneak preview of the new model were convinced that the new Transporter had succumbed to water treatment. In fact the grille concealed nothing more than air intake slots designed, as with the previous generation, to ventilate the vehicle's interior. The large grille's introduction successfully achieved two targets; a corporate look for the Volkswagen family of vehicles, the similarity in appearance even extending to the passenger-carrying Golfs, Polos and Passats; and incorporating the previously 'floating' headlamps as an intrinsic part of the design.

Loyal copywriters were eager to note that 'a Volkswagen roundel, the symbol of reliability, dependability, economy and quality, is now incorporated in the grille'. Perhaps somewhat diplomatically they failed to mention that the roundel was much smaller than the badge on the late second-generation model, which in turn had shrunk from the one it had had until its makeover

year of 1972. Considering that in many ways the T3 in old age would prove to be more prone to seam rust than its predecessors, the cynical might even go as far as to suggest that its small VW roundel symbolized the decline in standards from the days of Nordhoff!

Other frontal styling characteristics of the T3 soon provided subject matter for those devotees always determined to hark back to a golden era, imaginary or otherwise. In August 1967, for the 1968 model year, all but the base model 1200 Beetle had been endowed with much sturdier 'u'-profile bumpers. Came the 1972 revamp of the second-generation Transporter, similar technology was employed, Volkswagen variously referring to the bumpers as having been 'strengthened' or, more eloquently, as 'redesigned' with the aim of 'improving passenger safety and appearance'. Incorporating a curve that followed the contours of the second-generation Transporter's frontal profile, much of the strength of the new bumper was gained through a recessed central section. Painted off-white in true Transporter tradition, most followers of Volkswagen's ongoing programme of updates were suitably enamoured.

Compared to the Bay's bumpers, the girder-like fittings on the T3, although equally robust, appeared decidedly second-rate. Not only did they lack the second-generation model's expensive-looking contours, but also plastic end caps suggested a cheap alternative to properly fabricated metal. By 1979, the extensive use of black plastic was

A Vanagon transformed into a Westfalia Camper it might be, but this contemporary press image not only illustrates the T3's single grille but also the extremely small size of the VW roundel contained within it.

becoming prevalent, but somehow black-painted metal was more reminiscent of a cost-cutting exercise. It is worth noting here that the substantially larger exterior wing mirrors were also finished in black rather than the brightwork look of olden days. As the copywriters confirmed, the intention was 'to complement the black safety door handles'.

The irony behind three snippets of copywriters' text, each written just a few years apart, is hard to miss. When the second-generation Transporter was launched, a selling point was that the 'new turn indicators are larger, and curved round the sides of the body'. It might have been added that they were much lower down on the body than on the first-generation Transporter. In August 1972, referring to the second-generation Transporter's changed frontal appearance, the brochure text announced that 'this year we've … raised the indicators, so people can see where you're going …'. With the T3 Volkswagen came full circle, as not only did the brochure text refer to 'wrapround direction indicators', but also to a new location, 'lower down near the front bumper'!

Most journalists were more than happy with the frontal appearance of the T3 when it was launched. Nowadays, with enduring nostalgia for earlier times, the public's tastes have moved away from the angular lines of the late 1970s and the 1980s and consequently the appearance of the third-generation Transporter comes a poor second to the characterful, smiley 'faces' of its predecessors. Despite its somewhat serious, even austere, look, the T3 also lacks the sense of purpose displayed by its two successors. As yet, the appearance of its immediate successor, the T4, hasn't become sufficiently antiquated to make it undesirable, particularly on the later models, where the bonnet was elongated to accommodate the larger engines offered in the second part of its thirteen-year run. Similarly, most would acknowledge the current Transporter, the T5, to be well ahead of its competitors in the appearance stakes and as such streets ahead of the third-generation Transporter in visual appeal.

Another feature of the front of the third-generation Transporter, while intentionally not visible, was of significance. Throughout the history of the first two generations of Transporter the location of the spare wheel had been awkward, intruding as it did into either the cab area, or in the case of most of the second-generation models, the rear storage space above the engine compartment. Firms wishing to create camper conversions found the spare wheel particularly intrusive and some resorted to bolting it to either the front or to the rear of the vehicle. In the former instance, apart from ruining the aesthetics of the vehicle, the spare wheel impeded airflow to the cab, and contributed to more excessive fuel usage. Attaching the spare wheel to the tailgate, meanwhile, made opening it more difficult, in no small part due to the additional weight of an already heavy item. The designers' solution to this ongoing annoyance was to relocate the third-generation Transporter's spare wheel under the cab floor and to the rear of the front bumper. As it was securely housed in a solid cradle, the only drawback to the new arrangement, which had been made possible by alterations to traditional Transporter suspension methods, was that changing a tyre meant kneeling on the floor to access the spare.

As for the rest of the exterior design, there is not a great deal to say. The vehicle's 'wedge' nickname might imply a lack of aesthetic detailing, while the less common 'brick' appendage merely refers to its slab-like sides. Compared to its predecessors, the third-generation Transporter did indeed fall short in terms of the prominence of its swage lines, but they did exist. In keeping with

The T3's wrap-round direction indicators. To some the low location was a cause of amusement, as the second-generation Transporter's had been moved higher on the body to improve their visibility.

The spare wheel and its tray in the position it would occupy at most times.

The spare wheel with the cover clasp released. The black plastic in the photos forms part of the bumper or spoiler of the late-model T3 photographed.

ABOVE: Volkswagen were sufficiently proud of the side view of the T3 to show it in such a pose on the stand of one of the many motor shows where it was exhibited. The Wedge/Brick nickname came later!

ABOVE: The petrol cap's proximity to a seam that is prone to ugly rusting when deprived of its protective filling has been the undoing of many T3s in later years.

RIGHT: The T3's engine cooling louvres naked of trim (left) as was the practice until January 1981 and (right) with black plastic trim as fitted to a T3 dating from 1989.

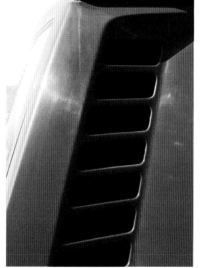

the times, the waist lines were angular to an extreme and noticeable in their proportions, although the addition of a second indentation that bisected the lower sections of the wheelarches and a substantial portion of the lower body was so delicate that it was easily missed. This line on the body was actually linked to a similar one below the turn indicators on the front panel, although was lost at the vehicle's rear, but it is doubtful if anyone picked up on this. On the other hand, the slab-sided nature of the third-generation Transporter's appearance was highlighted by more than a handful of journalists. The author of an article in the American magazine *Road and Track* successfully summarized the debate, both praising and condemning the third-generation Transporter in little more than a couple of sentences: 'The

cleaner, crisper styling results in a better looking van. Some may find that the Vanagon doesn't have the charm of the older VW bus design, but the familial resemblance is there …'.

To the rear of the side of the vehicle, horizontal cooling louvres similar in nature to those of the second-generation, but predictably more angular in the presentation of the surrounds and closer to vertical in their stacking, were much larger in overall size than those of their predecessor. Nevertheless, their work in helping to cool the engine was no more exacting, as will be made clear in the chapter covering the third-generation's air-cooled engines. Initially Volkswagen's design department offered the cooling louvres naked of trim as had been the practice previously, but from January 1981, in keeping with the trends of the age, a black plas-

tic cover was added and for once such an adornment added to rather than detracted from the overall appearance.

The fuel tank of the third-generation Transporter had been moved much further forward, to a position immediately behind the front axle line. As a result, the petrol filler cap was now sited below the right-hand cab door and behind the front wheel arch.

At the rear of the vehicle the only noteworthy feature so far not mentioned was the light clusters, which were reminiscent of the segmented style of those on the Golf and other members of the Volkswagen family. Horizontal and angular in style, rather than copying the vertical and slightly rounded structure of the second generation model, each function could be clearly seen and the cluster served its purpose more than adequately.

Exterior Specification by Model							
Exterior	**DV**	**HR**	**P**	**DCP**	**EPP**	**B**	**BL**
Two-speed self-parking windscreen wipers	X	X	X	X	X	X	X
Electrically operated windscreen washers	X	X	X	X	X	X	X
Full-width black-painted front bumper with plastic end caps	X	X	X	X	X	X	
Full-width black-painted rear bumper with plastic end caps	X	X	X	X	X	X	
Full-width chrome front bumper with rubber inserts and black plastic end caps							X
Full-width chrome rear bumper with rubber inserts and black plastic end caps							X
Front bumper mounted on deformation element	X	X	X	X	X	X	X
Dual-circuit brake system	X	X	X	X	X	X	X
Two exterior rear-view mirrors painted black	X	X	X	X	X	X	X
Safety door handles painted black	X	X	X	X	X	X	X
Sliding side loading door	X	X				X	X
Second sliding side loading door (nine-seater only)						X	X
Large, full-width pneumatic rear tailgate	X	X				X	X
Twin reversing lights	X	X	X	X	X	X	X
Under-body protection	X	X	X	X	X	X	X
Anti-rust treatment for body cavities	X	X	X	X	X	X	X
Hinged front doors with wind-down windows	X	X	X	X	X	X	X
Hub caps (chrome on Buses)	X	X	X	X	X	X	X
Engine access panel			X	X	X		
Under-floor locker with access panel			X	X	X		
Steel platform with wooden runners			X	X			
Wooden platform					X		
Steel drop-sides and tail board with safety bolts and step			X	X			
Wooden drop-sides and tail board with safety bolts and step					X		
Hinged door to rear compartment on nearside				X			
Four side windows in passenger compartment						X	X
Two side windows in rear cab (optional on version without rear seat)				X			
Radial ply tyres (optional on 1.6-litre versions but standard on all Bus Ls)	X	X	X	X	X	X	X
Lockable fuel cap							X
Two-tone paintwork							X
Chrome waist trim with decorative stripe							X
Window trim surround in bright work							X
Grille trim surround in bright work							X
VW roundel and badges in bright work	X	X	X	X	X	X	X

Key: DV = Delivery Van, HR = High Roof Delivery Van, P = Pick-up, DCP = Double Cab Pick-up, EXP = Extended Platform Pick-up, B = Bus, and BL = Bus L

Although the copywriters appeared to imply that such now rudimentary functions as reversing lights and fog-lamps were innovations specific to the T3, this was a definite case of enhancing the truth, as those conversant with a later, more luxurious, second-generation Transporter could easily testify.

'Colour your Choice from our Extensive Range of Exterior Colours'

The array of paint colours offered with the new Transporter was, to say the least, extensive. Volkswagen described some of the new options as 'exciting'. Several decades on, the general comment might be 'very 1980s', particularly so when it came to some of the two-tone combinations allocated to the Bus L. The range available for would-be UK buyers encompassed a full twenty options. However, an element of creative licence racked the numbers up to astronomic proportions. Buy a Transporter or a Bus in Ivory, for example, and that was a single colour as might be anticipated. Upgrade to a Bus L and specify Ivory once more and amazingly, at least according to the brochure, two colours had been selected, namely an ivory roof panel over ivory bodywork.

With such a plethora of colour, unsurprisingly some of the options were available to special order only (those marked with a 1 in the paint option chart). A few paint colours were carried forward from the latter days of the second-generation Transporter and these are indicated with a 2. Others were subtly amended, offering the same basic look but to a slightly altered recipe. Typical of these was the shade by which all three generations of Delivery Van were instantly recognizable, a light medium blue. In the days of the split screen Transporter this colour was named Dove Blue, which evolved into Neptune Blue in the era of the second-generation commercial models, and now became plain and simple Medium Blue. (As a footnote, the tradition of changing the basic shade of blue with each successive generation of Transporter was broken with the arrival of the T4, which kept Medium Blue in the list of available colours.)

Transporter (7 options)
Light Grey[1, 2]
Bamboo Yellow
Brilliant Orange[1, 2]
Orient Red
Medium Blue
Liana Green
Pastel White[2]

Bus (plus 4 additional colours)
Bamboo Yellow
Ivory
Brilliant Orange[1, 2]
Orient Red
Cornat Blue[1]
Liana Green
Pastel White[2]
Agate Brown[1]
Aswan Brown[1]

Bus L (9 options)
Bamboo Yellow/Ivory
Ivory/Ivory
Brilliant Orange/Ivory[1]
Orient red/Ivory
Cornat Blue/Guinea Blue[1]
Liana Green/Saima Green
Pastel White/Pastel White
Agate Brown/Ivory[1]
Aswan Brown/Samos Beige[1]

Exterior Colours.

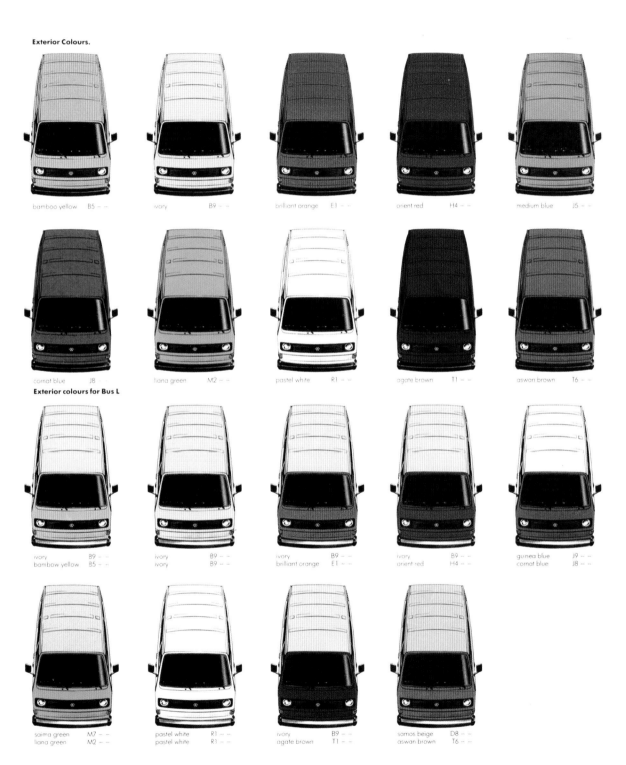

bamboo yellow   B5 – –   ivory   B9 – –   brilliant orange   E1 – –   orient red   H4 – –   medium blue   J5 – –

cornat blue   J8 – –   liana green   M2 – –   pastel white   R1 – –   agate brown   T1 – –   aswan brown   T6 – –

Exterior colours for Bus L

ivory   B9 – –   ivory   B9 – –   ivory   B9 – –   ivory   B9 – –   guinea blue   J9 – –
bambow yellow   B5 – –   ivory   B9 – –   brilliant orange   E1 – –   orient red   H4 – –   cornat blue   J8 – –

saima green   M7 – –   pastel white   R1 – –   ivory   B9 – –   samos beige   D8 – –
liana green   M2 – –   pastel white   R1 – –   agate brown   T1 – –   aswan brown   T6 – –

The rainbow of eighties colours offered for the various models within the T3 range.

LEFT: *Despite extensive modernization of factory processes, hand spraying remained an important element in the production of the T3.*

RIGHT: *A special vacuum device drew off paint excesses during the process of spraying the body shell.*

Paintwork Options for the Vanagon (US Market)

Vanagon 1980	Colour 'over'	Colour 'under'
	Ivory	Bright Orange
	Ivory	Agate Brown
	Guinea Blue	Cornat Blue
	Ivory	Ivory
	Samos Beige	Assuan Brown
	Ivory	Bamboo Yellow

Vanagon Camper 1980	Colour
	Medium Blue
	Ivory
	Assuan Brown

Reference to early Vanagon brochures indicates a somewhat more restricted choice of paint options (the workaday Transporters and their colour options weren't included). All Vanagons were only available in two-tone combinations, although again some might regard 'Ivory over Ivory' as stretching the concept somewhat! Vanagon Campers were presented in single colours only. There was also a slight variation in colour terminology between the UK market and the US.

Those who know that the German firm of Westfalia created the Campmobile out of the Transporter for VW of America will appreciate why Delivery Van and Kombi paint shades dominated this section. For a full explanation, *see* Chapter 6 and the story of the third-generation Transporter as a camper.

Paint – a Technical Guide

Volkswagen developed a reputation for their paint finishes as the Beetle became ever more prominent across the world. Inevitably, as the years went by technology advanced, and, with the advent of the T3, the dealerships were given a refresher course to help them clinch additional sales. From a simple summary confirming that the 'paint application process takes from four-and-a-half to five hours to complete, and involves some 12 to 15 pounds of paint' the following detail was added to make sure all were fully aware of what they were selling.

◆ A zinc phosphate bath is applied to both the inner and outer surfaces of all sheet metal. This bath prevents the rapid spread of corrosion to the sheet metal in the event of damage to the top finish.

◆ A zinc powder-based filler is applied to those body parts that are highly exposed. It provides extra protection against rust.

◆ Next, an electrophoresis primer is applied, using a dip method. The entire vehicle body is electrically charged, then submerged in a vat containing primer solution with an opposite electrical charge. The electrical attraction between the body and the primer solution increases both the amount of primer and the strength of the body between them. Cathodes are inserted in hollow body components to increase primer bonding by boosting the magnetic field in those areas. The vehicle's front end, so highly susceptible to corrosion, is dipped into the primer first for added protection.

◆ A filler coat is applied to give body surfaces a smoother finish, so that they are more receptive to the finish coat. It also provides extra corrosion protection.

◆ The finish coat is hand-sprayed for uniformity and smoothness. It is oven-baked for a hard, durable finish.

◆ … A wax preservative is applied to the vehicle's underbody. A polymer undercoating is applied to all wheels for water tightness. Undercoating protects against such road hazards as flying stones and corrosive salt.

The salesman's tutorial didn't end at that point, as the advantages of such attention to detail needed to be driven home.

The ultimate result of such attention to the Vanagon's exterior is a long-lasting finish. Such durability contributes to a higher resale value, as well as reduced maintenance during vehicle ownership – economical benefits your prospects are certain to appreciate.

Few if any at Wolfsburg and Hanover could have foreseen what the long-term fate of the third-generation Transporter's paintwork was likely to be in so many instances. All the care lavished on paint preparation and the additional steps taken to guarantee longevity were as nothing thanks to a fundamental flaw. While the benefits of injecting wax into the box sections were plain for all to see both then and now, the practice of filling the body seams with a thick, rubberized substance, while cosmetically pleasing when new was a killer as the years went by. Unfortunately such filler is prone to shrink with age, which in turn leads to cracking and even chunks falling out, thus allowing the tin worm access. Without doubt this single defect has made a major contribution to the demise of many a third-generation Transporter, or cost owners unrealistic amounts to rectify.

The Interior: 'The New Commercial's Cab. A Saloon Car Couldn't Ask for More.'

The most important story with regard to the interior of the third-generation Transporter should have been the additional amount of room – to store goods, to make seven or even nine people more comfortable than previously, or to allow Westfalia and others to create more versatile campers. *Car South Africa* certainly thought so in their first road test of the new Microbus 2.0, series 3.

> The enclosed versions – 10 seaters and vans – gain substantially in usable space: by something over 20 per cent, according to our own measurements. The luggage area in the tailgate is increased by more than 30 per cent to 1015dm³ net, with gains in all three dimensions, while total utility space (with seats removed) now measures nearly 5 metres cubed, making this the biggest of the 10-seater models inside.

Dashboard and Steering Wheel
Despite such a hot storyline at launch, the one that caught the journalists' eye and the marketing men's imagination was undoubtedly the dashboard and attributes of a similar aesthetic nature. Chris Barber of *Beetling* magazine

Careful attention was paid to the finish of the T3. The worker pictured was charged with inspecting the painted body shells.

Minor paintwork flaws became invisible in the hands of workers skilled at touching up any blemishes.

'THE ELEGANT "BUS L" HAS MANY DISTINCTIVE FEATURES …'

Although covered elsewhere, a timely reminder of T3 model terminology is called for when discussing the 'Bus L'. Volkswagen cleared the decks by announcing that if a T3's purpose was to be a workhorse, it would be labelled as a 'Transporter'. If it was intended to carry passengers it became a 'Bus'. Within this latter category, if the vehicle's badge bore the appendage 'L', it would carry more trim and extra luxuries as befitted its De Luxe status.

In an age when chrome and bright work generally was slowly but surely losing its glamour in favour of modern black plastics, it is perhaps a little surprising that the top-of-the-range passenger-carrying T3, known in Europe as the Bus L, should be bedecked with so much sparkle to complement what was not necessarily in-vogue two-tone paintwork. Chrome or general shininess extended to both the front and rear bumpers and the hubcaps, while bright work surrounded the front grille, and engulfed most, if not all, the windows, including the windscreen. Considering that in the heyday of Volkswagen chrome, namely the 1950s, 1960s and the early 1970s, even the most de luxe models of Transporter did not come with chrome bumpers as standard, such a move for the third-generation Transporter was distinctly odd. Volkswagen's text also touched on 'decorative stripes', while, although strictly speaking out of context here, chrome protection bars were offered 'inside on the rear door'.

The Bus L in Europe became the Vanagon L in North America. The two images depict the latter from both its front and rear and illustrate the amount of chrome and bright work lavished on the original top-of-the-range model.

FROM TOP TO BOTTOM: The process of adding the sparkly bits of trim was inevitably done by hand.
Never trust a press image – can this really be a regular assembly worker attaching the name badge to the rear of a completed T3?
Before bidding farewell to the environs of the factory, every T3 was subjected to a series of tests on the dynamometer.
Once approved for despatch, T3s were paraded in regimented rows, awaiting orderly dispersal via carefully loaded trains and ships.

The steering wheel and instrument binnacle of the T3, courtesy of Volkswagen's press office, and the dashboard in its entirety, courtesy of a Multivan at an enthusiasts' show.

summarized this the following way in the July 1979 edition of the magazine:

> The third-generation VW Transporter has much more 'passenger-car' type controls than before. The layout has typical 'water-cooled' similarities, and the entire dashboard is very functional. Even the radio is in easy reach of the driver.
>
> The heater/ventilation controls are also new, and 'Golf-like'. The three horizontal levers control temperature, amount and distribution of air. Interesting is that the heater now has several outlets in the rear of the vehicle (bus only), although we cannot at present judge the efficiency of these.

The key point was that the third-generation Transporter's dashboard could easily have been lifted out of one of Volkswagen's contemporary saloons. Admittedly, the steering wheel was somewhat large for the average 1980s family saloon but in both design and appearance the similarity was apparent. Made of hard plastic (effectively padded up when fitted to the Bus L), the rim featured hefty finger grips on the underneath and a two-spoke construction in the form of a central bar with a horn pad in its middle, which was surmounted by a moulded VW roundel. The dash itself was largely made of plastic and angular, in keeping with the Golf, Passat and Polo. Padded in parts and covered throughout in non-reflective grained vinyl, all key gauges and instruments were shrouded by a near rectangular binnacle, whose upper corners appeared to have been carefully sanded to take away any sharpness. More utilitarian models lacked such luxuries as a dash-mounted clock, its

place being taken by nothing more than an apparently blank dial, apart from a small segment allocated to a fuel gauge. As this was 1979, few would have taken umbrage at the thought that a radio was only available as an extra-cost option across the board, while such goodies as a fresh-air blower, dashboard pocket and 'additional' padding were either the preserve of the elite Bus L owner, or once again, items to be financed by the vehicle's owner.

The salesman's manual summed up all the dashboard's selling points with consummate ease:

> Volkswagen's interest in comfort and convenience is clearly reflected in the driver's seat and instrument panel. All gauges, instruments, and controls on the Vanagon's instrument panel are within the driver's field of vision. This makes driving easy, comfortable and convenient. The application of ergonomics – the study of how people fit into a driving environment – ensures that all controls are within easy and operable reach of the driver.

While the language in the handbook is undoubtedly more flowery, the bullet list that follows summarizes all the points the salesmen were advised to memorize:

◆ Non-glare colours and materials
◆ Padding and flexible construction
◆ The important gauges – the speedometer and the fuel gauge – easily checked at a glance
◆ Trip-meter – helpful for long-distance journeys – contained with the speedometer (not part of the specification of most models)

◆ Convenient rocker switches to operate headlights, emergency flashers and the rear-window demister (last item not standard to all models)
◆ Window demister switch lights up when on, to remind driver to turn off when function completed
◆ Fingertip control of indicators and windshield washer/wiper system by use of stalks either side of steering column
◆ Left-hand stalk also operates headlight beams
◆ Right-hand stalk also features an intermittent wipe position for use in light rain or drizzle (not standard to all models)
◆ Most important warning and indicator lights conveniently located between the speedometer and the fuel gauge
◆ Brake warning light to left of instrument panel glows during braking 'if a malfunction occurs in one of the Vanagon's dual braking circuits' (not all models)
◆ 'Benefit of convenience' – ashtray on the dash, glove compartment, vanity mirror on the front passenger's sun visor (not all models)

Gear Change and Pedals

Whether the Transporter was manual or automatic, the gear change arrangement was floor mounted. It was lengthy by necessity, given that this was essentially a commercial vehicle, and there were accusations that the manual version was floppy and imprecise to use, but that was nothing new under such circumstances. As for the automatic, its identifying feature was the equivalent of a 'T' handle by which the various driving modes could be selected.

TOP LEFT: *The basket-weave pattern leatherette-covered seats of the workhorses in the Transporter range.*

TOP RIGHT: *Leatherette upholstery for the Bus models mimicked real leather in true late 1970s/80s style. Decades later, this is probably the least desirable of any of the upholstery finishes allocated to early T3 models.*

LEFT: *The upholstery of the Vanagon L as depicted in a sales brochure to promote the new model. The material colour was named Topaz – the other option in the early days was 'Van Dyck', a darker shade of brown.*

A big plus was achieved with the T3 in countries where right-hand-drive prevailed. Both the first- and second-generation models in RHD guise were open to criticism when it came to the pedal arrangement, for in each instance, and particularly so in the case of the Splitty, the pedals were offset, making longer journeys decidedly uncomfortable for drivers. Thanks to the general roominess of the latest model, brought about primarily by its increase in cab and body width, awkward movement for the feet, and cramped legs and limbs, were a thing of the past.

Upholstery and Trims
Inevitably the specification of the interior varied from model to model, with the Delivery Van and the Pick-up being more basic in nature than the Kombi, which in turn looked spartan when compared to the Bus. This applied to vehicles built for domestic consumption, export to other European countries and even to the United States, although it should be borne in mind that not all markets received all models.

What isn't so straightforward is when, for example, carpet floor covering, cloth upholstery, even head rests, were part of a model's standard specification. The following text relates generally to the UK market, without totally overlooking America's Vanagon. In conclusion there is a summary UK specification chart, together with a list of optional equipment at extra cost, to dispel any remaining confusion.

The headlining was made of plain white vinyl and, in line with Volkswagen's general rule regarding tiers of trim levels, extended to more than the basics in the more expensive models. Hence, whereas the Delivery Van had little more than a square of lining covering the cab roof, the Bus L's material, if not necessarily the padding, extended to cover otherwise exposed metal pillars. Similarly, the cab floor and beyond (when it came to the passenger-carrying models) were covered with rubber matting, while for some countries, although not necessarily all (*see* table pages 58–59), the Bus L benefited from relatively luxurious but also hard-wearing carpet. To clarify here, the

floor of the cargo area of the Delivery Van had no covering; rubber, which always adorned a cab area – the most extensive being that of the Double Cab Pick-Up – covered the whole floor area of the Bus. Interior trim panels were made of vinyl throughout the range and this matched the colour, if not necessarily the material, used to cover the seats.

For many years, the seats of not just the Transporter, but those of the older air-cooled passenger cars in particular, had been covered in a basket-weave design of leatherette. While cloth-covered seats of varying degrees of luxury were standard in virtually all Volkswagen's car ranges by the end of the 1970s, basket-weave leatherette, either black or brown – officially 'Van Dyck' – remained standard for the workaday elements of the third-generation Transporter models. New, though, was a smoother, almost leather-look vinyl, again in black or Van Dyck, which was offered on the Bus. At the top of the range, in the Bus L, cloth was now standard, the darker of the two shades offered confusingly carrying the Van

The luxury of this late-model interior characterizes Volkswagen's attempts, throughout the production run of the T3, to make the top end of the people-carrying elements of the range more like a luxury car than utilitarian transport.

vehicle when it was driven at higher speeds, or in lower gears, but long before the days when air conditioning and controlled temperatures were commonplace as they are today, what owner of a vehicle with a water-cooled engine could deny that the longer they drove with the heater on, the warmer and stuffier the atmosphere became? Volkswagen was either of the opinion that the Transporter turned out enough heat in the cab – and the passenger area where applicable – or accepted that if a compromise had been made to perpetuate the life of air-cooled technology they had to suffer the consequences of any backlash of criticism when it came to heating. Was the salesman's handbook text somewhat over optimistic, slightly over-egging the system's capabilities?

Dyck label, but being supplemented by Topaz, a lighter, almost dark fawn shade of material.

Seats

Volkswagen claimed that the driver's seat had been ergonomically positioned to suit 95 per cent of the population, while the seat controls were 'anatomically designed' – whatever that meant. What was of genuine significance was the abandonment of conventional springs and their replacement by foam, a material claimed to be more comfortable.

The salesman's manual predictably took the story further. The following text was written for Vanagon dealerships, so the use of the word 'bucket' in the context of seats wouldn't necessarily imply racing car style, as it could well do to British eyes, but rather body-supporting, as in anatomical.

The driver's and front passenger's side bucket seats are contoured for good support. This provides the benefit of comfort, and, as a result, the driver is less likely to be fatigued on long trips, and is thus less likely to fall asleep at the wheel. So the benefit of safety is also offered by the Vanagon's front bucket seats.

The driver's seat allows for a great deal of comfort because it's adjustable, so there's no stretching to reach the foot pedals. As a result, no matter how long a driver's legs are, he or she will

still feel at ease in the Vanagon. The lever at the outboard base of the seat controls this adjustment. By opening the lever at the inboard side of the seat, the driver can adjust the seat back angle to his or her liking. Since the driver's is a bucket seat, the adjustment does not interfere with the comfort of the front seat passenger. Of course the passenger's seat may be adjusted tilt-wise and back and forth too. The major benefit offered by the Vanagon's dual front bucket seats is comfort.

Heating and Ventilation

The third-generation Transporter's ventilation saw a quantum leap forward when compared with that of its predecessor, but, as far as heating the vehicle went, journalists and air-cooled engine sceptics immediately raised the age-old chestnut of the ineffectiveness of heat exchangers. Admittedly, much more heat was pushed through the

The Vanagon's heating system provides for rapid warming of the passenger compartment. The fresh air that passes through entry ports at the rear of the vehicle passes through two high-capacity heat exchangers on the engine for quick warming. The warmed air is forced through vents into the passenger compartment.

Heating and ventilation nozzles were larger than previously and more plentiful in number. For some commentators the realization that Bus versions of the third-generation Transporter had 'several outlets in the rear of the vehicle' was of most interest, although whether passengers appreciated the ceiling-mounted vents forcing either hot or cold air down on them has to be open to question. Fortunately for those that did not, the settings could be adjusted. On the other hand, nozzles at either end of the dashboard were effective

While Volkswagen found it difficult to illustrate hot and cold air, the roof-mounted ventilation shots could be pictured. Ever helpful, graphic designers added idiot-proof guide arrows!

Equipment Summary – UK Specification

Interior Cab	DV	HR	P	DCP	EPP	B	BL
Drivers seat adjustable for reach and rake	X	X	X	X	X	X	X
Single passenger seat adjustable for reach and rake	X	X		X	X	X	X
Double passenger seat			X		X		
Leatherette seat covering	X	X	X	X	X	X	
Cloth seat covering							X
Safety belts on front seats	X	X	X	X	X	X	X
Floor fully lined with rubber matting	X	X	X	X	X	X	X
Door trim panels	X	X	X	X	X	X	X
Cab headlining	X		X	X	X	X	X
Non-reflecting instrument panel	X	X	X	X	X	X	X
Door pull-to handles	X	X	X	X	X	X	X
Interior light (door/manual operations)	X	X	X	X	X	X	X
Passenger grab handle	X	X	X	X	X	X	X
Coat hooks	X	X	X	X	X	X	X
Glovebox	X	X	X	X	X	X	X
Ashtray	X	X	X	X	X	X	X
Cab steps in door wells	X	X	X	X	X	X	X
Interior safety rear-view mirror	X	X	X	X	X	X	X
Adjustable fresh-air vents in dash panel	X	X	X	X	X	X	X
Door-mounted, draught-free, adjustable fresh-air vents	X	X	X	X	X	X	X
Heater, demister and warm-air outlets	X	X	X	X	X	X	X
Automatic choke	X	X	X	X	X	X	X
Floor mounted gearshift	X	X	X	X	X	X	X
Two-speed windscreen wiper/washer stalk with brief wipe setting	X	X	X	X	X	X	X
Twin indicator/headlamp flasher stalk	X	X	X	X	X	X	X
Anti-theft steering lock	X	X	X	X	X	X	X
Floor-mounted handbrake	X	X	X	X	X	X	X
Safety steering column	X	X	X	X	X	X	X
Steering wheel covered with vinyl (foam padded on Bus L)	X	X	X	X	X	X	X
Ignition switch with non-repeat lock	X	X	X	X	X	X	X
Heating and ventilation controls	X	X	X	X	X	X	X
Horn	X	X	X	X	X	X	X
Speedometer	X	X	X	X	X	X	X
Odometer	X	X	X	X	X	X	X
Fuel gauge	X	X	X	X	X	X	X
Warning lights for main beams, turn indicators, oil pressure and generators	X	X	X	X	X	X	X
Hazard warning light systems	X	X	X	X	X	X	X
Self cancelling turn indicators	X	X	X	X	X	X	X
Fusebox	X	X	X	X	X	X	X
Access to load or passenger compartment	X	X		X	X	X	X
Lockable glove box	X	X	X	X	X	X	X
Trip mileage recorder							X
Clock							X
Cigar lighter with socket							X
Vent wings in drivers cab							X
Door storage compartment							X
Padded armrests							X
Padded steering wheel							X
Interior load space/passenger compartment							
Ribbed steel floor (not on Double Cab with seats and floor covering)	X	X		X		X	X
Safety belt anchorage points						X	X
Spare wheel (under front cab)	X	X	X	X	X	X	X
Seating for up to six persons (middle bench on guide rail)						X	X
Seating for three persons in rear compartment (optional)				X			
Four fresh-air vents in ceiling						X	X
Additional hot-air outlets						X	X
Interior light with sliding door contact switch	X	X					X

	DV	HR	P	DCP	EPP	B	BL
Side walls reinforced inside (not on Double Cab with seats and floor covering)	X	X		X			
Roof reinforced inside (not on Double Cab with seats and floor covering)		X		X			
Storage compartment above cab (not with full-height partition)		X					
Side panels with trim (not Double Cab without seats)				X		X	X
Full-length headlining						X	X
Additional grab handles						X	X
Additional coat hooks						X	X
Ashtray						X	X
Rubber floor mat (not on Double Cab without rear seats)						X	X
Leatherette seat covers (not on Double Cab without rear seats)				X		X	
Sliding door with inside trim						X	X
Cloth seat covers							X
Folding backrest on rear seat						X	X
Carpeted luggage compartment floor						X	X
Interior trim panels with ornamental strips							X
Chrome rear protective bars							X
PVC trim panels on all surfaces (above waist)						X	X
Engine access panel in rear	X	X				X	X

Key: DV = Delivery Van, HR = High Roof Delivery Van, P = Pick-up, DCP = Double Cab Pick-up, EXP = Extended Platform Pick-up, B = Bus, and BL = Bus L

As a footnote, here are a few extracts from the Vanagon 'standard features' listing produced for the same model year, confirming country to country variations.

'The driver's and front passenger's bucket seats feature adjustable head rests as standard equipment ...'
- Seven-seater (two adjustable front bucket seats with head rests, two-seater centre bench, three-seater rear bench)
- Interior trim available: three colours in leatherette (black, brown, beige) two colours in cloth (brown, beige)
- Floor covering in rubber, black
- Carpeting throughout – Vanagon L package
- Electric window defroster

in directing warm air on to the side glass and clearing steamy windows faster than had been the case with the previous model.

Whatever the shortcomings of the new system of ventilation and heating outlets, it cannot be denied that Volkswagen did their utmost to improve the former at least. Here's the salesman's handbook text:

The operation of the flow-through ventilation system is quite straightforward. As the vehicle moves forward, outside air is forced into it through intake vents at the base of the windshield. A separator removes water droplets before the air passes on to the passenger compartment. Fresh air passes through the driver's and front passenger's door panels, then up the door posts to four outlets in the roof, to circulate through the passenger compartment. Stale air is discharged through adjustable exit vents at the base of the front doors. At maximum operation, this ongoing cycle provides a complete change of air for the driver and front passenger approximately every 18 seconds. Since the system uses the forward movement of the Vanagon to force air into the vehicle, it is extremely energy-efficient. It is also a quiet system, as it is not dependent upon open windows for a fresh supply of air.

Elsewhere the most extravagant claim of all was made. Volkswagen stated that the interior temperature of the T3 could be raised to a 'comfortable' 20°C (68°F) in no more than ten minutes from a cold start, even when the ambient temperature outside was around the freezing mark. Advocates of the effectiveness of heaters based on water-cooled technology must have stood with their mouths open in amazement at the extravagance of such a claim.

Curiously in an age when opening quarter-lights were more or less deemed a thing of the past, the Bus L was endowed with these, immediately improving the prospects for a steam-free vehicle. 'Volkswagen has thoughtfully included vent windows in the driver's and front passenger's doors to offer even greater personal comfort', announced the handbook text. One boast later, the writers added that 'operable' vents were 'a popular feature', which were 'costly' to manufacture and 'rarely found on competitive makes' as a result. Even more intriguingly, Vanagon passengers sitting in the rear of the vehicle were given 'sliding' glass in both the side door and the window opposite. This was not part of the UK specification; perhaps it was only the American salesman's handbook that could justify the inclusion of the statement that 'the Vanagon lets its occupants tailor the climate to their liking.'

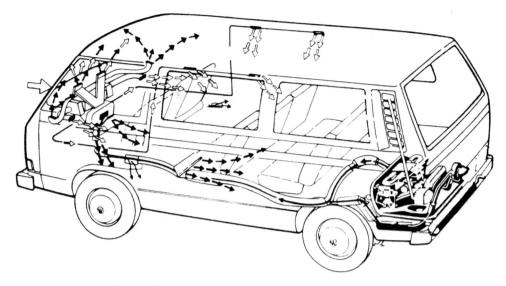

Vanagon salesmen were offered this diagram of air circulation – both hot and cold. The format is relatively crude, the sales pitch particularly effective!

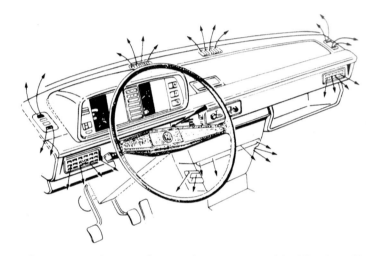

Drawn for the Vanagon salesman to refer to, even the most inexperienced should have been able to work out where the air outlets were on the dashboard!

Noise Insulation

Finally, a word or two ought to be said about noise levels. Chris Barber, writing immediately after being invited to the press launch of the new model, was definitely impressed.

> On starting the engine, it is immediately apparent that the new soundproofing is very effective indeed. The internal noise level is considerably reduced: so much so, that we found that the rev limiter (1.6 litre engine) kept coming in, as we inadvertently over-revved the engine.

Rubber mountings for axle assemblies, improved engine mountings, absorbent material diligently applied to metal panels to prevent vibration, and noise-absorbing roof lining material all helped a great deal, and in their quest to create a quieter Transporter than either of the earlier models, Volkswagen duly succeeded.

Optional Extras

Many additional items of equipment were available on the Transporter and Bus range, at extra cost, and a few are listed below.

All Models

- Laminated windscreen
- Lockable fuel cap (standard on Bus L)
- Heated rear window
- Automatic transmission (on 2.0-litre models only)
- Radial ply tyres (standard on 2.0-litre models and Bus L)
- Anti-glare interior rear-view mirror
- Trip mileage recorder and clock (standard on Bus L)
- Fresh air booster fan
- Vent wings in cab doors
- Head rests on cab seats
- Headlight washers
- Rubber inserts on bumpers (standard on Bus L)
- Convex exterior mirrors
- Independent auxiliary heater
- Radio
- Mud flaps

Delivery Van

- Second sliding door (not high roof)
- Dual passenger seat with half-height, full-width partition
- Various partitions for cab
- Side walls lined with board in load compartment
- Roof lined with board in load compartment (not high roof)
- Automatic side step

Pick-up

- Hoops and canvas tilt

Double-Cab Pick-up

- Hoops and canvas tilt
- Dual passenger seat with half-height, full-width partition

Bus and Bus L

- Second sliding door (standard on nine-seater versions)
- Automatic door step for sliding door
- Tinted windows all round
- Head rests in passenger compartment
- Sliding steel sunroof

Factory-Fitted Options									
Equipment	**DV**	**HR**	**P**	**DCP**	**B8**	**BL8**	**B9**	**BL9**	**Price**
Automatic transmission	X	X	X	X	X	X	X		£448.50
M013 Dual passenger seat (M500 mandatory)	X	X	std	X			std	std	£31.14
M102 Heated rear window	X	X	X	X	X	X	X	X	£38.62
M121 Fresh air booster	X	X	X	X	X	X	X	X	£64.78
M219 Ventilator	X	X							£19.55
M227 Front seat head restraints	X	X	X	X	X	X	X	X	£66.03
M500 Full-width, half-height bulkhead	X	X		X			std	std	£34.87
M520 Second sliding door on right-hand side (hinged on double cab)	X	X			X	X	std	std	£176.90
M544 Upper cab partition with fixed window (M219 and M500 mandatory)	X								£79.35
M560 Steel sliding sun roof					X	X			£313.95

Key: DV = Delivery Van, HR = High Roof Delivery Van, P = Pick-up, DCP = Double Cab Pick-up, B8 = Bus 8-seater, BL8 = Bus L 8-seater, B9 = Bus 9-seater, and BL9 = Bus L 9-seater

Factory-fitted optional equipment was fairly extensive. The factory-fitted options chart indicates what was available for a given model, whether it was part of the standard specification on other models, 'M' or *Mehrausstattung* optional extra code (for true enthusiasts), and for curiosity value, the price chargeable in 1980. Reference to the retail price list for all models listed above should at least offer comparative values.

PRESS COMMENTS

Having earlier used an article from the May 1980 edition of *Safer Volkswagen Motoring* to introduce the most noteworthy elements of the T3's specification, it appears logical to offer its author, Chris Burlace's, verdict on the new model before the opinions of others. Take care, though, and note that despite the very genuine claim of the magazine to be totally independent of Volkswagen, single-marque publications by their very nature do tend to offer a more favourable view of models in the range than other journalists.

For a couple of days, when commuting for a few miles along a local stretch of exposed motorway, the wind was considerate enough to reach Force 6 and the effects of the changes in weight distribution and suspension were amply demonstrated. Unlike its predecessors, this van ... handled easily and

Volkswagen's image of an early top-of-the-range Bus L parked alongside an equivalent late model illustrates how aspects of the T3's design progressed. Similarly, the change in fashion from two-tone paint and glittering chrome to the status value of a metallic finish and colour-coded and chunkier bumpers is obvious. (The early model is finished in Saima Green over Liana Green.)

predictably in crosswinds … On its 185SR 14 Michelin XZX tyres … [it] could be hurried around bends and hustled through roundabouts with confidence inspiring stability. Cruising at 65mph we travelled smoothly and quietly, engine noise is certainly reduced in the new VW …

Cab comfort is up to passenger car standards … The driving position of the older VW commercials was always good but the new van represents a significant advance in this respect. The revised steering wheel angle sets it ideally for a comfortable ten-to-two grasp and everything is to hand. The gear change is more positive with shorter travel between positions …

A great improvement is the handbrake arrangement, with a pull-up lever beside the seat replacing the inconvenient 'umbrella handle' which protruded from beneath the fascia.

There is a marked increase in efficiency as well as accessibility. Stalks on the steering column cater for headlamp dipping and flashing, indicators and wipers and washers, while the main light switch is a rocker unit on the facia. …

Our long journeys on motorways and A-class roads and our meanderings on the byways of Derbyshire confirmed the performance … as being in the limousine bracket. … Some vans can provide an equal or marginally better ride in the front, over good roads, but none can match the Volkswagen when the going gets rougher, and none will provide a better ride over any type of surface than the … [T3] gives its rear seat occupants.

Another Chris, on this occasion one Chris Barber, future author of what would prove to be a definitive work on the road to production of the Beetle and a journalist whose words of wisdom with regard to the T3 have been noted every now and then throughout this chapter, was invited to the launch preview of the third-generation Transporter at Wolfsburg in May 1979. He reported for *Beetling*, another single-marque magazine that one day in the future would develop into *VW Driver*, and it is his concluding paragraph that is of most interest here.

From first glance, the VW company have not forgotten how to make superb, air-cooled, rear-engined vehicles. We were very, very impressed and look forward to driving one for a longer period in the future. It seems, from our somewhat biased viewpoint, such a shame that the passenger cars from VW have left this 'old fashioned' principle, because VW have proved without a shadow of doubt that they know what they are doing in this area, and a vehicle for the eighties can also have the works in the tail. The price is interesting too. The retail recommendations on the home market … are only five per cent higher than before. But that five per cent is, in our opinion, more than justified for this excellent Transporter for the 1980s.

Robin Wager, of *Safer Motoring* and for a good number of years its illustrious editor, took the new third-generation Transporter out on test on the Grand Prix circuit at Silverstone and duly reported his findings in the magazine. As a variety of Volkswagen's contemporary exotica was also ready and waiting with keys in the ignitions, perhaps Robin's opening comment isn't that surprising.

A press shot undoubtedly taken to emphasize the T3's substantial tailgate – affording shelter from the wet when open and, more importantly, easy access to the interior without the need to heave and struggle.

The Cornat Blue paintwork of this twelve-seater Bus, described as 'another new passenger carrier' from Volkswagen, somehow epitomizes the early days of the T3 and the type of vehicle the motoring press were evaluating in their reports.

I was the only person at the event who took out the new VW Transporter. Hardly the vehicle for the Grand Prix circuit, you may think, but I overtook a surprising number of cars in this splendid carry-all, the only air-cooled survivor in the range.

This 2-litre version (like its 1600 alternative) has more or less the old engine

… but everything else about it is new, from the all-round coil spring suspension to the Golf/Polo derived instrument panel …

The old characteristics are still in the engine, which will rev happily (I saw 70mph/112km/h in third) and helped me to take advantage of the van's new-found cornering power …

Away from the cocooning of single-marque magazines and typical English restraint, the third-generation Transporter still didn't fare too badly, although one or two rather unusual assertions were made that the average Volkswagen follower would have been quick to attempt to shoot down in flames. Take, as possibly the most

Although the T3 wouldn't sell in the hefty numbers achieved by the second-generation model before the oil crisis of the mid-1970s, Leiding and his colleagues needn't have worried. The picture shows Carl Hahn, Director General of Volkswagen in the 1980s, speaking on the occasion of the production of the six-millionth Transporter in January 1986.

controversial example, the words of the German magazine *Mot*: 'With its 1.85m [width] handling isn't quite as good as the old model … Parking is easier though, with a 2.0m smaller turning circle balancing out the wider body.'

The American magazine *Road and Track* started off in condemnatory tone in its report from September 1979, as the following extract from the first paragraph illustrates. However, the author soon mellowed and seemed genuinely to warm to the Vanagon. The magazine's words pertaining to air-cooling are repeated at reasonable length at the start of Chapter 4.

The new model is out, and those who insist on something new will be disappointed. VW has stuck with tried-and-true layout … despite the fact that, in Germany at least, VW no longer produces a single model of this genre. Now, is that any way to maximize profits?

Aside from the traditional engine

drive-train … the Transporter is virtually an all new vehicle. … The front grille gives it a strong family resemblance to the LT series … Inside, the redesign is as complete as it is outside … The steering column is more raked, giving less of the bus-driver effect. Instrument and warning lights are set into a pod above a typically contemporary moulded-plastic dash; everything is clean logical and legible … Efforts [have been] … directed toward increased comfort, through the progressive-rate spring-ing and improved sound insulation. … The feeling is much more carlike now, thanks to the new steering wheel angle and instrument panel design. Still the seats are tall and the gearshift long, just to remind us that we're not in someone's slinky station wagon. … Wind noise … is high, but quality is so good that there's no hint of air leaks, much less rattles or squeaks. … I tried a little hard cornering – something one normally does not do with a VW Bus. Sure enough, it was well up to whatever I subjected it to: strange as it may

sound, speeds over winding roads will not be limited by cornering ability. … As for performance, well, not much change here. These vehicles were always best suited to a leisurely driving style. A good deal of shifting is required to coax the bus along, but this is by no means unpleasant …

Motor Trend glowed in their praise for the Vanagon. What reader of the following review could have failed but to ditch their current wagon in favour of Volkswagen's latest offering?

The Vanagon is one of the best utilitarian vehicles ever to take to the highway. Its efficient use of space, attention to ride comfort and sedan like handling position it as the new high mark the industry must strive to equal.

Car South Africa was lavish in its conclusions – sufficiently so that Volkswagen should have considered re-publishing such glowing testimony.

The new model is a remarkable achievement: not only is it more modern, more spacious than the Kombi/Microbus we have known for more than two decades, but our test has shown that its fuel economy at steady speeds is improved by an average of eight per cent – at the expense of a small loss of performance.

There are scores of detail improvements on this handsome new Microbus – wrap indicators, improved mirrors, better instruments, and inertia-reel belts in new housings, to name a few – and all contribute to making it a practical, modern and very pleasing vehicle. It's a bit up-market from the Kombi of past years, but it is far superior in almost every department. Even more than with earlier 10-seater models, this is the VW for people with a lot of living to do!

America's *Pickup Van and 4WD* gave an unbiased appraisal, which led them to come to what can only be described as a glowing conclusion. Rather than regurgitate plus points already picked out of other magazines' reports, the negatives have been tracked down to help throw a little light on a comment contained within the summary, which, of course, is reproduced in full:

What instruments there are, are nicely visible; we're not wild about the headlight switch arrangement however, which is a VW Rabbit/Scirocco rocker-type switch mounted to the left of the instruments. Neither are we wild about the heater control markings … Frankly, even after puzzling over the owner's manual for some time, we never were really certain which lever did what.

The one negative comment we can come up with as regards this suspension system is one which will be important to those of you wondering about the Vanagon's off-road potential … The Vanagon is as poor out in the dirt as it is excellent on the pavement. Even slight variations in the level of the road surface will cause one of the Vanagon's rear wheels to lose traction, and a moderately abrupt bump – or dip – on one side or the other will cause a rear tyre to come clean off the ground … if you're going slowly, trying to pick your way over rough terrain, you'll stop immediately, well and truly stuck in a place where no other vehicle we can think of could get stuck. This, we feel, is a truly sorry state of affairs, and we surely hope Volkswagen's engineers can address themselves to it.

The only other negative in the report related to the Vanagon's air-cooled engines, their heavy fuel consumption and pedestrian performance, a topic to be covered in the next chapter. In conclusion:

What Volkswagen has done with this vehicle, is that it once again has beaten the competition. The Vanagon is very comfortable (if quite pricey), very stable, very well built, and fun to drive. It has a couple of problems, to be sure; what all-new vehicle doesn't? Still, consider how the Germans work; those problems, on a domestic vehicle, might logically be expected to live for the life of the vehicle. The Germans undoubtedly will refine, refine, refine, until road testers can't find anything major to complain about. That, we think, is the way it ought to be done.

Hardly the spotlessly shiny press image one might expect of an engine. However, this picture of the T3's air-cooled engine was taken by Volkswagen in recent times!

4 air-cooled, diesel and water-cooled engines

Where to start when it comes to the engines offered at the time of the launch of the third-generation Transporter will always be something of a quandary. Although the reasons behind the simple reissuing of the power plants that had propelled the later Bay models are known, as is Volkswagen's 'when funds allow' longer-term strategy, the surprise of some journalists and the relief amongst the ranks of the Transporter's devotees, is of greater significance than a regurgitated and no doubt exceedingly familiar specification of past air-cooled engines.

FOCUS ON THE PRESS

Ever loyal, Chris Burlace wrote in *Safer Volkswagen Motoring* of the T3 remaining 'true to tradition' and of 'unchanged' engines, while the similarly staunch Chris Barber, scribe for *Beetling*, referred to the power plants continuing 'in more-or-less the same form', while noting that it wasn't 'very often these days that the Volkswagen Company introduce a new air-cooled vehicle'.

American magazine *Car and Driver* attributed a novel explanation for the use of outdated technology to Volkswagen generally, without naming any specific spokesperson, or even whether this alleged insider information had filtered through from Germany, or had been deliberately leaked by the US satellite operation.

The engine chosen for the job is ... surprising, given VW's switch to and promotion of water-cooled power-plants. It's a two-litre version of the familiar air-cooled flat four that powered every Vee Dub until the Rabbit [Golf]. Volkswagen claims that it would have preferred to use a Rabbit-derived engine lying on its stomach, but because of the flood of orders for the Rabbits, the VW engine foundry simply couldn't supply enough extra engines for the Vanagon. So that change will have to wait a few years ...

Ron Wakefield of *Road and Track* was at best bemused by the choice of engine, and immediately leapt into questioning the viability of what Volkswagen appeared to be trying to achieve.

The new model is out, and those who insist on something new will be disappointed. VW has stuck with the tried-and-true layout, the traditional Boxer-motor behind the transaxle, driving the rear wheels. This despite the fact that, in Germany at least, VW no longer produces a single car model of this genre. Now, is that any way to maximize profits?

With the bit firmly between his teeth, Wakefield set out to demonstrate why Volkswagen had taken the decision to retain the air-cooled engines, showing an apparently remarkable knowledge of the workings of the marque. Whether this was a result of his own detailed research, or came to him from the ethereal sources at Volkswagen of America, or was simply imaginative speculation, is not clear.

People from the Transporter engineering departments ... assured me of the correctness of the decision. They have spent decades perfecting the concept, making the pancake engine durable enough ... and now you want us to throw all that out of the window?

Logical enough, but there is a 2-litre engine in the VW family that's already been converted for truck use: it powers the LT and, in other forms, the Porsche 924 … But here VW engineers elaborate that 2 litres is the upper limit of the Transporter range, and that they want to continue with a 1.6 option for the European and other markets. This displacement exists in their water-cooled line too, but adapting the engine and/or modifying one of the car power-trains for heavy duty use would have cost enough to wipe out the benefits of increased interchangeability for years to come. So the basic decision was made to keep the air-cooled engine.

Clearly inspired by Ron Wakefield's initial report, *Road and Track* returned to the subject of the Vanagon less than a year later. While the July 1980 article heading must have warmed the cockles of any anxious PR men's hearts at Volkswagen, when it came to the engine story Schmücker and company would no doubt have been disappointed that an unclear financial future and necessary caution with the pennies a few years previously was now resulting in the wrong message being broadcast about the Transporter.

Speculation was rampant that this third version of the VW van … would be totally different from its predecessors and would be powered by a water-cooled version of the VW Rabbit inline 4-cylinder engine. But, while VW says the Vanagon is new from the ground up, the drive-train is a carryover and represents the last bastion of VWs built in the homeland with air-cooled pancake engines. … The engine, then, is the same 1970cc overhead-valve flat-four as before with Bosch K-jetronic fuel injection. It develops 67bhp (SAE net) at 4,200rpm and 101lb/ft torque at 3,000, which propels the Vanagon in reasonable fashion considering its roughly 3,500lb test weight: 0–60mph in 21.2 seconds; the quarter mile run covered in 21.5 seconds at a speed of 60.5mph. Clearly, this is not acceleration that will elicit gasps of glee …

Motor Trend somewhat unusually had little to say about the vehicle's engine, preferring to concentrate on all the advantages of the third-generation Transporter over its predecessor, and restricting itself to one often trotted-out remark.

The Vanagon feels spry enough, but when you put a watch to it, the acceleration proves to be well in the snoozer class. Our tests showed the … [manual model] to deliver a 0–60mph run in a lengthy 23 seconds.

Negativity on the whole seemed to have been fairly contained, and while the old air-cooled engines hadn't exactly been showered in glory, similarly the press did not with one voice damn Volkswagen for prolonging their already lengthy lifespan. One magazine, however, was set to spoil the near unblemished story. *Pick-up Van and 4WD* would have definitely been off Schmücker's Christmas card list, almost from the first words uttered in the engine section of an otherwise nearly wholly favourable review:

The Vanagon is a delight to drive – as long as the driver is expecting no more than typical VW van performance. Because that surely is what he's going to find after he turns the ignition key and that flat-four wheezes into life with the sounds familiar to what must be a couple of generations of Volkswagen drivers. … In this day and age of emissions regulations, VW vans have not been particularly long on fuel economy, and the Vanagon was no exception, recording an average of 16.44mpg. Even dropping the low figure of 10.4mpg and the high figure of 19.0mpg from the overall average, which would then be figured over seven tankfuls instead of the nine tankfuls used to get the 16.44 mpg average, the number goes only to 16.9mpg. Now, fuel economy in the range of 16.0 to 17.0mpg wouldn't be bad if the Vanagon was capable of providing fearsome performance, but it is not; it remains a Volkswagen, and performs like one, reaching 60mph from zero in 21.2 seconds, and touring the quarter mile from a standing stop in 21.6 seconds, with a terminal speed of 60.1mph. First gear is short, so gives a good push off from rest; it's deceptive though. Once you hit second, then

third, then finally fourth gear, it becomes difficult to stifle a yawn.

To make matters worse, *Pick-up Van and 4WD*'s reaction to what was uncannily accurate information with regards to the Vanagon's future methods of propulsion was not flattering to Volkswagen's hierarchy either.

That grille up at the front of the machine hints at something other than the old air-cooled motor, 'tis true. We're told, however, that while it will eventually provide ventilation for a radiator, that that radiator will cool an in-line diesel. Diesel power may improve economy somewhat, but chances are it won't do much for the vehicle's performance capabilities – unless by some chance it is turbocharged.

T3 ENGINE SPECIFICATIONS AT LAUNCH

Snippets from Volkswagen's promotional material demonstrate two entirely different dilemmas for the company. First and foremost, in those sparkling days of unveiling and revelling in all the significant advances that distinguished the third-generation Transporter, everyone must have been conscious of how little there was to say about the engines. Secondly, aware of what was planned for the future, how far could Volkswagen's bosses allow their marketing men, their gifted copywriters, to go on praising the air-cooled concept without appearing decidedly hypocritical in a few short years' time?

Of just over a thousand words written about the exciting new developments of the third-generation Transporter at its launch, just thirty-eight were allocated to the engines. A year later, when the word count had escalated to 2,400, the engine allocation still covered no more than five short sentences and fifty-five words.

The drive concept, which has proved to be so successful … has been retained. So too, has Volkswagen's air-cooled engine, renowned for its reliability and durability. … There are two air-cooled engines available. The miserly 1.6-litre (50bhp DIN) or the powerful 2.0-litre (70bhp DIN). They both run on 2 Star (minimum 91 RON) petrol.

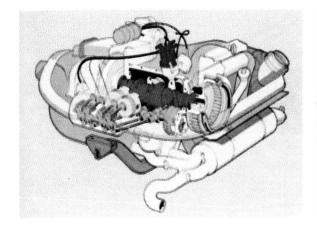

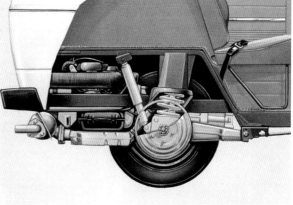

Images of the T3's air-cooled engines were singular by their absence from promotional material. ABOVE LEFT: This tiny and rather badly reproduced outline is better than most. The message wasn't one of air-cooled supremacy, but rather a story of the engines being made 'lower and flatter' to allow more space in the luggage compartment. ABOVE RIGHT: The line drawing – hardly the best for engine enthusiasts – illustrates the point reasonably well and has been taken from a full T3 cutaway drawing.

LEFT: Volkswagen of America relied on a photographer to reproduce a satisfactory image of the 2.0-litre air-cooled engine. This picture illustrates the suitcase nature of the engine better than any other.

Perhaps Volkswagen of America were cleverest in their approach to the Vanagon's engine, for while their collective conscience allowed them to praise the air-cooled motor's heritage, they tended to concentrate more on what had been done to old technology to advance it in the style Volkswagen had once always advocated. This quote is from August 1979 (Vanagon, Vanagon Camper, 08/79):

Volkswagen has always remained at the forefront of economical power-plant development. Take Vanagon's proven, air-cooled, two-litre, flat, four-cylinder engine. Although it has an enviable heritage of over five million predecessors, today's Vanagon engine offers space age engineering. Example: a digital idle stabilizer. It has been designed to maintain constant RPM under all engine operating conditions. In addition, Vanagon's engine is fuel-injected and the ignition system is electronic – virtually maintenance free …

Without doubt, the dealers were given the greatest amount of information in their salesman's handbook, just as they were about every other aspect of the new Transporter. Curiously, there was little if anything about the air-cooled units' 'proven' track record. Instead, space was allocated to listing the things not required when an engine is air-cooled and the additional burdens and cost of fitting water-cooled units. As the people with direct customer contact, it would be the self-same individuals who were destined to look the silliest in just a few years time if, as they must have done, they repeated everything they had been told parrot fashion. Those with a conscience must have been delighted when water did make its debut that at least it was poured into a boxer motor!

The engine … a horizontally opposed, 2-litre, flat-four design, provides a lower centre of gravity for less body lean in cornering. The benefit offered is better handling. By using horizontally opposed cylinders – two on either side of the crankshaft – Volkswagen has ensured both less vibration and reduced engine wear. Hydraulic valve-lifters also reduce noise. In addition, they require no routine adjustments for reduced maintenance and greater economy.

Due to the horizontal design of the engine, combustion vibrations offset each other. As a result, crankshaft rotation is more even, and wear on crankshaft bearings and engine mounts is reduced. The most meaningful benefit for prospects [would-be buyers] is durability, in terms of longer engine life. The design also provides improved performance.

The … Vanagon uses air-cooling, the most direct method available, to keep engine temperature down. To increase air circulation, cylinders are separated from one another and finned. The aluminium alloy cylinders heads are likewise fitted with fins, which increase the amount of surface area exposed to cooling air for more rapid heat dissipation.

Cooling air enters the engine compartment through openings in the rear of the Vanagon. A blower fan is driven directly by the crankshaft on which it is mounted. Direct drive means no V-belts that require adjusting or replacing. The fan forces the air through shrouds which surround the engine; the shrouds funnel the air over cylinders and cylinder heads. The fins on the cylinder heads radiate heat to the cooling air, which is then vented to the outside. A thermostat regulates the direction of air according to engine requirements. It provides for quick, dependable, engine warm-up. This direct approach to engine cooling means no radiator, hoses, or water pump to require maintenance – a savings [sic] for the Vanagon owner.

The technical specification chart is taken from Volkswagen's UK technical data listing as of August 1979. Details pertaining to the last year of production of the second-generation Transporter are shown in brackets for comparison purposes, while further down the technical specification for the launch model Vanagon is also reproduced.

The Vanagon was only available with a 2.0-litre engine. VWoA made no attempt to distinguish between the four-speed manual and automatic gearbox in performance terms.

Even the less than eagle-eyed will have noted that all but the most rudimentary performance figures were absent from even the most allegedly comprehensive of technical specification charts produced for the UK market. The same was true of listings provided for home consumption, while the Vanagon data lacked what to many was, to say the least, interesting information too. Of course, motoring journalists were quick to come to the rescue of fact-stranded would-be buyers, and the reason that such information was kept to a basic minimum soon became clear to anyone sufficiently interested to stroll to their local newsagents. Although America was spared the sloth-like capabilities of the 1.6 engine, even with the 2.0-litre

Air-Cooled Engine Technical Data – UK Source, August 1979

Air-cooled, four-cylinder, four-stroke, horizontally opposed, rear-mounted, petrol engine

	1.6 litre	2.0 litre
Bore	85.5mm (85.5mm)	94.0mm (94.0mm)
Stroke	69.0mm (69.0mm)	71.0mm (71.0mm)
Cubic capacity	1584cc (1584cc)	1970cc (1970cc)
Compression ratio	7.5:1 (7.5:1)	7.3:1 (7.3:1)
Output – kW	37kW (37kW)	51kW (51kW)
DIN	50bhp (50bhp)	70bhp (70bhp)
@ rpm	3800/min (4000/min)	4200/min (4200/min)
Maximum torque – Nm	103Nm (108Nm)	137Nm (143Nm)
SAE	71.0lb ft (74.5lb ft)	94.5lb ft (98.6lb ft)
@rpm	2400/min (2800/min)	3000/min (2800/min)
Fuel rating (RON)	91 (91)	91 (91)

Performance

		1.6	2.0	2.0 Automatic
Maximum speed – generic		68mph (109km/h)	79mph (127km/h)	76mph (122km/h)
		(68mph)	(79mph)	(76mph)
Maximum speed	Van/Bus L	68mph (109km/h)	78	7
	Pick-up	68mph (109km/h)	76	74
	Dble Cab	69mph (111km/h)	76	74
	High Roof	65mph (105km/h)	71	69

Fuel consumption – generic		24.5mpg (11.5ltr/100km)	23.7mpg (11.9ltr/100km)	(21.7mpg or 13.0ltr/100km)
		(24.8mpg or (11.5ltr/100km)	(23.7mpg)	21.5mpg (13.1ltr/100km)

Fuel consumption

With half permissible payload at constant [3/4] of max speed plus 10 per cent

	Van	25.6mpg (11.0ltr/100km)	21.3mpg (13.3ltr/100km)	19.7mpg (14.4ltr/100km)
	Pick-up	25.4mpg (11.1ltr/100km)	21.0mpg (13.5ltr/100km)	19.6mpg (14.4ltr/100km)
	Dble Cab	26.3mpg (10.8ltr/100km	21.3mpg (13.3ltr/100km)	20.0mpg (14.1ltr/100km)
	High Roof	24.7mpg (11.5ltr/100km)	23.5mpg (12.0ltr/100km)	23.2mpg (12.2ltr/100km)

Fuel consumption – official government figures

	Bus/L Urban	17.9mpg (15.8ltr/100km)	16.8mpg (16.8ltr/100km)	19.6mpg (14.4ltr/100km
	Bus/L 56mph	23.7mpg (11.9ltr/100km)	25.0mpg (11.3ltr/100km)	23.2mpg (12.2ltr/100km)

Hill climbing ability

On good roads, fully laden and in first gear	26%	29%	23%

Vanagon/Vanagon Camper Specifications – Engine and Performance

Engine

Number of cylinders	4
Bore and stroke	3.70in × 2.89in
	(94mm × 71mm)
Compression ratio	7.3:1
Horsepower, SAE net	67hp @ 4,200rpm
Maximum torque, SAE net	101lb ft @ 3,000rpm
Engine type	4-cylinder, opposed; rear mount
Cylinder head	Aluminium alloy
Valve train	Push rods, overhead valves, hydraulic lifters
Cooling medium, drive	Air-cooled, crankshaft-mounted blower
Fuel/Air supply	Electronic fuel injection, Air Flow Control (AFC)
Cylinder firing order	1-4-3-2
Fuel requirement	Lead-free only (all states)

Performance

Top speed	75mph
Hill climbing capability	1st gear: 29.1% grade
(with maximum payload)	2nd gear: 15.2% grade
	3rd gear: 8.7% grade
	4th gear: 5.6% grade
	Automatic transmission: 27.0% grade

model the third-generation Transporter was struggling to keep pace with the opposition.

Even *Beetling*'s air-cooled addict, Chris Barber, had little option but to include a condemnatory line in his marque-biased report. For Barber 'the straight-line performance' was 'about the same as before, but on our 1.6-litre bus, we thought it a bit sluggish, the top indicated speed being 110kph [68.4mph].' Fortunately, he redeemed himself when writing of the 2.0-litre, for in Barber's eyes it 'fairly flew along', leaving him with 'no reservations in recommending that latter for most users, particularly for motor caravan owners, with extra weight on board.' Admittedly writing nine years after the third-generation Transporter's demise, when it was clear what could have been achieved, author Laurence Meredith summarized what had been said in the summer of 1979. 'Considering the additional weight of the Wedge, the 1600 was wholly inappropriate. With this power unit, changing gear was a constant necessity and very wearing.' That was in his Crowood Press volume, *Volkswagen Transporter: The Complete Story*, while elsewhere he noted that:

> The 1.6-litre unit was capable of driving the Wedge along at a comfortable, if

slightly strained, 65 to 70mph. But an uphill gradient saw this figure slip appreciably downward and most drivers got fed up with having to change down a 'cog' in an attempt to maintain anything resembling reasonable pace.

The unkindest cut of all, though came from *Car South Africa*, who lined up three of the third-generation Transporter's rivals, incidentally all of which were manufactured in Japan, and left conclusive evidence for their readers of the air-cooled 2.0-litre engine's struggle to keep up. To add insult to injury, the result was published in tabular form; only an inability to read across the lines could have saved the VW!

ENGINE IMPROVEMENTS

When you consider what Volkswagen had in mind regarding the engines of the third-generation Transporter it may appear odd that neither the 1.6- nor the 2.0-litre engines were merely hooked out of the second-generation Transporter and lowered into its successor. Instead, even in the twilight days of air-cooling, at Wolfsburg and more particularly at Hanover, technicians behind the scenes were dedicated to improving the product.

Probably of most significance was the introduction of hydraulic tappets, a first on any Volkswagen, and a move which at a stroke did away with the tedious business of manually adjusting traditional tappets. While some diehards criticized hydraulic tappets for their tendency to clatter for some minutes after first starting the engine, overall they made for quieter running.

Performance Comparison Chart: Volkswagen T3 Versus Japanese Models

'A dozen years ago, you would have bought a Volkswagen Kombi because that was THE Minibus … you are now confronted with four attractive minibus options …'

	Datsun Ekonowagon	Mitsubishi Canter L-300	Toyota Hi-Ace Super Ten	VW Microbus
Engine size (cm³)	1770	1597	1968	1970
Power output (kW at rpm)	68 at 5,000	55 at 5,200	64 at 5,000	51 at 4,200
Acceleration (seconds) 0–100 km/h	21.3	24.2	22.4	33.6
Acceleration (seconds) 1km sprint	40.9	41.3	41.0	44.7
Price (in Rand)	R 11,995	R 11,355	R 12,345	R 12,500

Electronic ignition was the second innovation, a feature that in theory meant that both engines should have stayed in tune longer. The third advance illustrated how the emergence of computers as part of everyday existence was influencing all aspects of life: the third-generation Transporter was the first Volkswagen to utilize a microcomputer as a tick-over stabilizer. 'Digital Idling Stabilization', or DIS, played a large part in stabilizing the essential mixture of fuel and air, resulting in the virtual elimination of the age-old annoyance of the engine cutting out on a frosty morning, or conversely failing to restart when hot, after, for example, a good thrashing on the motorway. Visually nothing more than a small box fitted on the left-hand side of the engine compartment, its additional advantage was a much reduced CO value in the exhaust gases.

Pertinent to the 1600 unit only, as the 2.0-litre was already of such a design, and as a direct demand created from the useful lowering of the loading/luggage platform at the T3's rear, the cooling fan was driven directly off the nose of the crankshaft, while the engine's ancillaries were moved to positions lower on the sides of the block. In other words, the last upright air-cooled engine became what has been referred to by many as a 'suitcase' engine, first developed when the larger air-cooled passenger cars joined the range and specifically engineered to make greater space for luggage in what was essentially a conventional boot at the rear of the car, but with a flat engine underneath. Despite the obvious benefits of this reshaping of the 1600 engine, the more mechanically minded enthusiasts complained about the accompanying 'pestiferous many part exhaust', which was a necessary consequence of such a rehash.

As snippets from the motoring press will have revealed, there was a fundamental difference in the engine specification of European T3 models and that of the American Vanagon. This diversity had emerged during the lifespan of the second-generation Transporter and came about as a result of America's fascination, bordering on obsession, with emissions ahead of the rest of the world. Hence, whereas third-generation Transporters intended for the

European market were fitted with carburettors, Vanagons were fuel-injected. Catalytic converters were the exclusive preserve of the Californian market.

The 2.0-litre European market third-generation Transporters were fitted with twin Solex 34 PDSIT carburettors; the 1600 engine had a single Solex 34 PICT-4 carburettor. Reference to the Vanagon dealers' handbook not only puts Bosch fuel injection into context and inevitably illustrates its advantages, but also outlines its composition in detail.

Volkswagen has … made use of the latest in automotive technology to increase fuel efficiency. The … Vanagon uses air-flow controlled (AFC) fuel injection, rather than conventional carburetion. The system offers precise control of fuel/air mixtures for good performance at all engine speeds. As a result fuel waste is minimal.

In fuel injection, the system's air intake manifold branches to each cylinder. Separate fuel injections spray finely atomized fuel into each branch of the air intake manifold. Because fuel enters the cylinders as a mist, rather than as droplets, combustion is more complete. The timing of the injection is controlled by several factors: the driver's foot on the accelerator pedal, engine temperature, outside temperature, and the volume of air flow past a sensor plate in the intake manifold. The electronic control unit is the system component which monitors injection timing in milliseconds.

The fuel/air mixture, then, is varied to meet differing requirements. For example, when idling, the Vanagon requires a richer fuel/air mixture; at normal road speeds, the mix is leaner; for acceleration and full throttle driving, an enriched mix is used. Finally, the system provides for rapid fuel reduction during deceleration, for minimal fuel waste. The benefit here is economy.

The system needs no choke. Instead, a cold-start valve ensures added injection into the intake manifold in cold weather. As a result, the Vanagon offers easy, dependable starting in all weather conditions. In warm weather, constant pressure on the fuel supply eliminates vapour lock.

In addition to fuel economy, AFC fuel injection improves performance: with

less fuel left unburned, exhaust emissions are cleaner. In addition, the Vanagon offers a relatively flat torque curve for adequate pulling power over a wide engine rpm range.

Exhaust emissions were similarly dealt with in two different ways depending on which side of the Atlantic the market lay, while by definition the catalytic converter fitted to California-bound Transporters illustrated a third variation. Essentially the conventional system involved closed-circuit crankcase ventilation, a mechanism which allowed emissions from the crankcase to be recirculated to the air cleaner. Fumes were directed to the air cleaner via a breather pipe on the crankcase. Here they mixed with fresh air intake and thus were eventually burned within the engine.

The alternative system was given the abbreviation of EGR, which, when expanded to 'exhaust gas recirculation' becomes virtually self-explanatory. Small quantities of exhaust gases were channelled back into the inlet manifold via an EGR valve, which controlled the amount and where they were blended with the fuel/air mixture. Inevitably, this made the combustion process much cleaner, even reducing the emissions of nitric oxide.

WHY VOLKSWAGEN ABANDONED AIR-COOLING

Many decades after Volkswagen moved from its traditional stance of air-cooled flat four engines to what had become near universal acceptance of water-cooled supremacy, the decision remains controversial in more than just diehard enthusiast circles. As the topic has already been covered at reasonable length in Chapter 2, the story here is restricted specifically to the Transporter.

With the increased weight of the third-generation Transporter compared to that of its predecessor, the elderly 50PS 1600 engine, a product whose origins dated back to the summer of 1967 and a unit which had been eclipsed by increasingly powerful larger air-cooled engines, finally met its match. Correctly, the smaller of the two T3 launch engines was not inflicted on America, but on the home and other

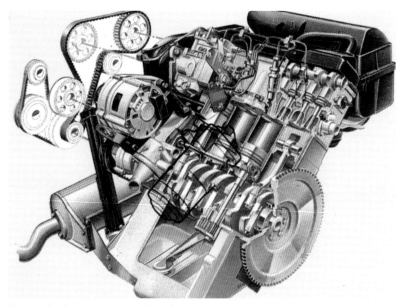

The 50PS diesel engine was squeezed into the engine compartment of the T3 at a 50-degree angle.

Two workaday T3 models: the blue Delivery Van, above middle, has one grille and is air-cooled; the yellow model would either have been a water-cooled petrol engine model, or a diesel. Both demanded a second grille to accommodate a radiator at the front of the vehicle.

European markets it no longer served an effective purpose. Its decidedly pedestrian performance could not be excused on the grounds of fuel economy. Even the 2.0-litre engine, which fared better, did not have performance that could be described as startling.

The nub of the matter was the relentless development of emissions equipment, which apart from creating a complexity not known before and by so doing inescapably added substantially to repair cost whenever something went wrong, had the effect of sapping all engines of their power. To date, all the Transporter's larger engines had been at worst borrowed or at best developed alongside those needed for other air-cooled models. Both the second-generation Transporter's 1700 and 1800 engines had been designed for and then shared with the VW 411/412. The 2.0-litre engine was bestowed on the Transporter as a result of the introduction of the joint project car with Porsche, the mid-engined VW Porsche 914. While at one stage rumours of a 2.2-litre air-cooled engine persisted – though certainly not by the time that the Transporter might have benefited from it – the only realistic air-cooled option open to Volkswagen at the time of the T3's debut would have been to add two more cylinders and a minimum of a further 400cc. Prohibitively expensive to build, potentially producing an unacceptable level of cab and passenger area noise, and no doubt soaking up ever more costly fuel in disproportionately large gulps, such a development was not on Volkswagen's agenda.

DIESEL DEVELOPMENTS

When Chris Barber of *Beetling* magazine put pen to paper for his April 1981 launch report on Volkswagen's diesel-engined Transporter, he confirmed that knowledge of its impending arrival had been widespread almost since the third generation made its debut.

> Since the introduction of the third-generation of VW Transporter in 1979, it has been a badly kept secret that VW have been working on a diesel unit for it. Almost a year ago the German Post Office received the first of hundreds of these 'Transporter D' vehicles

Diesel Engine Technical Data, 1981

Engine

Number of cylinders	4, in-line
Bore and stroke	76.5mm x 86.4mm
Cubic capacity	1588cc
Compression ratio	23.5:1
Horsepower/output	50PS @ 4,200rpm
Maximum torque	75.9lb ft @ 2,000rpm
	103Nm @ 2,000rpm
Fuel rating	45CN
Fuel supply	Indirect, swirl chamber
	Distributor injection

Performance

Top speed – all models except High Roof	68mph (109km/h)
High Roof	65mph (105km/h)
Fuel consumption (1.6-litre petrol engine shown in brackets)	
Delivery Van	32.8mpg (8.6ltr/100km) (25.6mpg or 11.0ltr/100km))
High Roof Van	28.0mpg (10.1ltr.100km) (24.7mpg or 11.5ltr/100km)
Pick-up	32.1mpg (8.8ltr/100km) (25.4mpg or 11.1ltr/100km)
Double Cab Pick-up	32.1mpg (8.8ltr/100km) (26.3mpg or 10.8ltr/100km)
Hill climbing ability, on good roads, fully laden and in first gear (1.6-litre petrol engine shown in brackets)	24% (26%)

and they have been really tried and tested in the most extreme conditions. Other fleet users have also had them for some time now, and in February 1981 the company announced that full scale production has started: orders can be taken.

Initially it appeared that the diesel engine was to be confined to the home market, perhaps for twelve months, conceivably longer, despite immediate availability across the range of vehicles in Germany. Once a byword for a less than palatable combination of unacceptable noise levels and incredible crudity, diesel engines had become more appealing as a result of the Middle East oil crises of the mid-1970s. Car manufacturers – and Volkswagen was no exception – were galvanized into producing a palatable diesel engine option. The new generation of engines was not going to set the world alight in performance terms, but they were economical – so thrifty indeed that Volkswagen soon decided to sell its oil-burning Transporter not just in Europe, but in North America too. Curiously, with such thriftiness to hand and for the first time ever a water-cooled engine in a Transporter, little space was allocated to the innovation in contemporary marketing material. At least

Undoubtedly originally released to illustrate the conveniently large size of the T3's tailgate, the vehicle's badge is of interest. The model shown is described as a Transporter 'D' – the letter standing for diesel.

Volkswagen of America had the decency to include what European publicity lacked. All pointed out that the diesel engine was water-cooled, but only in the USA was reference made to 'an extra grille up front'.

Origins of the Diesel Engine

With understandable caution, the money required to develop an appropriate diesel engine for the T3 had been kept down by adapting the four-cylinder engine first produced in late June 1976 at Volkswagen's Salzgitter factory for use in the Golf and Passat. This engine had been created out of the 1471cc petrol engine and carried a bore and stroke of 76.5mm and 80mm respectively and a compression ratio of 23.5:1, while maximum torque of 60.2lb ft was achieved at 3,000rpm. Developing 50PS at 5,000rpm, the diesel engine mustered 60mph in a laid-back 18.0 seconds. Once suitably wound up, in the Golf the engine could be persuaded to propel the car at a maximum of 87mph (140km/h), a figure which lagged a little behind all but the most basic of petrol engines, but the real benefits of oil-burning ownership came in miserly fuel consumption. According to figures issued by Volkswagen at the time, an average of 43.5mpg (6.5ltr/100km) could easily be achieved, while a Scrooge-like figure of 62.6mpg (4.5ltr/100km) was quoted if the Golf was to travel at a constant 50mph (80km/h).

During the course of 1980 the basic diesel engine was upgraded. Although bore remained at 76.5mm, the stroke increased to 86.4mm. Compression was unaltered, but maximum torque rose to 73.4lb ft, with 54PS being developed at 4,800rpm. The 0–60 time in the diesel Golf dropped to 16.8 seconds, while the car's top speed crept up to 88mph (142km/h), barely faster than previously. It was this revised diesel engine on which the power unit for the T3 was based. Balanced precariously in the T3, more of which shortly, maximum power was reduced back to 50PS, but the compensation was that revs were also reduced by 600rpm, making for an even longer-lasting motor. With maximum torque of 75.9lb ft (103Nm) at 2,000rpm, a figure which was slightly higher than that of the Golf, greater

flexibility was achieved in a vehicle, which, weighing nearly twice as much as the car, really needed it.

The figures shown in the specification chart are all from Volkswagen. Perhaps not altogether surprisingly, straightforward 0–60mph times are absent although a 0–50mph time of 22 seconds was officially leaked to a thankful audience. Testing a diesel-aspirated T3 for *Safer Motoring* magazine, Chris Burlace had the following to contribute to the performance debate, although he did point out that the vehicle he was driving had no more than 1,400 miles (2,250km) on the clock.

> I was able to record 23 seconds to an indicated 50mph. To achieve that figure, and to get acceleration in typical traffic conditions which matched that of the petrol van, I found that I was exceeding the recommended change-up speeds marked on the speedometer (about 14, 26 and 42mph) by about 5mph, but the engine sounded quite happy at the higher speeds and was not held back by its governor …

The Diesel T3

Cramming the diesel engine into the limited space available in the rear of the T3 was no mean feat and demanded that it was tipped by over 50 degrees to the left, which demanded a new cast aluminium sump, which was bolted to the crankcase and bell housing to increase rigidity. One incidental benefit of this arrangement was that aluminium alloy aided cooling. To avoid problems of vibration, the exhaust system was bolted straight onto the engine, while, again thanks to space issues, a special air filter had to be fitted. The Transporter was a heavy vehicle in comparison to the Golf and Passat, so a stronger flywheel was fitted, as was a heavier-duty clutch. Pre-empting any problems caused by heavy load conditions, an oil-cooler was fitted to regulate engine temperature. The starter motor's output was increased to 1.7kW and the engine-located battery was upgraded from the normal 43amp hour unit to a 63Ah version with a special cold current test producing 380A instead of 300A. Both were devices designed to cope with the greater starting demands of a diesel engine.

Input air for the engine was drawn in through the left-hand air intake, while airflow was made quieter and fitted with a water trap.

Conscious that diesel engines were even noisier than the frequently criticized air-cooled units in this respect, extra care was taken to keep clatter down. The engine was mounted with a three-point fixing made of double rubber elements, while the two tubular members, one at either side of the power block, were supplemented by a gearbox mounting larger than that fitted to the air-cooled petrol engines. According to press information released by Volkswagen, the net effect of these amendments to the standard package was equivalent to three decibels, while the interior of the T3 was thoroughly insulated from both noise and vibration. In similar vein, Volkswagen added a galvanized sheet metal tray, lined with polyurethane, under the engine to reduce exterior noise. It could be removed when work on the engine was required.

Visually, the most distinctive feature of the diesel T3 was the appearance of an extra grille at the front of the vehicle. Set below the existing one, which some described as a dummy, despite its role of disguising the vents through which fresh air entered the Transporter, the new grille sat almost immediately above the bumper; its purpose was to feed the radiator, which was positioned directly behind it in an almost purpose-built cavity cradled between the cab and the front panel. The constant supply of cooling air afforded to the radiator through the grille was supplemented by a twin-speed electric fan, which was automatically controlled by a thermostatic switch. The attendant corrosion-proofed coolant hoses wove their way through and were protected by the under-frame of the Transporter. The capacity of the cooling system amounted to 16 litres (3.5 gallons), which worked under pressure increased by one bar, while frost protection down to −25°C (−13°F) was guaranteed. Both the expansion tank and filler were situated in the engine compartment and, in the unlikely event of either the coolant becoming too hot or some or all of it being lost, a warning light flashed in the temperature gauge dial.

A by-product of water-cooling was a revision to the heating arrangements, which were now identical to those installed on the Polos, Golfs and Passats of modern-day Volkswagen. A three-speed fan ensured warm air – or cool air, if the heater was switched off – circulated freely in the relevant parts of the T3's interior.

For once the dealers' comprehensive handbook of T3 selling points seemed to lack the conviction to make the case for buying a diesel invincible. Perhaps this was because the diesel-engined Vanagon was an optional extra to the core range, while the claim that the 'EPA mileage rating of 29 miles per gallon' made it 'the best mileage van sold in America' may have been deemed irrelevant in a land where fuel was so cheap to buy.

The dealer handbook lingered on the 'specially engineered' glow plugs which were designed to heat up extremely fast compared to those of other manufacturers. Indeed, the handbook went so far as to claim that while 'conventional' diesels might take up to 60 seconds to start and 'longer in cold weather', 'in temperatures as low as 0°F, the Vanagon Diesel will start in a mere 12 seconds'. Conversely, there was virtually nothing said about the merits of water-cooling; perhaps the attendant increase in the overall weight of the vehicle proved a sufficient deterrent. Instead, though, lines were devoted to the thermostatically controlled radiator fan.

This fan only runs when it is needed, as it is controlled by a thermostatic switch. When the engine becomes hot enough, the fan switches on. A benefit from the electric cooling fan is that no energy is drawn from the engine to run the fan. This is unlike conventional belt driven fans that can sap up to 5% of an engine's output. So it's no wonder the diesel Vanagon's thermostatically controlled fan increases the engine's performance. It also helps save gas, reduces engine noise, and allows the engine to warm up faster in cold weather.

Probably the most useful and by implication, educational, part of the whole dealer handbook related to the actual working of the engine, which it is worth repeating in full here.

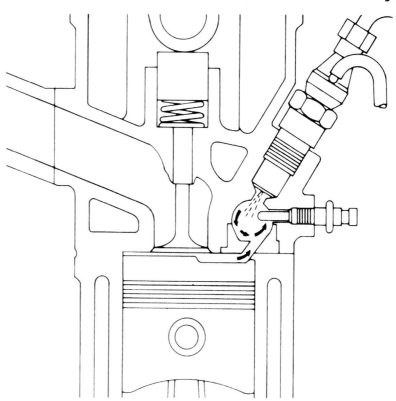

'The diesel engine features swirl-type combustion chambers where air is properly mixed with injected fuel. Fast warming glow plugs will allow cold starts in less than 12 seconds at 0°F' – Volkswagen of America.

The fuel pump injects fuel into the cylinder via an injector. A fine spray of extremely high pressure diesel fuel is shot into the combustion chamber by the injector. The engine is engineered with a swirl-type combustion chamber. The swirl-type combustion chamber allows for the optimum mixing of air and fuel. This results in total combustion, meaning greater fuel economy, greater performance, less noise, and less smoke.

Diesel: the Contemporary Verdict

A little of Chris Burlace's findings from the December 1982 issue of *Safer Motoring* magazine has already proved invaluable in confirming the lacklustre speeds achieved by the T3 diesel engine. His verdict on the merits, or otherwise, of the diesel in general make fascinating reading.

The diesel seemed to produce its power remarkably smoothly without a trace of a flat spot, and the wide high-torque characteristic served to mask any effects of the extra weight. Overall the diesel was not quite so brisk as the conventionally powered van, itself not renowned for performance, but redeemed itself by its very smoothness … As in the normal 1600 Transporter it is necessary to make frequent use of the gearbox … in order to get the best from the vehicle. Examination of the power curve showed why it is necessary to keep the revs up, for there is fairly pronounced fall-off in power below 3,000rpm.

Although the good low-speed torque allows a smooth pull-away from a much lower speed in each gear, one can employ the early change-up technique only if satisfied by the most gentle acceleration! Hill climbing was acceptable in those situations where the revs could be kept up and the 'attack' made at 50mph or more, but approach too slowly, or change down too late on the hill, and the diesel is soon buzzing away to maintain a modest pace in second gear. Once in second, however, the … [diesel T3] will climb most things, and is often able to reach maximum revs but does not have power in hand to cope with an upward change. Diesel and 1600 petrol versions of the Transporter could both benefit from the 5-speed gearbox that is to be offered on the 1983 Transporters …

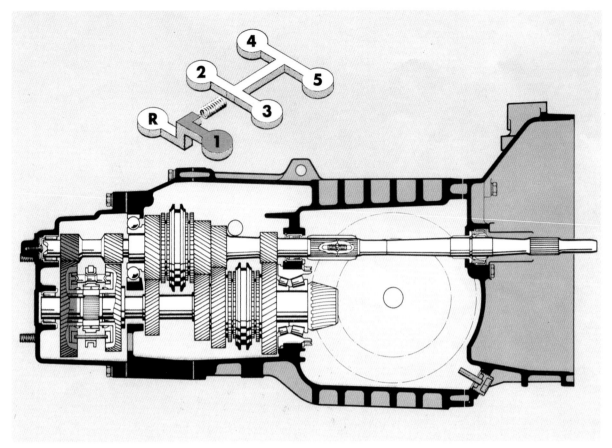

The arrival of a five-speed gearbox precipitated comments such as 'spoilt for choice' from Volkswagen's marketing department. The wily remark that the gearbox and final drive were housed in the same weight-saving unit was probably of more interest.

Paul Harris, editor of *Beetling*, produced a similar verdict after a two-week excursion with a diesel Bus L in Southern Germany and Switzerland, where, apart from a reasonable amount of *Autobahn* travel, he found a surfeit of 'rather hilly country'. It is in his conclusion that the inevitability of what Rudolph Leiding had originally planned for, and which was now only a short time away, was revealed. The diesel might be as dull as ditchwater slow on hills, and inevitably took some considerable length of time to wind up to maximum speed on the level; that

was the price to be paid for unprecedented fuel economy. However, if economy wasn't the first priority, the air-cooled engines did not give performance either. With water now ducted through the once Sahara-like body of the third-generation Transporter, there was nothing to stop the victorious march of performance and economy with an army of modern water-cooled engines.

The version we tested, with L pack plus about 15 other extras ... [weighed in at] over 1600kg. Bearing that in

mind, we would rate the performance [of the diesel engine] as 'satisfactory' all round. In the towns, and short runs, it was quite all right, but on long runs, particularly on Autobahns, a few hp more would often come in handy. This is noticeable when overtaking lorries and when climbing hills. ... We noticed how on inclines we often needed to slip into third gear to maintain even a reasonable speed of 80kph, and that with hills of no more than 1 in 15 (6%). With steeper hills, 2nd gear was called for. On the level we obtained a mean maximum of

Gear Ratios, 1983				
Gear ratios	**1.6-litre** **petrol – manual**	**2.0-litre** **petrol – manual**	**Automatic** **3-speed petrol** **automatic**	**1.6 litre** **Diesel 5-speed manual** **(4-speed figures in brackets)**
1st gear	3.78:1	3.78:1	2.55:1	4.11:1 (3.78:1)
2nd gear	2.06:1	2.06:1	1.45:1	2.33:1 (2.06:1)
3rd gear	1.26:1	1.26:1	1.00:1	1.48:1 (1.26:1)
4th gear	0.82:1	0.88:1	–	1.02:1 (0.85:1)
5th gear	–	–	–	0.77:1
Reverse gear	3.78:1	3.28:1	2.46:1	3.67:1 (3.28:1)
Final drive	5.43:1	4.57:1	4.09:1	4.86:1 (5.43:1)

The double grille paraded on all models – this geometrically arranged line-up for the European market also shows the engine access cover in the Pick-up's loading platform.

114kph, at which speed the bus was beautifully stable.

Although the maximum power is not so high, the engine is quite torquey over a wide range of engine revs. The acceleration figures (0 to 80kph 18 seconds and 0 to 100kph in 35 secs) are, for what they are worth, not impressive, but this does not seem to worry the driver, for there is a distinct lack of fuss … What really impressed us greatly was the incredible economy achieved with the diesel Bus. Type 2 VWs are not normally renowned for their economy, being so big and heavy. But we reckon you save between 30 and 40% of your fuel costs with the diesel version and in most countries on the continent where diesel is much cheaper than petrol the savings are even greater.

America's take on the water-cooled story came in the form of a photograph of the new engines.

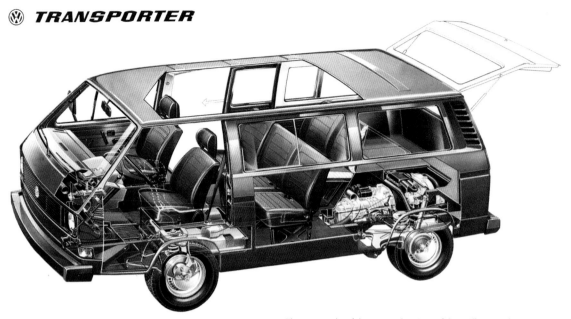

These two colourful cutaway drawings of the T3 illustrate the progression from air- to water-cooling and the associated pipework and paraphernalia required with the new generation of engines.

We did not find a great difference in the fuel consumption in our test. Being driven 'around town' we achieved 34mpg … and being driven on normal country roads 36.5mpg. On the Autobahn, at top speed, 33mpg was achieved. All in all, during our 1,000km test we got an incredible average of 35.5mpg!

The slight lack of performance, noticed really only on longer runs, was more than compensated for by the extraordinary fuel economy, bettering the air-cooled Bus by between 30% and 40% in comparable conditions, and 50% or even more where diesel fuel is much cheaper than petrol.

A GEARING DIVERSION

Reference was made in the previous chapter to the disappointing lack of a fifth gear for the third-generation Transporter when it was first launched – a definite minus point for two distinct reasons. Firstly, Volkswagen weren't keeping up with the Joneses, as most manufacturers had already taken the plunge to add the equivalent of an overdrive fifth ratio. Secondly, in an age when the cost of fuel had recently become much more of an issue than it had ever been before, four gears equated to heavier consumption than five.

Belated though it was, at least for the

1983 model year diesel-aspirated Transporters acquired a fifth gear, as shown in the updated gear ratio chart on page 76.

THE ADVENT OF
WATER-COOLED ENGINES

Was the motoring world really taken by storm when the announcement finally came that the third-generation Transporter's two air-cooled engines were to be phased out? The answer is a resounding 'no'. The advent of the oil-burning diesel engine, in itself a badly kept secret, put paid to the prayers of air-cooled aficionados, while everyone else following the fortunes of Volkswagen – who had been surprised, possibly even disappointed, to see traditional VW engine technology survive the model change of August 1979 – could no longer see a reason why modern water-cooled engines should not be levered into the T3. What proved to be a revelation was the nature of the new engines. The leading VW marque magazine of the day at first reported the news and then, in the next issue, like many others, raised the questions on everyone's lips.

Air-cooled engines axed

The air-cooled engines currently available in the Type 2 – the only air-cooled VW still in production in Europe – are to be phased out over the next few months in favour of a 1.9-litre water-cooled power unit. The move, made for reasons of production costs, fuel efficiency and noise levels, ends an era of air-cooled engines going back well over 40 years to the original KdF-Wagen. The new flat-four water-cooled engine, which made its debut at the Paris Show, is more powerful, more economical, and quieter than its predecessors. Remaining rear mounted, it has a high (8.6:1) compression ratio, and it is cooled via a front mounted aluminium radiator. A new, all-synchromesh five-speed manual gearbox will be offered as an option, and the existing 1.6 litre diesel engine will continue to be available.

News Round-Up, *Safer Volkswagen Motoring*, November 1982

Considerable VW interest in the commercial vehicles hall was focussed on the luxury 7-seater bus, known as the Caravelle, which housed the new 1.9 litre water-cooled engine. Astonishingly this is a flat four, looking like a water-cooled reincarnation of the VW air-cooled engine. The new unit has all the installational [sic] advantages of the air-cooled motor, whilst being quieter, more powerful, and more economical. There is a 60bhp version with a single choke carb, and a 78bhp version with a twin-choke carb; both have 8.6:1 compression. The cooling system is piped via a front radiator. In view of the fact that VW have already successfully installed the Golf type engine in the

rear of the Type 2 (the diesel version being found in the diesel Transporter and Bus), the question in everyone's mind is why is the water-cooled flat-four necessary and will it be seen in other vehicles?

Peter Noad reporting from the NEC Car Show, *Safer Volkswagen Motoring*, December 1982

What Volkswagen had done was most unusual. Having proved they could tip a conventional water-cooled engine on its side for the T3 and, even more importantly, utilize a power unit that already had a place and an important part to play in the modern line-up of VW passenger cars, they had instead decided to create a separate genre of engines and swallow all the consequent costs. Peter Noad asked the obvious question regarding the new engine's role within the Volkswagen empire of vehicles, but must have known the answer: with the huge success story of the Golf, Passat and Polo on Volkswagen's hands, a story not only of ingenious design, but also of a perfect combination of frugality and performance, the water-cooled flat-four was doomed from the start to be a one-off wonder.

Volkswagen's PR and press office was inevitably on overtime and offered three not entirely convincing reasons for the T3 water boxer decision. A pre-

amble designed to explain why air-cooled technology had to go was largely irrelevant, as it did nothing to justify the choice of a one-off engine. Press and public were painfully aware that to stay competitive Volkswagen needed more economy from their Transporter and particularly so in an urban environment. Equally, everyone was familiar with the company's struggle to keep up in the commercial vehicle power-game. And few would have been shocked to discover that in a world where the dreaded demands of health and safety were beginning to encroach on freedom of choice, the old air-cooled engines were set to fall victim to proposed European Community restrictions on noise, something which non-participatory Switzerland had led the way with by introducing new vows of silence legislation which took effect in October 1982.

With such prefaces discarded, the official line was that a boxer engine had certain distinct advantages over more familiar water-cooled technology. First, the flat-four was both low in its overall height and compact, particularly in its length. This made it ideal to slip into an engine space that had been deliberately reduced in size to facilitate easier loading at the rear of the Transporter. This argument could be countered by noting the diesel engine's build was conventional. Secondly, there was desire to continue making flat-four

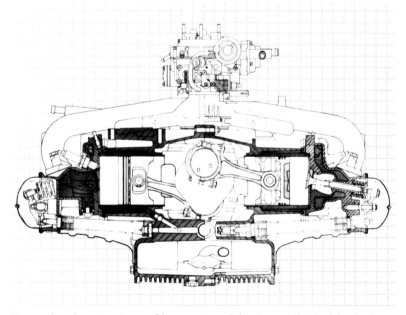

However clever the cutaway images of the new water-cooled engines were, this simple line drawing illustrates the composition of the water-boxer to perfection.

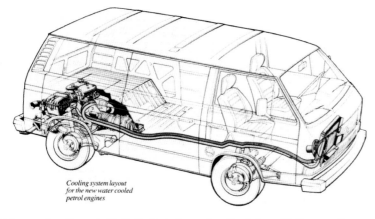

Cooling system layout for the new water cooled petrol engines

Volkswagen's caption embedded in the illustration confirms the obvious, while the ease with which a radiator could be sited at the front of the vehicle confirms the strategy that Leiding had in mind almost a decade earlier.

The 1.9-litre 44kW 60PS engine.

engines as the company that had built its reputation on the reliability of 30 million such units, albeit all of them air-cooled. Again, on its own, this argument did not really make sense, as logically the last previous flat-four would not have been designed in 1968 for use in the air-cooled VW 411, as Golfs, Passats and Polos would have been similarly endowed. Thirdly, with balance being an integral part of the flat-four design, even, silky running was guaranteed, potentially offering smoother characteristics than many six-cylinder engines.

While this last point couldn't be easily denied, there were other more important reasons for the water boxer engine's introduction, and they were clear to anyone who cared to look.

Marketing material was not neces-sarily as glossy as once it had been (in keeping with the spirit of the times), VAG (United Kingdom) Limited's mate-rial to promote the new range of water-cooled engines must have come as a bit of a shock to dealers when it first thudded through the letterbox. The covers looked essentially like graph paper, on which outlines of the vehicles – and in the case of the 'technical information' edition a cross-sectional drawing of the new engine – were superimposed. Fortunately, for future generations of devotees and historians alike, the text was both wordy and overtly technical in comparison to the average offering.

Before confirming, or should that be admitting, the real reasons for the switch to water in the Transporter, yet another preamble was required. This

one had a logic that only the hierarchy at Wolfsburg would know was slightly suspect.

The introduction of the third Commer-cial generation in 1979 with a modern running gear … was followed one year later by the first step towards a new engine generation: the water-cooled, inclined, in-line diesel engine. On account of the economy it offered as a result of favourable fuel consumption, the 4-clinder diesel engine met with immediate acceptance and now accounts for a good half of the produc-tion volume.

The second and decisive phase in the conversion of the Volkswagen Commercial to a new engine tech-nology is the presentation of the brand-new water-cooled carburettor engines.

The next paragraph provided the core reasons for water-cooled engines, but although they remain easy to under-stand without in-depth knowledge, some of the language is clearly intend-ed to deceive would-be purchasers into believing that all the changes had been made primarily for their benefit, rather than really being to do with Volk-swagen's need to provide economy in fuel consumption and more power if they were to stay as market leaders, while reducing noise to levels to com-ply with current, or proposed, European legislation.

Requirement-orientated output, econ-omy, comfort and the satisfying of legal requirements as regards less envi-ronmental impact were foremost when planning the new carburettor engines. The economy aspect and the utilisation of existing production facili-ties as well as the logistics and the han-dling of the new engines in practice were also of prime importance for Volk-swagen. The company's many years of experience with boxer engines also played a part in the decision in favour of the power concept to be used. In the past 37 years more than 30 million such four-cylinder power units have come off the production lines in the Federal Republic of Germany and in the various production facilities belonging to the VW Group. All this is backed by an immeasurable know-how potential in terms of foundry, processing and production engineering: a wealth of knowledge which is worth a lot and for which we are envied. The Boxer concept with central crankshaft and opposed cylinders offers numerous technical advantages and is ideally suited to the Commercial with its direct rear-wheel drive. The decision to develop a new 4-cylinder boxer engine for the wide-ranging Commercial line was thus not only consistent but also an obvious step.

By way of a timely diversion, of all the research documents collated during the writing of this book undoubtedly one of the most impressive was *Road and Track*'s road test of the Volkswagen Vanagon 'Wasserboxer'. Not that the report's conclusions differed from those of other magazines and journalists; where it stood out was in its overture to the demise of air-cooled technology. Here, at long last, was a skilful piece of writing comparing the approach of one former bastion of air-cooling to that of another – a company that bore the surname of Volkswagen's forefather, Ferdinand Porsche.

What does the 1983½ Volkswagen Vanagon have in common with Porsche's legendary 935 Turbo racing car? If you guessed that both have rear engines, you're right. And if you guessed that both engines are boxers – a flat-4 in the VW and a flat-6 in the Porsche – you're right again. But did you know that like its racing cousin, the Vanagon's latest 4-banger has water cooling? Volkswagen's reasons for turning on the waterworks are not unlike Porsche's, at least on one count – thermodynamic efficiency. When Porsche began turning up the boost on its turbocharged racing 6-cylinders, it found itself reaching the limits of the air-cooled engine's performance. Simply put, the factory discovered that even the most effective fan could move only so much air past hot cylinder barrels. So the wizards of Weissach devised water-cooled cylinder heads used with air-cooled cylinders to bring operating temperatures within optimum levels and make the turbocharged Porsche racing engine one of the most powerful in the world. Meanwhile, back in Wolfsburg, VW had been having similar problems with its air-cooled Vanagon power-plant. Displacing almost 2.0 litres, the 4-cylinder

Water-Cooled Engine Technical Data – UK source, September 1982, and US Source, 1983 Model Year

4-cylinder horizontally opposed OHV water-cooled

	1.9-litre (single carburettor)	1.9-litre (twin carburettor)	1.9-litre Vanagon (fuel injection)
Bore	94.0mm	94.0mm	94.0mm (3.70in)
Stroke	69.0mm	69.0mm	69.0mm (2.72in)
Cubic Capacity	1915cc	1915cc	1915cc (117.0cu in)
Compression ratio	8.6:1	8.6:1	8.6:1
Output – kW	44kW	57kW	82bhp (SAE net)
DIN	60bhp	78bhp	
@ rpm	3,700	4,600	4,800
Maximum torque – Nm and lb ft	140Nm	141Nm	105.5lb ft (SAE net)
	105.5lb ft (SAE net)	103.9lb ft	
@rpm	2,200	2,600	2,600
Fuel rating (RON)	91	91	Unleaded only
Fuel air supply	Solex 34 PICT – 5 carburettor	2E3 carburettor	Fuel injection, digital air-flow controlled

Performance – based on Delivery Van, UK source

	1.9-litre 60bhp		1.9-litre 78bhp		
	4-speed	5-speed	4-speed	5-speed	Auto
Maximum speed	73mph	73mph	81mph	81mph	77mph
	(117km/h)	(117km/h)	(130km/h)	(130km/h)	(124km/h)
Acceleration 0–50mph (at half load capacity)	19.1 secs	18.2 secs	15.7 secs	15.1 secs	N/A
Fuel consumption (at half payload, constant ¾ maximum speed, + 10%)	25.9mpg (10.9ltr/100km)	25.9mpg (10.9ltr/100km)	24.1mpg (11.7ltr/100km)	24.7mpg (11.5ltr/100km)	22.6mpg (12.5ltr/100km)

Performance – Vanagon

	Manual (4-speed only)	Automatic
Maximum speed	84mph (135km/h)	81mph (130km/h)
Acceleration 0–50mph	12.2 secs	13.0 secs
Acceleration 0–60mph	17.3 secs	21.3 secs
Estimated fuel consumption (inc California)	19.0mpg (14.9ltr/100km)	19.0mpg (14.9ltr/100km)
Estimated Hwy fuel consumption (inc California)	27.0mpg (10.5ltr/100km)	24mpg (11.8ltr/100km)

Water-Cooled Engine Gear Ratios			
Gear ratios	4-speed manual	5-speed manual	Automatic 3-speed (78bhp only)
1st gear	3.78:1	4.11:1	2.7:1
2nd gear	2.06:1	2.22:1	1.50:1
3rd gear	1.26:1	1.48:1	1.00:1
4th gear	0.85:1	1.02:1	–
5th gear	–	0.77:1	–
Reverse gear	3.67:1	3.67:1	2.43:1
Final drive – 60bhp	4.57:1	4.86:1	4.09:1
78bhp	4.86:1	4.81:1	

was at the ragged edge of efficiency. At 67bhp, the Type 4 (located at the rear of a large box and subject to less than ideal airflow) was doing all an air-cooled engine could to propel a 3,300lb vehicle and stay alive. Something had to be done and that something was water cooling, not just the cylinder heads, but the cylinders as well ...

Water-Cooled Engine Specifications

The two new engines were identical save for the carburettor. Contrary to some assertions that they were little more than air-cooled units clad with a water jacket they were almost entirely different internally. In overall size the new engines were shorter than the air-cooled blocks as the cylinders were closer together than previously. The cylinder blocks, with wet cylinder liners and heads, were made of light alloy, while the crankcase was split and no

longer required the finned barrels of the air-cooled engines. The centrally located crankshaft was also new and came with a shorter stroke than that of its predecessor at 69.0 compared to 71.0mm. It had three main bearings and drove the similarly located camshaft drive by gears. The larger intake and exhaust valves, reshaped for better flow, were operated by push rods and hydraulic tappets. The Transporter's heating and intake manifold heating were connected to the coolant circuit, utilizing pump and thermostat controls to regulate the operating temperature. As established with the introduction of the diesel engine, the aluminium radiator was located at the front of the Transporter and was fan-aided.

The combustion chambers lay partly in the cylinder head and in part in the – unique for Volkswagen – Heron-type pistons. This combination of bowl in piston combustion chamber and the

combustion chamber in the cylinder heads, together with close production tolerances, made a very narrow squish gap between the piston and cylinder head at piston TDC, resulting in a very high squish figure and, as a further consequence, a very effective fuel/air mix. Thus, alarming 'pinking' was totally avoided and a high energy yield ensured.

Pre-heating of the fuel/air mixture was achieved in the warm-up phase by 'hedgehog' electrical heating in addition to warming the intake manifold with coolant, the net result of which was to lower fuel usage in urban driving conditions. The cylinder capacity of 1913cc was realized from a bore of 94mm and a stroke of 68.9mm. The mean piston speed at rated engine speed was 8.5m/s for the 60PS engine and 10.6m/s for the more powerful 78PS engine. Such ratings suggested long life for both engines.

The less powerful of the two engines was fitted with a Pierburg 34 PICT downdraught carburettor (also noted to be a Solex 34PICT-5 in VAG's Service and Training Manual for employees, dated September 1982). The secret behind the extra power of the 78PS engine was the Pierburg 2E3, a newly developed downdraught unit with double choke.

The detailed specification chart gives all the figures. However, it is worth noting that for reasons of emission controls if nothing else, the American-specification Vanagon, although moving from air to water like the European models, continued to benefit from fuel injection – an upgraded system. 'Digi-Jet' fuel injection used digital rather than analogue technology and generally speaking was simpler than the previous first-generation Bosch L-Jetronic system. (Rumour had it that the earlier

The 1.9-litre 57kW 78PS engine.

arrangement had been bedevilled by electronic gremlins.) VW of America noted in one of their typically well-produced sales brochures that 'Digi-Jet fuel injection monitors the fuel and air mixture for maximum output'; the new system also limited the engine's speed to 5,400rpm by shutting off the fuel pump when this was achieved.

Fuel Efficiency, Less Noise and More Power

Volkswagen's press office pushed home the key advantages of the water-cooled engines over those of their predecessors. Of these, probably the most significant was the additional power of both engines, although without doubt better fuel economy was also a big selling point. Nearly as significant was the reduction in noise levels. Brochures produced for different markets across the world told the same story, but on occasions figures differed!

The claim in Germany was that the 60PS engine, which replaced the 50PS air-cooled version, realized an average 16 per cent improvement in fuel economy, with 21.8mpg (13.0ltr/100km) being achieved on the city cycle and 29.0mpg (9.8ltr/100km) at a constant 90km/h (56mph). The 78PS unit, which replaced the 2.0-litre 70PS engine, boasted an average 12 per cent advance in fuel cutbacks, with a figure of 20.3mpg (13.9ltr/100km) being given for the city cycle and 29.8mpg (9.5ltr/100km) at a constant 90km/h. Referring to this latter engine, Volkswagen of South Africa suggested a 23 per cent improvement in 0–100km/h times, a 14 per cent reduction in fuel consumption and an easily measurable 10 per cent increase in output. Volkswagen of America responded to the customers' thirst for information by telling them that power had increased by 22 per cent, while the new engine was 19 per cent more economical generally and 23 per cent less thirsty on 'the highway'. A VAG UK publication cited a 20 per cent boost in power and, with its 'flexible, evenly balanced engine', an increase in miles per gallon of up to 15 per cent.

Leaving aside the discrepancies arising from figures being produced using different benchmarks, all were agreed that improved torque was of great significance. VAG UK even claimed a

delivery of 36 per cent more than previously, although without confirming which engine this pertained to. Both engines developed their maximum torque in the medium speed range, 'where flexibility and the ability to pull hard are most needed'.

> With a torque of 140Nm (103.1lb ft) at only 2,200/min engine speed, the 60bhp (44kW) engine easily surpasses most engines of greater power. The driver will be glad of this torque when accelerating from a low speed in 4th gear, or starting away with a heavy load on a hill. The 78bhp (57kW) engine develops no less than 141Nm (103.9lb ft) of torque at 2,600/min. Throughout the lower engine speed range it produces the same willing flow of power as the 60bhp unit, but the additional output at higher speeds means that the vehicle can be driven at 81mph (130kph) and over when necessary. This is the ideal power unit for regular runs at high average speeds.

VAG UK claimed a staggering 50 per cent reduction in cab noise thanks to 'increased sound insulation just about everywhere. Not least around the engine itself.' In reality the engine's water jacket accounted for a good proportion of the reduction in noise. Another noise-reduction measure undoubtedly helped as well. Instead of the old four-bolt mounting system of the engine, a new three-point arrangement incorporating massive rubber blocks was introduced, reducing at a stroke the transfer of both noise and vibration to the interior of the vehicle. The net result was a reduction of 3dB, which tallies with the seemingly highly optimistic claim made by VAG UK. Crucially, the reduction from 80dB of the air-cooled T3 to the 77dB of the revised vehicle ensured compliance with Swiss regulations, which came into effect in October 1982, and with proposed European regulations due to be imposed in October 1985.

Related Improvements

A criticism always levelled at any Volkswagen fitted with an air-cooled engine was that the heater was ineffective. Aftermarket heat exchangers with simplified or even cost cutting

construction shortcomings undoubtedly played their part here, as a genuine exchanger was certainly capable of taking the shine off a shoe placed too close to the heater outlet, but only a real air-cooled diehard would seriously argue equity between air- and water-cooled heating capabilities.

To implement this heating miracle, all Volkswagen had to do was filch the system they had already installed in the diesel. This, as outlined earlier, was borrowed from the Passat, Golf and Polo, and consisted of a three-speed fan, sliding temperature controls – to mix warm and cold air – and separate controls for the windscreen, the front footwells and, where applicable, the balance of the passenger area.

Other detail improvements included a hydraulically operated clutch on all models, a vacuum brake servo on all petrol models and, although nothing to do with the change of engines, an upgrade in tyres to 185 R 14C 6PR radial tyres on all models.

Press Reaction

Writing many years after the event, much-respected author Laurence Meredith summarized why Volkswagen had to move on from air-cooling. He argued that the 'Wasserboxer' was conventional thinking from Volkswagen, however much they endeavoured to suggest that the new engine was part of their evolutionary process.

> The 'Wasserboxer' petrol engine continued to sound like a flat-four, but not an air-cooled flat-four. It had something of a muted growl about it that smacked of convention. The Bus was no longer a product of unorthodox thinking, but of a new age in which compliance with the norm became an economic necessity for all manufacturers, including Volkswagen.
>
> (*VW Bus*, Laurence Meredith, Sutton Publishing, 1999)

Finding a British review of the new engines in the archives proves to be a remarkably difficult task, in spite of all the hype the average Volkswagen enthusiast might have anticipated. Fortunately, ever loyal, ever faithful, Chris

Burlace, a stalwart of *Safer Volkswagen Motoring*'s team of writers and a man with a particular interest in campers, was on hand with a report he compiled in October 1983.

What the VW lacked was power, and to a woeful degree in the 1600 model. The new engines, flat-fours with water jackets, looked set to rectify the one shortcoming of the Transporter.... At speeds of up to 70mph the engine is scarcely audible, and the twin carburettor version of the 1.9 litre flat-four obviously has plenty in hand for speeds well above the legal limit (with the optional, five speed gearbox the 4th-to-5th change-up point is marked at 75mph). In the 78bhp, 4-speed version of the water-cooled model the 2nd-to-3rd change-up point is marked at 40mph, and 65 is the speed for selecting top. The speeds feel right for the power and torque characteristics of the motor and I soon found there was no temptation to try to exceed them ... I rated the acceleration exceptional by motor caravan standards, bettering the manufacturers' quoted 0-50 mph figure of 15.7 secs, by just over a second. ... The 78bhp VW proved itself a more nimble climber than the former top-of-the-range 2-litre air-cooled model.

A little later than many countries in the world, in 1984 the Australian market accepted delivery of its first water-cooled 'Kombis', a one-time generic name for all Transporters down under. For Volkswagen's dealers, its arrival should have been much earlier, at least if one of the first press reports, courtesy of *Motor Manual*, from December 1984, was anything to go by:

One can hardly argue that VW has not done a Good Thing with this new engine as, more than ever, it makes the transporters the 'Mercedes' of the light van class. Topping out at $18,995 for the automatic Caravelle GL model, you certainly have to pay a premium for the best, but then again you are the owner of something special, that even the best of the Japanese people-movers have to accept has no peers.... It's hard to say that the engine sounds any different to the familiar air-cooled rush simply because it's so muted you hear very little above other sounds entering

the interior. ... Inside, it's so smooth, you'd honestly be pushing to say it wasn't a six, rather than a four. The combination of the inherent balance characteristics of a horizontally opposed four, and the distance between it and the driver, make the engine remarkably non-intrusive. With the very latest in fuel injection technology, which is the Digi-Jet L-Jetronic Bosch system developed by VW, using digital rather than analogue technology and incorporating things like deceleration fuel shut-off, the Caravelle starts instantly hot or cold and performs smoothly at all times. ... The power from the engine doesn't go unnoticed, either. Torque reserves, specially with the lower set of intermediate ratios, are generous enough to allow the VW to motor comfortably around in the higher gears, yet the actual speeds are quite adequate... Running the VW against the stopwatch, we found ourselves bettering the factory-claimed figures, specially up the top end, where we managed to reach 100km/h in just under 20 seconds, rather than the 21.1 suggested by the people from Wolfsburg. And over 400 metres, it managed 21.2 seconds, which, even though the vehicle was admittedly a manual, sure beat hell out of the 23.5 seconds recorded in our last Kombi test. Fuel economy over a hard-driven 300km averages out to 12.6 litres per 100km, or 22mpg, which was once again a big improvement ... So the VW Caravelle swishes along quite economically, rushing up hills with ease where an air-cooled version would have been struggling ... No, the VW isn't about to be deposed from its throne as the best one tonne people-mover around. A bit like the Range Rover, its been around for years, but no even seems to have made a serious effort to match it, yet alone better it. Up the eurocars.

America's crème de la crème of water-cooled Vanagon reviews (from *Car and Driver*, June 1983) came with the appropriately title, 'Volkswagen Vanagon GL, just add water.'

There's no question that wetter is better. As a result of the refurbishing programme, the Vanagon drinks less fuel, makes more power, and gets off the mark better – something VW vans have

perennially been lackadaisical about. These improvements actually have little to do with the new cooling system. Water cooling does allow better cylinder-to-cylinder temperature control, more precise fuel metering, and tighter emissions calibrations, but most of the engine's new found sinew was developed elsewhere. While the engineers were designing the cooling passengers for the cylinder heads and piston sleeves, they also went through the all-alloy engine from valve covers to oil pan. In the process, the combustion chambers, valves, camshaft, pistons, and electronic fuel-injection system were altered for better power and efficiency. ... [The increase in horsepower] ... translates into more relaxed 65-to-75mph cruising and some extra power for passing that wasn't there before. They haven't invented the Vanagon that will crack sixteen seconds in the zero-to-sixty dash, so the VW is still no threat to your average Subaru. Luckily, though, the Vanagon has the gift of feeling quicker than it is. It always seems to have enough oomph to keep traffic from breathing down your neck. Better still, you ... can get where you are going on significantly less fuel than before ...

FURTHER DEVELOPMENTS

Two developments later in the history of the T3's engines are worthy of detailed analysis. One took the diesel from a sloth-like workhorse, inevitably designed to clatter and grind its way around town rather than to belt along the Autobahn, where petrol competitors and other diesels with a certain magic ingredient would have left it wallowing in its own cloud of obnoxious vapours. The easily predictable addition of a turbocharger gave the oil-burner a purpose and pointed to a time when powerful VW diesels would outshine all others in the world of commercial vehicles.

Of equal significance was a yet more powerful petrol engine, a unit which broke the 2.0-litre barrier for the first time for a Transporter, and one which once and for all confirmed that the days when Volkswagen's small commercial vehicle and large people carrier was eminently loveable but always a little underpowered were well and truly over.

However, in what can only be described as a period of frenzied activity at least one other power unit came and went, while the legislative march of the catalytic converter created subdivisions of 'with' and 'without'. There was even a PS postscript to the non-turbo-diesel story, which while hardly of news-breaking headline significance at least has to be charted. To this end, the engine range tables duly list what was what and when, and includes those diesel and water-cooled engines already discussed in detail purely for the sake of clarity. However, it should be noted that engines with comparable cubic capacities were available for specific countries with varying output, while most markets didn't carry every engine available. For example, the Vanagon could only be specified with a diesel engine for three model years – from the oil-burner's inception through to and including 1983. America had voted with its feet as far as the diesel was concerned and there was no move to add the turbo-boosted engine to the range when that became available.

TD – TWO POWERFUL LETTERS?

While confirming in print what had been known since the non-turbo-diesel engine emerged as an 'an ideal unit for short trips', Volkswagen heralded the introduction of a more powerful diesel engine for the Transporter in 1985 as a convincing advance. They promoted its performance, its relatively low fuel consumption and lower noise levels, in that order, and, for once, Volkswagen were entirely right.

As had been the case when the 50PS diesel made its debut in the Transporter, the idea of a turbocharger wasn't new to Volkswagen, and it had already proved successful elsewhere in the range. Nor will it be a surprise to learn then that when the Golf Mk2 made its entrance on the home market in 1983, a turbo-diesel, the GTD, was included in the range of vehicles offered. The hatchback managed a top speed of 99mph (159km/h), while a 0–60mph sprint of a respectable if not awe-inspiring 13.5 seconds was possible. However, any notion that the Golf's turbo engine was merely prised out of the car and spooned into the Transporter would be misplaced. Volkswagen's engineers had to alter the specification to ensure compatibility with the T3.

As an example, and a significant one at that, the turbocharger was completely new. Branded as the KKK turbo, it been specially developed by Kühnle, Kopp and Kausch to lessen the lag in response of a system that would normally build pressure only at high revs, and as such offered a boost of 0.2 atmos. at 1,450rpm, and 0.6 atm. at 2,000rpm. Substantial changes to the exhaust turbine side were complemented by minor revisions to the 'cold compression' part, while the injector pump had a steeper cam, thus increasing injection velocity. New Bosch injectors with different jets were fitted; the piston cooling system, the piston rings, the oil pump, even the oil capacity (now 4.5ltr/1.2 gallons), were all changed to help restrict engine wear concurrent with the extra stresses caused by forced charging. Equally significant were the use of high-grade materials for the cylinder head and other components, plus the strengthening of the crankcase.

Turbocharging had the effect of increasing the maximum power from 50PS at 4,200rpm to 70PS at 4,500rpm, while torque became lively, with enough of it low down to make the move up from the 103Nm (76lb ft) at 2,000rpm of the naturally aspirated diesel to138Nm (102lb ft) at 2,500 rpm smooth and easy. The overall result was a vehicle capable of 79mph (127km/h) when coupled to a five-speed gearbox, and 74mph (119km/h) if fifth was lacking. In their sales literature, Volkswagen, as usual, were somewhat coy about the turbocharged T3's ability to sprint, quoting 17.1 seconds for a 0–50mph test with a delivery van at half-load capacity, compared on this occasion to 25.7 seconds for a 'normal' diesel of the same type. *Safer Volkswagen Motoring's* Chris Burlace, on the other hand, appeared to have special insider information when he revealed that 'Volkswagen's figures from rest to 50, 60, 80 and 100km/h (31, 37, 50 and 62mph) are respectively 6.5, 9.0, 15.9 and 26.5 seconds.'

Fuel consumption was good but, as might have been expected, not comparable with that of the non turbo engine. Figures vary, the Wolfsburg press office suggesting 32.5mpg

Diesel Engine Range

	1600	1800	1600
	50PS	57PS	70PS (Turbo charged)
Produced	1981–87	1987 onwards	1985 onwards
Bore	76.5mm	79.5mm	76.5mm
Stroke	86.4 mm	86.4mm	86.4mm
Compression	23.0:1	23.0:1	23.0:1

Water-Cooled Petrol Engine Range

	1.9-litre	1.9-litre	1.9-litre	1.9-litre	2.1-litre	2.1-litre
	60PS	78PS	83PS (Cat)	90PS	95PS (Cat)	112PS
Produced	Throughout	Throughout	To mid-1985	To mid-1985	From 1985	From 1985
Bore	94.0mm	94.0mm	94.0mm	94.0mm	94.0mm	94.0mm
Stroke	69.0mm	69.0mm	69.0mm	69.0mm	76.0mm	76.0mm
Compression	8.6:1	8.6:1	8.6:1	8.6:1	9.0:1	10.5:1
Carb/injection	Single Carb	Twin Carb	Bosch Digi-jet fuel injection	Bosch Digi-jet fuel injection	Bosch Digi-jet fuel injection	Bosch Digi-jet fuel injection

The 70PS turbo-diesel engine enhanced both the performance and the reputation of the oil-burning T3.

(8.7ltr/100km) for the city cycle, and 36.0mpg (7.9ltr/100km) at a constant 56mph (90km/h), while with a half payload delivery van at a constant ³/₄ speed, plus 10 per cent, Volkswagen UK quoted 29.4mpg (9.6ltr/100km) overall. Using the same criteria a five-speed without a turbo recorded 37.1mpg (7.6ltr/100km).

Safer Volkswagen Motoring's Chris Burlace was one of the first UK journalists to test the new turbo-assisted diesel and his enthusiasm for the product is immediately noticeable in his report.

The extra power of the turbo unit was immediately noticeable, and progress strikingly more brisk than in the rather stodgy standard diesel with its 50bhp. Performance, not unexpectedly, seemed to fall between that of the 60bhp and 78bhp versions of the petrol-powered Transporter. But it takes practice to learn the technique of keeping the turbo 'on song' … The turbo boost starts quite low down the rev range, 0.2bar at 1,450rpm, but the influence of the turbo really starts to be felt as revs come up to 2,000, at which speed a boost of 0.6bar is produced. Maximum turbo pressure is 0.7bar and over the range from about 1,800 to 3,700rpm torque exceeds 90lb ft. For the best performance, and the best economy, therefore, it pays to make

good use of the turbo boost by keeping the revs above the 1,800 mark – and that often means staying in a gear which, when driving a normal diesel, one would feel to be too low.

Towards the end of the era of the T3, the normally aspirated diesel engine grew a little in size. While stroke remained the same at 86.4mm, the bore was increased from 76.5mm to 79.5mm, with a resultant enhanced cubic capacity of 1716cc, a more important boost in power from the 50PS of old to 57PS at 4,500rpm, but no change to the maximum torque of 76lb ft.

When VAG (UK) Limited added the 'Transporter 800' to its commercial vehicle offer as a 'no-nonsense van at a realistic price' for people who needed 'neither the payload or performance of the standard one tonne van' in the summer of 1989, two engines were offered. If the petrol unit was the basic 60PS unit, the lowly status of the 57PS diesel engine was fully revealed as, sure enough, it was the alternative engine offered on this budget van.

'THE MOST INTERESTING OPTION'

It is doubly fitting that the 2.1-litre T3 engine is the one that brings this study of probably the greatest talking points of the third-generation models to a

close. Apart from being the first engine to be installed in any Transporter to exceed 2.0 litres in capacity and to have maximum output exceeding 100PS, it was a unit that at first was only bestowed upon the Caravelle Carat. This paves the way towards the next chapter and the evolution of the T3 in terms of an ever-more luxurious specification.

Compared to the short-lived 90PS engine it replaced, the 2.1-litre engine exhibited a number of changes. The crankshaft stroke stood at 76mm compared to the 69mm of the 1.9 litre, and came with new bearings, while the crankcase was made stronger in several areas. While the valves remained unaltered in size, the timing had changed and the manifolds were larger, resulting in a better gas flow. The efficiency of this engine was unparalleled, according to Volkswagen who, perhaps with a hint of wishful thinking, suggested that it compared well with a diesel, particularly when it was taken into account that the compression ratio of 10.5:1 demanded the use of 98 octane fuel.

The net result of the changes outlined was a fuel-injected (Digi-Jet) engine that produced a maximum of 112PS at 4,800rpm, and 128lb ft of torque (174Nm) at 2,800rpm. At launch Volkswagen issued generic fuel consumption figures of 22.5mpg

(12.6ltr/100km) for city use, 31.5mpg (9.0ltr/100km) at a constant 56mph (90km/h), and 21.5mph (13.1ltr/100km) when driven at 75mph (121km/h). Later this was slightly revised to 23.5, 32.1 and 21.6mpg (12.0, 8.8 and 13.0ltr/100km) respectively, while overall fuel consumption with a half payload, at ¾ maximum speed plus 10 per cent was calculated at 21.9mpg (12.9ltr/100km). In terms of sprint performance, Volkswagen remained a little shy, issuing 0–50mph times when pushed, but omitting them from the technical data sheets attached to many a sales brochure. However, compared to the 1.9-litre, the 2.1-litre engine was approaching three seconds faster in the run-up to 50mph, producing a comparatively healthy result of 10.3 seconds. The maximum speed was given as 94mph (151km/h) for the standard five-speed model, while the automatic option rolled in at 91mph (146km/h).

When mated to a catalytic converter and run on lead-free petrol, maximum PS dropped to 95, while the compression ratio stood at 9.0:1. The top speed fell to 84mph (135km/h).

Other new aspects of the 2.1-litre engine, which did not have a bearing on performance or were not a necessary change to cope with the increase

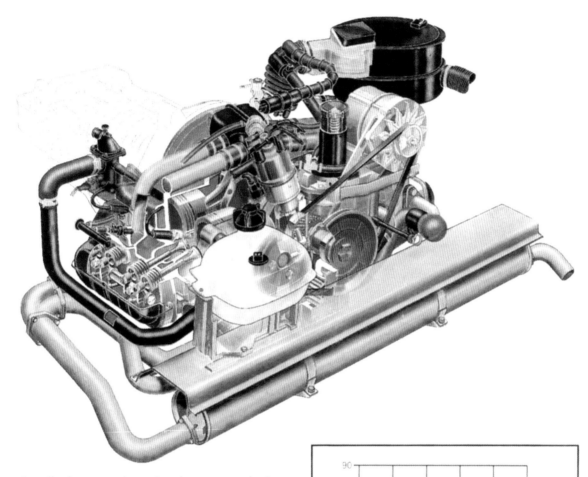

4-cylinder petrol engine (water cooled, horizontally-opposed), displacement: 2,109 cm^3, compression ratio: 10.5 : 1, output: 82 kW (112 bhp) at 4,800 rpm. Maximum torque: 174 Nm at 2,800 rpm.

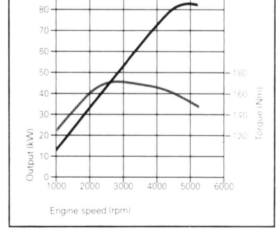

'Immensely free-revving and flexible', was Volkswagen's own verdict on their top-of-the-range power plant for the T3, the 2.1-litre engine.

The complexities of the water-cooled engines in the T3 – this is the 2.1-litre version.

Volkswagen of Canada's text to accompany this 1986 image advised that 'all [models] are powered by Volkswagen's proven 2.1-litre 95-horsepower engine', which for European-specification Transporters would not have been the case. (Note also the twin headlights and their rectangular cases – another feature not applicable to workhorse models for the home and European market at this time.)

in size, included a water-cooled oil-cooler as per the turbo-diesel, and a glass-fibre and plastic case for the thermostat, which was located by cylinder number three to keep it cooler.

Despite the 2.1-litre's leap forward in performance, praise was far from universal, and with the benefit of hindsight it is easy to see that the automotive world beyond Volkswagen had once again moved on. While the marque-specific magazines recognized in the 2.1-litre an engine that fellow enthusiasts and Volkswagen followers could cling to as the crème-de-la-crème of T3 performance, others had no reason to be loyal to the T3.

Volkswagen Audi Car contributor and one time air-cooled devotee turned water-cooled champion Peter Noad, spent a week behind the wheel of a 2.1-litre Caravelle and was suitably impressed, noting to start with the engine's similarity to one powering a car.

This is a particularly interesting powerplant. It develops 112bhp at 4,800rpm; the same as the injection in-line engine which powers the [Golf] GTI, but at much lower revs. It develops a maximum torque of 129lb ft at a very low 2,800rpm. This compares with 113lb ft at 3,500rpm for the GTI engine … This, then, is a powerful, gutsy flat four capable of pulling hard from very low speeds … Acceleration in the 50–70mph overtaking band is particularly good … [The] overall effect is to give this big vehicle the responsiveness one expects from a car and, if the heavier fuel consumption can be accepted, indulging performance to the full is a thoroughly enjoyable pastime.

In complete contrast, this short extract from Autocar written in June 1989 was about as bad as it could get for Volkswagen's marketing men.

At town speeds the … [2.1litre] engine feels brisk enough but out on the open road acceleration is sluggish. The Carat's 16.9secs 0–60mph time is good for a van, but by car standards … it is simply

not good enough. Beyond 60mph the rate of acceleration is even less acceptable. It takes almost 10secs to climb from 60 to 70mph and a further 20secs to reach 80mph. Given enough road, it will eventually reach 90mph.

Moving swiftly on to a time when American magazine *Road and Track* was fully aware that the Vanagon's days were numbered, the swansong review is surprisingly generous. While denigrating it as 'one of the slowest vehicles on the road', the author of the article, 'You don't know what you've got til it's gone', nevertheless portrayed the catalyzer-bound 2.1-litre engine as 'smooth', and decided that despite the plethora of vehicles with V8 torque on American roads, perhaps there was a

place for a Vanagon with this power plant after all.

As most of us know, the 3,500lb Vanagon struggles to sustain fast-lane speeds up to freeway grades. But to the surprise of those accustomed to V8 torque, it's not all that big a deal to drop down a gear and join the trucks in the right lane for a while. Driver and Vanagon will be more relaxed anyway. And on flat land, the Vanagon maintains freeway speeds with ease. Treated right … the flat-4 will provide continued good service.

The specification chart for the 2.1-litre endeavours to include as many details as possible, in line with those charts produced for other engines.

2.1-Litre Petrol Engine Technical Data, 1985–End of Production

112PS fuel-injected petrol engine

Bore	94.0mm
Stroke	76.0mm
Cubic capacity	2109cc
Compression ratio	10.5:1
Output – kW	
DIN	82kW
	112PS
@ rpm	4,800
Maximum torque	174Nm
	128lb ft
@rpm	2,800
Fuel rating (RON)	98
Fuel air supply	Digital controlled fuel-injection system (Digi-Jet)
Maximum speed	94mph (151km/h)
Acceleration 0–50mph	10.3 sec
Fuel consumption (at half payload, constant ¾ maximum speed, + 10%)	21.9mpg (12.9ltr/100km)

2.1-Litre Petrol Engine Gear Ratios

Gear ratios	5-speed
1st gear	4.11:1
2nd gear	2.13:1
3rd gear	1.48:1
4th gear	1.02:1
5th gear	0.77:1
Reverse gear	3.67:1
Final drive	4.57:1

The text written by Volkswagen to accompany this press image of a pre-production Caravelle refers to an air-cooled engine. Emerging as the changeover from air to water was occurring, the error was perhaps understandable.

5 increasing luxury and an off-road dimension

Whereas the previous chapter was devoted to the progression from classic air-cooling to the introduction of a diesel lump, to modern water-cooled engines, this one is devoted to two very different aspects of range development. The first theme is one of evolution, from late 1970s simplicity to ever-increasing luxury; the second is a tale of technological development, with the emergence of a new strain of T3, the dynamically versatile off-road models – the syncro vehicles.

RISE OF THE CARAVELLE

Hot on the heels of the switch to water-cooled engines, other departments at Volkswagen turned their attentions to rebranding the passenger-carrying elements of the T3 range, no doubt with the intention of fighting back in true Germanic style against Japanese bus imports and their inherent magpie-attracting gadgetry and gimmickry. Those hardest at work were the stylists, the makeover moguls, who once upon a time Volkswagen's management only tolerated at arm's length, but who, in an

age where additional sales and revenue could be achieved by offering a touch of luxury, were now at their busiest.

When the T3 was launched, the passenger-carrying elements of the range were endowed, or perhaps more accurately lumbered, with the collective title of 'Bus', hardly a word destined to endear the more affluent European to the concept. (Americans were saved from such a fate, as the newly created term Vanagon disguised a multitude of sins.) Clearly, if trim was to be enhanced and luxury embraced, a new name was essential, and from this was born the concept of the Caravelle. A toe-in-the-water tactic of a special launched at the IAA motor show in Frankfurt in September 1981, which found its way neither across the Atlantic nor to the British market, was sufficiently well received that by the time the 1983 model year's publicity material was available, the Caravelle had invaded the UK and America, albeit known in the latter as the Vanagon GL.

The special German edition forerunner's main attributes had been listed as:

two-tone paint; chrome bumpers with rubber trim; rear window wash/wipe system; driver and passenger head-rests; improved seat upholstery and padding, with foldable armrests on all seats; full carpet; additional storage compartments, protective bars for rear windows; driver and passenger door quarter-lights and 185 SR 14 radials. Now *Safer Volkswagen Motoring*'s November 1982 edition appropriately reproduced a press release with which to compare details of the Caravelle that would make its debut at the British Motor Show.

The Caravelle, a luxury specification Transporter, is making its first appearance on the Volkswagen light commercials stand at the NEC Motor Show. Seating a total of seven in considerable luxury, the Caravelle is an executive-style Transporter. The individually-contoured seats all have armrests for the central pair of seats and two for the rear triple seat. The interior is trimmed with plain and patterned velour and the floor is fully carpeted. Four controllable for direction fresh air outlets are mounted in the headlining above the side windows. A two tone paint finish distinguishes the exterior. The specification includes a laminated windscreen, rear wash/wipe, trip-meter and clock, cigar lighter and locking petrol filler cap. The Caravelle is available with either the 2.0 litre four cylinder air-cooled petrol engine or the 1.6 litre diesel.

Ignoring the communication faux pas between Wolfsburg and VAG (United Kingdom) Ltd with regard to engines, the path to luxury was clear; the thinking behind the special had clearly worked. Volkswagen of America told their version of the Caravelle launch story particularly effectively even though the name was never mentioned. Instead the story was of the by now classic Vanagon L and an all-new more luxurious level of trim, branded the GL.

Their opening gambit was to emphasize the solidity of the Vanagon and to suggest that such ruggedness was unlikely to be paired with a luxurious interior. In this respect the Vanagon GL broke the mould: the GL had an 'impressive ambience', its credentials focusing on the entirely frivolous comfort of contoured seats, the peculiar luxury of arm rests tailored for every seat, and the aesthetic pleasures of a colour-coordinated headlining, door trims and side panel materials.

Apart from describing the component list that made the Caravelle special, *Volkswagen Audi Car*'s Paul Harris drew an interesting analogy with top-of-the-range Transporters from previous generations, an approach that the marketing men devoted to promoting the Caravelle as a new concept would probably have deprecated.

The Type 2 range has seen many changes during recent years … The Caravelle is very much a luxury version of the Type 2. It is a seven seater vehicle with very generous amounts of luggage space, a high level of luxury for the occupants and yet all the utility of purpose which one expects of a Type 2 vehicle. This combination has been used before in the much earlier Samba and the Microbus de Luxe.

Volkswagen's press release to accompany this image referred to a feeling of 'elegance and solidity' and the Caravelle's 'affinity to a large passenger car'.

Many of Volkswagen of America's publicity images featured Vanagons in action. This image dates from 1984 and is of a Vanagon GL.

The 1985 model year Vanagon GL. Note how Volkswagen of America were eager to illustrate the vehicle's interior as well as its exterior.

In the main body of the vehicle there is a full-width seat for three occupants, separating off the rear luggage compartment and, adjacent to the nearside sliding door, a narrower bench for two. These bench seats feature fold down armrests … Both driver and front passenger have well shaped, if somewhat firm seats, with fold down armrests on either side. One of the features of these vehicles is the height at which one sits and the amount of roll which occurs if they are driven vigorously. For these reasons, these armrests are a boon. Both seats are adjustable fore and aft and both have a lever which allows one to adjust the backrest angle. As we have noticed on previous vehicles, sliding out of the driver's seat often depresses the lever so that the backrest shoots to its vertical position.

… The floors are carpeted with a good quality pile carpet and the trim panels have sections of upholstery material let into them. The Type 2s still have a traditional, flexible headliner and all interior appointments are very well conceived. Each seat has a headrest and both main side windows have sliding sections to increase ventilation.

… The Caravelle certainly takes the Type 2 into the luxury market. Not only will it accommodate six people plus the driver in comfort, but it provides them with much more living room and space to spread their legs than one ever gets in an equivalent car. We can foresee lots of organisations for whom a Caravelle would be of much more use than a company luxury car …

Such was the impact of the Caravelle that with effect from the start of the 1984 model year, in August 1983, Volkswagen went one large step further in all places except North America, where the Vanagon name would remain at the core of marketing strategies until the end of T3 production. At last the increasingly undesirable Bus

Caravelle script adorned the rear of the vehicle. Note how the style changed over the years, the upright version being the earlier of the two.

The liftstyle portrayal in this image was undoubtedly deliberately chosen to assist in the promotion of the Caravelle.

terminology was banished to its rightful place in the dusty and hopefully forgotten archives, while the once model-specific name of Caravelle embraced all passenger-carrying T3 models, which were now carefully divided into three trim levels of ascending luxury: C, CL, and GL.

Dedicated publicity material placed full emphasis on the GL element of the range – passenger transport at its most luxuriant! Volkswagen were committing to changing the way people thought of the vehicle that had been known as the Transporter for over thirty years and they had no intention of harking back to the days of the Samba, as *Volkswagen Audi Car* had suggested. Their message was one of a new concept in personal transport, a limousine that could carry more than the normal four, or possibly five, people; luxury transport that remained so even when fully laden with the paraphernalia of a

weekend break or a longer holiday, unlike the more cramped conditions experienced under such circumstances in even the most lavish of estate cars.

Volkswagen claimed a first in their creation of an opulent vehicle for the 'larger family', the 'sporting fraternity' and the executive business class. Sadly, however understandable such an assertion was in its attempt to belittle the offerings of rival manufacturers, in so doing Volkswagen denigrated their ancestry by overlooking the much-loved Microbus De Luxe of first- and second-generation Transporter fame. To a lesser extent they also denied the heritage of the standard Microbus of earlier years and possibly even the shining star of the range, the ubiquitous Kombi. The proclamation that the Caravelle ranged from the 'practical' to the 'downright luxurious', which the earlier models in their various guises had similarly done, was undoubtedly

The T3 Caravelle Range 1984 – UK market		
Model	**Engine**	**Gearbox**
Caravelle C 8-seater	60PS and 78PS petrol, 50PS diesel	5-speed and automatic
Caravelle CL 8-seater	60PS and 78PS petrol, 50PS diesel	5-speed and automatic
Caravelle C 9-seater	78PS petrol, 50PS diesel	5-speed and automatic
Caravelle CL 9-seater	78PS petrol, 50PS diesel	5-speed and automatic
Caravelle C 12-seater	60PS and 78PS petrol, 50PS diesel	4- and 5-speed, plus automatic
Caravelle GL 7-seater	78PS petrol, 50PS diesel	5-speed and automatic

careless, while a boast that there were now twelve-, nine-, eight- and seven-seat configurations, however impressive it might be to new members of the larger Volkswagen community, was hardly shiny, tempting and new to the old hands, who were only too aware that it had all been done before.

All that having been said, little helps to identify the scope of the Caravelle range more clearly than reference to the specification details, which highlight the differences between the luxurious GL, the intermediate CL and the comparatively comfortable base

From left to right the images show the front ends of the Caravelle C, the Caravelle CL, and the Caravelle GL – base model to top of the range when these images were produced in the mid-1980s.

Caravelle Specifications by Model

Caravelle C 8- and 9-seater

Trim Full-length headlining, rubber matting on cab floor and passenger area, interior trim in vinyl, cab door arm rests, luggage compartment insulated and carpeted.

Seating Driver's seat adjustable for reach and rake; 8-seater version – passenger seat as driver's, 9-seater version – static dual passenger seat in cab. Centre bench secured on rails for easy removal. All seats covered in textured leatherette.

Windows Heated rear window.

Access Passenger compartment in 9-seater – additional sliding door on offside.

Storage Storage compartment under passenger seat, large lidded and lockable glove box.

Heating and fresh-air system 3-speed heater fan, 4 slide controls for distribution and heat selection, side window demister vents, 4 controllable fresh-air vents in roof of passenger area, sliding air extraction in cab doors.

Exterior Black-painted bumpers with plastic end caps, chrome hubcaps.

Caravelle C 12-seater – specification as Caravelle C with the following alterations

Seating Fixed dual passenger seat as per 9-seater. Three rows of three benches in the passenger compartment, all static.

Windows Sliding doors have sliding windows.

Access Dual sliding doors.

Caravelle CL 8- and 9-seater – specification as Caravelle C with the following additions

Trim Side panels with ornamental strip.

Seating Seats covered in hard-wearing patterned cloth materials. Front and rear head restraints.

Windows Opening quarter-lights, sliding windows, rear wash/wipe.

Equipment Chrome rear window protection bars, cigar lighter, padded steering wheel, dashboard padding, driver's door stowage pocket.

Instruments Quartz clock, trip mileage recorder.

Exterior Chrome bumpers with rubber protective inserts, additional exterior bright work, rain gutters to side of windscreen, lockable fuel cap.

Caravelle GL – specification as per CL with the following alterations

Trim Carpets fitted in cab and passenger area, cab doors and passenger compartment trim panels with velour inserts.

Seating for seven – driver's and passengers' seats equipped with folding arm rests. Centre row in passenger compartment accommodates two seats individually contoured. Outer arm rests are static, the centre rest is folding. The rear row seats three. Two folding arm rests, individually contoured seats. All seats are covered in a rich velour cloth and equipped with open-style head rests.

Windows Sliding windows in side door and in opposite panel, heat-insulating tinted glass.

Equipment Three interior lamps.

Controls Washer/wipe stalk operates rear wash/wipe and has a position for intermittent windscreen wiper operation.

Caravelle Standard Paint and Upholstery Combinations – UK, Early Years					
	Velour Saiga	Velour Balear	Cloth Black	Leatherette Black	Leatherette Van Dyck
Caravelle C					
Pastel White					✓
Capri Blue				✓	
Bamboo Yellow				✓	
Marsala Red				✓	
Caravelle CL					
Capri Blue/Damus White			✓		
Marsala Red/Damus White			✓		
Navy Blue/Capri Blue			✓		
Caravelle GL					
Dove Grey					
Metallic		✓			
Savannah Beige					
Metallic	✓				

model, the C. However, note that the particulars produced in the specification chart have been extracted from UK market publications and minor variations between countries could well exist. Similarly, year-by-year revisions to the specification of each model might make the list, which dates from the second year of the adoption of Caravelle range terminology, appear inaccurate. Really obvious elements of the basic specification have been deliberately overlooked.

Additionally, the exterior paint finish and upholstery helped to distinguish trim levels without reference to a badge. This can be broadly summarized as: single-colour paint with leatherette upholstery – C trim; dual colour paint with cloth upholstery – CL trim; and metallic paint with velour upholstery – GL trim. For the UK at least, some paint options were offered as standard in each trim level, while further options were available to special order.

Optional paint colours for the Caravelle C were: Ivory, Timor Beige, Navy Blue, Escorial Green and Merian Brown. These shades were offered with Van Dyck, or brown, leatherette upholstery, other than the Navy Blue shade, which came with black. The Caravelle CL was available with the following optional paint shades, all of which came with Van Dyck cloth upholstery: Bamboo Yellow/Damus White, Escorial Green/May Green, Merian Brown/Tuscan Beige. The Caravelle GL could be specified with two additional metallic paint options, which were Flash Silver (mated with Balear velour) and Bronze Beige (paired with Saiga velour).

Allowing for the transposition of imagery to make a T3 photographed in Germany appear suitable for the cover of a right-hand-drive market brochure, two simultaneously published and at first glance identical

Model Options, 1986 – Netherlands versus UK	
Netherlands	**UK**
De gesloten bestelwagen	The Delivery Van
(including high roof version)	(including high roof version)
De Pick-up	The Pick-up
(including extended load platform)	(extended load platform version not available)
De Pick-up met dubbele cabine	The Double Cab
De Combi	
(including high roof version)	
De Caravelle C	The Caravelle C
De Caravelle CL	The Caravelle CL
De Caravelle GL	The Caravelle GL
(available with two-colour paint and metallic finishes)	(available in metallic paint finish only)
De Caravelle Carat	
De Transporter en Caravelle syncro	The Transporter and Caravelle syncro

There were 15 upholstery options for the Netherlands, as opposed to 11 in Britain, while overall the number of paint shades available varied by just one in favour of the Netherlands; but when matching paint to upholstery the choices were strictly limited.

model range guides, one for Holland and the other for Britain, soon demonstrated the disparity in available options between nations and markets (*see* chart on page 94).

TOP OF THE RANGE – THE CARAVELLE CARAT

Virtually simultaneously with Volkswagen's adoption of the Caravelle brand for all passenger vehicles, another special made its debut on the home market. This was the Caravelle Carat, an even more luxurious luxury vehicle than the Caravelle GL and one that carried features that would in later years be integrated across the range. Thanks to the special's sales performance, the Carat was added to the range with effect from September 1985, although not all markets benefited from it immediately, while in the USA the badging remained strictly in the familiar realms of Vanagon and Vanagon GL. Nevertheless, one modernizing characteristic of the Carat, its rectangular twin-bulb headlamps, were added almost instantaneously.

Having used contemporary publicity material and reviews about various vehicles written at the time throughout this volume, for once it's appropriate to crib from one of last issues of *VW Motoring* (November 1985) magazine. With fellow editor of the day, Ken Cservenka, we came across a Caravelle Carat in near immaculate condition and to our delight, the owner, Fritz Yarwood, turned out to be something of an expert on the model.

The fuel injected, 2100cc, boxer engine developed 112bhp and, as the vehicle had a gross weight of 2500kg, power steering was standard. This was a luxury reserved for the Carat, for although … [other] Caravelle [models] weighed just as much, muscular owners had to tug away to get the vehicle to go where it was supposed to when requested. Power assisted steering, not to mention electrically heated and adjustable door mirrors, plus electric cab windows and lip-licking alloy wheels were all Carat exclusives, without anyone having to delve into a costly accessory list.

Fritz's T25 Carat, however, which had allegedly started life as a fleet vehicle

'The special class of the new Caravelle Carat is emphasized externally by twin halogen headlights, a front spoiler, front and rear bumpers in flexible glass-fibre-reinforced plastic, side protectors, newly styled alloy wheels and matched two-tone metallic paintwork' – Volkswagen AG.

With six individual seats covered in velour upholstery, velour carpeting, a trimmed luggage space, cloth inserts in both doors and trim panels, fully upholstered roof, posts and window caps, Volkswagen had created a true luxury vehicle in the Carat.

Another press image of the Carat confirms a number of features unique to the model, the most obvious of which were twin rectangular headlamps and the moulded fibre-glass-reinforced plastic bumpers. Gradually these and other parts of the Carat package would filter down to other models.

This image shows a Vanagon Camper and dates from the 1987 model year.

used by Volkswagen to ship top executives about, contains even more goodies than most, for while some can soon be determined as part of the standard package, others would have required a mooch around the accessory bins. Herr Yarwood want[ed] the world to know the full list of features and had even had a display board made to proclaim his Carat's pedigree. Of that list and in no particular order, the following are recognised Carat attributes or acknowledged accessories for this vehicle: ABS; a roof mounted air-conditioning system; cruise control; central locking; auxiliary under-floor heating; a factory body kit; suspension lowered at the factory by 30mm; headlamp washers; two side storage lockers added to an already generous luggage area; and a tinted windscreen and windows ...

Scouring through a list of the equipment special to the Caravelle Carat dating from the start of the 1989 model year, the following additional items, or perhaps slightly differently described attributes, are to be found:

Additions
- Spotlights (reading lights) with rotating control
- Illuminated ashtrays and cigarette lighters
- Front passenger's sun visor with illuminated make-up mirror
- Telltale light for dual circuit brakes and handbrake

- Reading light on front passenger's side
- Automatic light on step
- Luggage compartment lights
- Protective grille for rear window

Volkswagen's official descriptions
- Rectangular halogen twin headlamps
- Front spoiler
- Bumpers and trim surround colour co-ordinated
- 6J × 14 light-alloy wheels with 205/70 R14 tyres

As the T3's lifespan drew to a close, one or two attributes once unique to the top-of-the-range Caravelle Carat were carefully passed through to the lower-specification models. Intentionally or not, such filtering mimicked the modern tradition of loading run-out models with extra goodies at little extra cost. In today's parlance, whenever the trim

Twin rectangular headlamps on what started life as a Delivery Van and became a Camper – this vehicle was first registered in June 1989.

level 'Match', or 'Highline' is listed, it is a sure sign that Volkswagen are planning at least a facelift sufficient to brand the model as 'new' and more likely the introduction of a new genre of whichever model has been so designated. With the T3, however, it is more likely that trends and tastes were gradually changing and that the inclusion of such items as twin rectangular headlamps and moulded bumpers was simply a way of keeping the now aging third-generation Transporter relatively fresh in the eye of potential purchasers.

Despite the loss of some of its unique attributes, the Carat could still be described as 'pure luxury for six'. The final-year specification included the following (wherever possible Volkswagen's own terminology has been used):

- Metallic paintwork standard
- Colour-keyed lower body panels
- Alloy wheels
- Electrically adjustable, heated external mirrors
- Electrically operable cab windows
- Power steering
- Swivel and lock rear-facing centre seats for 'conference on the move' facilities
- Each seat provided with arm rests and individual back rest adjustment
- Deep pile carpeting throughout – linked to additional soundproofing designed to make the Carat exceptionally quiet
- Additional heater for the rear seat passengers to boost the output of the main system
- Optional full air-conditioning
- Top-of-the-range stereo radio cassette
- Side lockers in luggage area for stowing smaller, more vulnerable items

Despite such a lip-smacking description of the Carat, modern-day readers of Volkswagen's now almost classic literature would have been shocked to discover that the years of Caravelle brand building now appeared to have been in vain. Once again, a new story had emerged, and while the Caravelle name had survived, and would continue to do so throughout the lifespan of the third-generation Transporter's successor, the T4, and beyond, the term

Three images showing how all models had inherited characteristics once the sole preserve of the Carat, and how even the base model of the passenger-carrying range had progressed in terms of comfort.

was no longer the all-embracing concept of a few short years earlier. Instead the copywriter wrote of 'the new face of Volkswagen … Carat, Caravelle, Coach, Bus … a new range of vehicles designed to carry people in comfort and style.' Hence, whereas the Carat – the Caravelle prefix had been dropped

Branding on the front of a late base model in the passenger-carrying range.

– was 'the executive limousine with space, comfort and performance', the single model Caravelle had returned to its roots as, 'executive transport for seven people', while the eight- or nine-seat Coach was 'the general purpose people carrier', with hallmarks such as 'easy to clean wheel trims' and a floor 'covered with practical rubber matting for convenience' marking it out as the successor to the Caravelle C. As for the Bus, this was what Volkswagen described as 'a purpose built shell supplied to … converters'. Perhaps the most telling remark came after the copywriter had listed a host of possible conversions. 'They all have one thing in common. They are based on the Volkswagen Bus'. Talk about coming full circle!

VANAGON GL – THE FINAL MODELS

Having largely overlooked the progress of the Vanagon in North America in the latter years of the T3's production run, using the excuse that the range remained more or less unaltered, at least in terms of models available, a quick glance at the '1991 Vanagon

Specification', taken from a brochure printed in June 1990, illustrates that such a pretext could lead to less than a complete story being told. Certainly as far as the Vanagon GL was concerned, it had stayed put, not only at the top of the range, but with the same name it had always had. With an explanatory narrative making reassuring references to 'rich velour upholstery, front and rear heating, an electric window defroster and front and rear intermittent wipers', as well as 'reclining, body-contoured front seats featuring adjustable fold down armrests' the text appeared to confirm that little had happened. Perhaps a catalogue of the paint shades available at this late stage was indicative of Volkswagen's progression with their American people-carrier. How many of the following would have been offered a few short years earlier? Of the two straightforward paint shades – Navy Blue and Pastel White – neither had been available as recently as 1987, while Volkswagen had reacted to the growing trend away from dual-colour vehicles by deleting all reference to the often brash colour combinations of years gone by. Now the story was dominated by metallic paints, and here there was at least a semblance of continuity, as both Dove Blue and Flash Silver were popular survivors of a few years standing. Now the choice of fashionable colours was extended to include both a fruity Bordeaux Red and an oceanic Orly Blue.

The big change in the United States and Canada however, was the deletion

The 1991 model year sales brochure for the Vanagon GL included this carefully posed image. Note that Volkswagen of America were still selling the Vanagon after production had ceased on all models but the syncro offerings, and that the top-of-the-range vehicle was still referred to as the GL.

in the final years of the straightforward Vanagon and the introduction of a most interesting concept, the many-purpose Vanagon Multivan. Without wishing to pre-empt the storyline of the next chapter, in which the Vanagon GL Camper plays an exceedingly important part, the Multivan was something of a cross between a people carrier and a Camper. As such, it had an important role to play in Volkswagen's by then rapidly dissolving American dream.

THE MULTIVAN

The path to production of the Multivan started with its presentation at the September 1985 IAA show in Frankfurt as a special Camper study compiled at Volkswagen's behest by close outdoor partners, Westfalia. Such was the interest expressed in the concept that within twelve months the Multivan had been accepted into the range and would reach many a market. Essentially, the Multivan was a simple Camper with sufficient seats – seven in total – to convey the largest of families comfortably on a trip to the shops, or on safari if so desired. The rear bench seat was designed to fold down and, together with a cushion over the engine bay, converted into a generously proportioned bed. A storage drawer under the same bank of seats, a cool box stored behind the passenger cab seat, a flush-fitting foldaway table and various more minor attributes, like cup-holders and

carpets overlaid with plastic mats, more or less completed the package.

After the original Multivan variations inevitably emerged with, for example, US models including an elevating roof as standard, while alloy wheels certainly wouldn't have graced the home market product. The US Multivan came with the 2.1-litre engine as might be expected, but elsewhere it could be specified as a turbo-diesel, with the 78PS petrol engine, or as either a 112PS 2.1-litre or 95PS 2.1-litre with catalytic converter.

The complete list of equipment for the Multivan over and above that of the basic specification for all T3 models was listed as follows in a Technical Data and Equipment list dated August 1988 (for the 1989 model year):

- ◆ Painted bumpers
- ◆ Wheel trim covers
- ◆ Cloth seat upholstery
- ◆ Door trims with arm rest and door pull handle
- ◆ Front seats with folding arm rests
- ◆ Carpeted cab floor
- ◆ Wooden floor with plastic coating in passenger compartment
- ◆ Folding three-seater rear bench seat with head rests
- ◆ Storage compartment beneath rear bench seat
- ◆ Padded safety steering wheel
- ◆ Second battery with cut-off relay
- ◆ Fresh air outlets for passenger compartment

Der Volkswagen Multivan.

Special literature was produced to promote the Multivan.

- ◆ Side panel trims with folding table, integral arm rests, ashtrays and drink can holders
- ◆ Transistor light above folding table
- ◆ Individual seat with storage compartment behind the passenger seat (LHD vehicles)
- ◆ 12-volt icebox with plug socket
- ◆ Button-on curtains in passenger compartment
- ◆ Roof lining
- ◆ Luggage compartment lined at left and right
- ◆ Tailgate lined
- ◆ Wide cushion with fabric upholstery on luggage compartment floor

LEFT: Tailgate badge denoting the Multivan.

BELOW LEFT: An enthusiast's Multivan on display at a Transporter meeting.

BELOW RIGHT: The versatility of the interior of the Multivan is demonstrated in this VW Press Office image.

- Heated air outlets for passenger compartment in centre aisle (not on models with automatic transmission and turbo-diesel engine)
- Heat exchanger under rear bench seat on models with automatic transmission and turbo-diesel engine
- Through-flow ventilation behind rear side windows

As a concept, the Multivan was destined to outlive the T3, and rightly so. Here was a vehicle that avoided the intricacies of the full-blown camper, which were and are by their very nature a type designed to appeal to a specific market. Instead, the Multivan offered all-year-round, no-compromise facilities for passengers, while also encom-

passing sufficient attributes to make a regular home-from-home picnic enjoyable, and an occasional midsummer night under the stars decidedly pleasant. With the North American add-on of an elevating roof and a skylight, few would have been able to resist the Multivan's temptations. Volkswagen were aware they had another winning combination on their hands, and under the jurisdiction of the T4 the company made sure that the concept was kept up to date and meaningful.

THE WHIMSICAL WORLD OF THE T3 SPECIALS

Having started life as a design study and product with an anticipated short shelf life itself, just like the original Car-

avelle and the equally one-off Caravelle Carat, the Multivan spawned its own special – the Multivan Magnum. For anyone diligent enough to wish to know about every special model, market-specific peculiarities, invaluable 'accessories' for specific applications and more, Volkswagen catalogued the lot, recording the extras on every vehicle to leave Hanover in the form of a plate under the passenger seat, stickers by the driver's pedals, or a label attached to the front page of the service book. Brief reference has already been made to 'M' codes, the letter 'M' being an abbreviation for *Mehrausstattung* (factory-fitted extras, or occasionally deletions, from a specification), in Chapter 3, to these it is now necessary to add 'S' codes, short for

Like its predecessors, the third-generation Transporter deliberately spawned many special-purpose models. A reasonable percentage of such vehicles could be found under a Volkswagen 'S' code, alongside special-edition packages more related to trim than purpose. An 'S' code denoted that either the factory built the variant itself, or had officially delegated the task to an approved agent. Other established converters and adaptors continued as they had done previously to buy Transporters from Volkswagen and then carry out their own conversions. The manufacturer of the ambulance shown in colour was the well-known conversion firm of Binz.

Sonderausführungen (special models). Nevertheless, in the topsy-turvy way Volkswagen chose to record its models, it was equally possible for a limited edition to be listed under an 'M' code on the basis that most such vehicles were little more than standard models with additional trim.

The accompanying table is not intended to be exhaustive – far from it – but merely to illustrate how the factory identified its own products, while setting the scene for a little more detail regarding a couple of particularly interesting limited edition models. Constituent parts contributing to particular specials are included as well, as are specifics to illustrate, for example, how in the production of a right-hand-drive vehicle use of particular equipment was essential.

Multivan Magnum

S741, the Multivan Magnum, was conceived in February 1987 and continued in production until the end of the 1988 model year on 31 July. A special sales

Selected 'M' and 'S' Special Order Codes	
Note: codes might be reallocated and no code was necessarily applicable from 1979 to 1990	
M18	Padded steering wheel
M20	Speedometer in mph
M58	Bumper and spoiler applicable to the Caravelle Carat
M61	Speedometer in mph, temperature gauge in Fahrenheit, headlamp dim and full-beam setting suitable for British market
M73	Opening in roof for Campmobile
M106	Cloth upholstery instead of leatherette
M127	Tailgate without window
M137	Prepared for Camper conversion firm
M201	Pick-up with enlarged wooden platform
M299	Four-wheel drive syncro package
M314	Limited edition model 'TriStar'
M521	Caravelle Carat
M542	Special equipment for German armed forces
M552	Additional heater in the passenger compartment
M568	Green tinted side windows
M693	Driver's seat swivel
S735	Limited edition model 'Bluestar' (body-coloured mirrors, folding table, provision to collapse rear seats to make a bed etc.), based on Caravelle GL
S741	Limited edition model Multivan 'Magnum'
S746	Limited edition model Caravelle C 'Coach' (body kit, spoiler, big bumpers, light grey interior)
S773	Limited edition model 'Caravelle'

TOP: *The Multivan Magnum. The vinyl decal above the headlamp hardly shows in the main picture, and a close-up shot demonstrates why.*

LEFT: *The German market limited edition Bluestar.*

BOTTOM: *A side shot of the BlueStar and the large but subtle decal used to identify the special.*

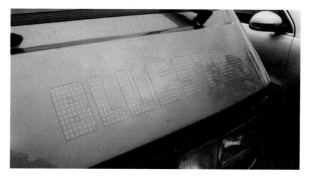

brochure was duly released but all this revealed was a regular Multivan with a smattering of additional equipment or trimmings, which included Carat-style lower body kit and moulded bumpers, plus dual light rectangular headlamps.

TriStar

Available from the last days of February 1988, the TriStar was to all extent and purposes a luxury version of the increasingly popular Double Cab Pick-up, which by the time of the special's launch had been available with Volkswagen's revolutionary four-wheel drive system for the best part of three years on the home market at least and is the only remaining major T3 development by Volkswagen yet to be covered in this chapter. Unquestionably, here was a forerunner of the luxurious four-wheel drive giant pick-ups built in ever-increasing numbers to satisfy the needs of businesses, who, in the UK at least, had been able until recent years to avoid paying company car tax by opting for a high spec pick-up with plentiful seating for the family and a reasonable load area. Of course, if questions were asked, such vehicles could be hastily crammed with the attributes of the Monday to Friday job, confirming their status as a van or workhorse, and thus releasing an owner or driver from any liability when it came to the punitive taxes imposed on the car-using employee or boss of any business.

The TriStar proved a popular special model, so appealing that Volkswagen saw considerable financial gain coming their way through the extension of the four-wheel drive people-carrier to many markets, including Britain. Inevitably special sales literature was demanded and printed and it is from this source that a list of its special attrib-

Publicity material for the Multivan Magnum included the stage-style backdrop depicted here.

utes is taken. Top of the range in all respects, the TriStar inevitably sported either the 112PS fuel-injected petrol engine, or the 70PS turbo-diesel power plant. Power steering was handed over from the Caravelle Carat too.

Exterior 'extras'
◆ Twin rear doors with sliding windows
◆ Moulded front bumper system
◆ Front and rear wheelarch protection
◆ Lower panels painted black

◆ Front grille with twin headlight rectangular lamps
◆ Headlight washers
◆ Halogen front fog lights
◆ 6J × 14 alloys (6J × 14 steel wheels optional)

Interior 'extras'
◆ Front seats (adjustable for reach and rake) with arm rests, head restraints and map pockets
◆ Contoured rear bench seat for three passengers incorporating storage locker

Volkswagen released a wealth of imagery in the UK to promote the TriStar, from the distinctly quirky to the decidedly matter of fact.

- Light grey cloth upholstery
- Pile carpeting throughout the cabin
- Additional heater for rear bench passengers
- Padded steering wheel
- Illuminated vanity mirror
- Heated rear window
- Rev counter and digital clock
- Padded dashboard
- Bottle stowage facility

Optional extras included a variety of so-called bull bars, roll bars and air-conditioning, as well as various additional shades of paint, including Cherry and Titian Red in the plain colours, and two metallic choices in the form of Flash Silver and Dove Grey. The standard paint colours were Capri Blue and Pastel White.

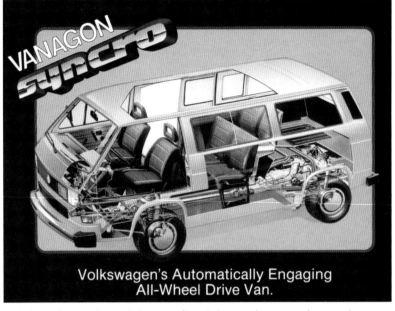

Volkswagen's Automatically Engaging All-Wheel Drive Van.

While the wording was clever on Volkswagen of America's postcard to promote the syncro the illustration would only have meant something to those aware of the principles behind the technology.

FOUR-WHEEL DRIVE TRANSPORTER

Volkswagen's desire to dabble with four-wheel drive was definitely a theme of the 1980s. The Passat was the first to be endowed, its debut being announced in October 1984, and within months the third-generation Transporter had joined it. In the minds of some journalists, never had a vehicle been more appropriate for such a development, and amidst the excitement, bordering on hype, a few even forgot that the T3 wasn't the four-wheel drive pioneer for Volkswagen they claimed it to be. Here is Chris Burlace writing in *VW Motoring*, in July 1985:

> The VW Transporter has long been a favourite vehicle for use in out-of-the way places where, off-road, its excellent traction resulting from the rear-engine layout has been highly valued. Now, however, with a profusion of 4-wheel drive vehicles available worldwide the Transporter's rivals are many. It is not surprising, therefore, that VW have chosen the light commercial as the first in their range to benefit from 4wd.

Despite such a transgression, Chris Burlace had made two important and intrinsically linked points. Due to the diversity of the Transporter/Caravelle and Camper range, Volkswagen's T3, more than any other vehicle produced at Wolfsburg, Hanover or elsewhere, was the one that would best benefit from four-wheel drive; the sales potential was far greater than with the Passat, for example. Secondly, the upsurge in Far Eastern and particularly Japanese seemingly high-tech and certainly high-spec products, combined with the adoption of four-wheel drive by many a European manufacturer, looked set to topple the T3 from the pivotal place its predecessors had held from the concept's birth more than thirty years earlier.

Some commentators said Volkswagen appeared to have been asleep, that a march had been stolen. The reality of the situation was completely the opposite, despite a couple of oddities later in the story; Volkswagen's associations with a four-wheel drive Transporter stemmed back more than a decade. In the mid 1970s, unbeknown first to Leiding, and later to Schmücker and their respective boards of management, two enthusiastic engineers, Gustav Mayer and Henning Duckstein, clandestinely created an all-wheel drive version of the second-generation Transporter. Referred to as project EA 456/01,

The launch of the syncro saw Volkswagen issue a further version of the already amended cutaway drawing of the T3. As the essence of syncro technology was out of view it was necessary to produce a mirror image of the underside of the T3.

testing of the vehicle started prophetically on Christmas Day 1975, with the Sahara and areas where ferociously tricky sand dunes might easily extend to over 400m (1,300ft) in height duly targeted as ideal terrain. The total mileage on this pioneering trip extended to a gruelling 800km (500 miles) and the prototype accomplished every task with consummate ease. With the vehicle's existence difficult to disguise in the light of its success, it wasn't long before Wolfsburg's sale's department requested the development of a further 'Allroad', as the four-wheel drive Transporter had been named, and by the time production of the second-generation model ceased in the high summer of 1979, a total of five off-roaders had been built – three Kombis and two Westfalia Campers.

The demise of the second-generation Transporter inevitably scuppered further progress towards production with that model. However, when the press announcements broke in early 1985 that production of four-wheel drive T3s, to be known as syncro models, had begun 'officially' at the Steyr-Daimler-Puch factory in Graz, Austria, it became clear that development work had been in progress for some time. *VW Motoring*'s News Round-up of February 1985 carried the information release issued by Wolfsburg to journalists more or less verbatim.

> The Austrian company, which has particular expertise in the field of specialised transmission systems, have developed the all-wheel drive Transporter in conjunction with Volkswagenwerk under an agreement signed in May 1982, and will be responsible for assembling the series production vehicles, using their own transmissions in

combination with CKD parts kits supplied by VW's Hanover commercial vehicle plant. Production of the four-wheel-drive Transporters is being gradually increased to an average of 40 vehicles per day in readiness for the planned launch in March …

A further release, this time covered in depth in the April 1985 edition of *Volkswagen Audi Car*, illustrated the severity of the rules and the depth of thought behind the contract with Steyr-Daimler-Puch. Clearly not the result of a whim of the latest Director General, Carl Hahn, who had assumed office on 1 January 1982, the only queries to emerge retrospectively related to the perfunctory dismissal of the second-generation prototypes and the somewhat unusual decision to reject both the experience and design technology of Volkswagen's wholly owned subsidiary, Audi, whose endeavours with the Quattro had rocketed them to the forefront of attention on a number of fronts.

Nevertheless, a look at the ground-rules for Steyr-Daimler-Puch's work provides an insight into the management and development style of the Volkswagen Company rarely afforded elsewhere.

- The four-wheel drive system had to fit into the body of the T3 without changing it
- As few new parts as possible were to be involved
- Optimal reliability was demanded even under difficult conditions
- A minimum of service requirements was essential
- The already well-known road-holding properties of the T3 were to be improved upon

- The system must work without requiring further action from the vehicle's driver
- The comfort afforded by the T3's radical new suspension had to be maintained

'syncro' – the Specification

Steyr-Daimler-Puch were masters of their craft and leaders in their specialist field, previous successes ranging from the then well-known, but tiny, Haflinger, to the Mercedes 'G-Wagen', the most luxurious off-road vehicle then imaginable. At the heart of their work for Volkswagen was a British invention, the 'viscous coupling', which had been developed by Ferguson and used by Jenson and on the race track using the 'Ferguson Formula' four-wheel drive arrangement.

The viscous coupling, built into the front differential unit, was filled with a thick silicon oil and hermetically sealed in a drum-shaped unit. Comprised of two sets of independent series of discs, each perforated with holes and slits, the coupling acted as an automatic clutch engaging and disengaging front-wheel drive as and when necessary. One set of discs was connected to the pinion shaft of the front-wheel drive; the other was joined via a splined shaft to a stub shaft at the rear. Under typical road and driving conditions, when the front and rear axles were rotating at roughly the same speed, the front-wheel drive effect hardly engaged, with in excess of 90 per cent of the drive going to the rear wheels. However, in less forgiving road or track circumstances, where either loose materials predominated, or a combination of glutinous mud, thick snow and treacherous ice prevailed, as soon as

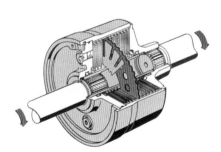

The self-contained viscous coupling was housed in the front final drive.

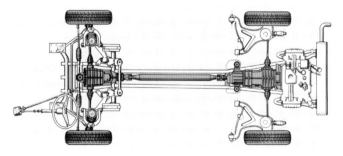

The modified running gear ensured power was directed to the rear axle and, via a prop shaft and the viscous coupling, to the front axle so that the driving force could be directed evenly to the rear and front wheels as required.

the rear wheels started to lose their grip and rotate faster than the front ones, the fluid coupling locked, not by the discs coming together, for they always remained equidistant from each other, but only via the silicone oil, instantly providing the vehicle with the equal 50/50 drive characterized by all methods of four-wheel drive. Under extreme circumstances, where the back wheels were temporarily out of commission, say, for example, embedded in particularly thick snow, all power could be delivered to the front wheels. As the system was permanent, the coupling being able to sense differences in speed between drive and output and react accordingly without provocation, the driver had nothing to do.

Originally planned as an extra, and remaining so for some markets, pneumatically actuated, manually operated, differential locks for both front and rear did require the driver to estimate when they should be used, which for most would be never, as they were only really needed on excessively steep or slippery surfaces. Although they could be engaged at any time, even when the vehicle was moving, the front differential adversely affected steering ability when the syncro was being driven on a hard surface.

Drive to the coupling was provided by a Cardan shaft from the front of the rear-mounted gearbox and differential unit. The gearbox, while providing the standard four ratios of a four-speed box, even first being retained, was duly modified at its forward end to accommodate a flanged output shaft and gear train for reverse and what amounted to an off-road or crawler gear. Volkswagen described this modified unit as their new '4+G gearbox', the fifth ('Gelände') gear being a cross-country ratio, some 60 per cent lower than first and identical to reverse.

Volkswagen today continues to release imagery of the syncro in action. This picture is available to journalists across the world.

4 + G Gearbox Ratios	
1st gear	3.78:1
2nd gear	2.06:1
3rd gear	1.23:1
4th gear	0.85:1
G gear	6.03:1
Reverse	6.03:1
Final drive ratio	4.86:1 with 185 R 14 C tyres
	5.43:1 with 205 R 14 C tyres

Although the front axle arrangement demanded a new sub-frame structure to accommodate the front final drive and integrated viscous coupling, the suspension type, utilizing double wishbones and coil springs at the front and semi-trailing arms with coil springs at the rear, was basically the same. However, the suspension movement was 20mm (^{3}/$_4$in) greater, while all syncro models stood 60mm (2^1/$_4$in) higher than usual. The ground clearance was some 190mm (4in) more than normal. Thus, with the 78PS engine in situ (the standard offering in the early days of the four-wheel drive model), and with the T3 syncro fully laden, the angle of approach could be up to 21 degrees, the angle of leaving up 19 degrees, while the potential maximum angle of climb was no less than an impressive 54 degrees.

The rear axle remained unchanged. Guard rails were fitted on the left and right to protect the prop shaft. The engine, gearbox and front axle were also protected from damage by special guards.

Changes to the bodywork were minimal, both the propeller shaft and the coupling being so compact that combining them within the existing body framework presented no problems. Hence changes as such were epitomized by the apparently trivial relocation of the fuel filler cap from its normal location behind the front wheel to one behind the rear wheel, a move necessitated by moving the 70ltr (15.4-gallon) plastic fuel tank back to the traditional

Transporter location over the rearward transmission. The revised arrangements at the front were responsible for the tank's move, but with the necessary removal of the spare wheel from its position under the cab at the front to a once standard location at the side of the rear luggage area, the weight of the syncro was neatly distributed 40/60 front/rear.

The additional weight of any syncro model compared to its two-wheel drive opposite number, some 140kg (308lb) in total, could be largely explained by the protection afforded underneath, with a front plate and parallel bars to protect the front axle, two heavy struts running to the rear under the engine and a substantial engine sump plate – a necessity for this kind of vehicle.

A 'Superior Concept'

To say that Wolfsburg's marketing gurus spent a considerable amount of time and money on promoting the syncro is, strange as it may sound, an understatement. Despite the gloomy predictions of the then marketing manager of commercial vehicles for VAG that such vehicles had 'only a limited potential market in Britain', the prediction was clear: the syncro would take sales from both traditional people-carriers and larger estate models.

Complete sales brochures were printed to advertise this essentially niche market concept, while no T3 promotional material could be deemed a syncro-free zone. The intention was clear – Volkswagen were going to make certain that everyone knew that the syncro would become available rapidly across the whole range of Transporters, with Caravelles and even 'official' Campers offered with off-road ability. The reasonably hefty price increase over and above the RRP of the two-wheel drive versions was considered well worth it for the advantages gained. The syncro story might best be summarized in marketing terms as follows:

◆ Exceptional directional control, particularly on smooth, slippy road surfaces with little grip.
◆ Optimum off-road performance and improved tractive power on difficult terrain, unpaved roads and on building sites.
◆ Outstanding tractive power particularly on snow and ice and for moving off and tackling steep, difficult mountainous routes, for instance.
◆ Essentially neutral cornering with improved safety reserves in marginal areas.
◆ Positive influence on braking performance even in winter road conditions.

In conclusion, driving was a safer business, a destination could be reached more easily and, crucially, owners of syncro models were better equipped to deal with critical situations.

Excited by the marketing department's not totally unwarranted hype, a lengthy queue of dribbling journalists were only too eager to test syncro incarnations of any model of Transporter or Caravelle. Most of the resulting reviews were highly complimentary and, mimicking the euphoria of the day, these are reproduced here as a chapter-closing highpoint. On the other hand, the harsh reality was that by March 1989, a full four years after production had commenced at the Steyr-Daimler-Puch works only 25,000 syncro models had been built, or just 4 per cent of total T3 production over the same period. Perhaps Volkswagen's own harbinger of doom in his commercial vehicle marketing office was right after all – but surely not!

… [We sampled] the versatility of the system in snowy conditions on the Scottish launch. Here we discovered

ABOVE AND OVERLEAF: Inevitably Volkswagen's press office at Wolfsburg issued a whole selection of images of the permanent four-wheel drive syncro models, each depicting models tackling off-road conditions totally beyond the scope of a two-wheel drive Transporter and Caravelle. While some were particularly dramatic as with the example depicted at the top, many illustrated the syncro in a manner likely to be experienced by the average driver in winter.

Traction on mud, snow and ice is very impressive and the Caravelle syncro can keep going on slippery surfaces and rough terrain which would stop any conventional vehicle. High ground clearance together with 4wd enable the syncro to transverse deep ruts, soft mud and steep slopes. We drove across mud that would have bogged down a classic trials car, accomplished a start on an icy gradient that was almost impossible to walk on, and easily negotiated a ford crossing a river with a soft sandy base.

Volkswagen Audi Car, 'Bus GTD', May 1987

I chose a track which climbed at a modest gradient from the road but which had a cross-fall to force one's wheels into the troughs of mud left by tractors. The syncro came through all without hesitation. I stopped intentionally with one pair of wheels in a particularly soft and slimy patch at the side of the track. The syncro pulled away impeccably. I stopped next with the rear wheels in a gulley and again the VW started off as if on a metalled highway …

VW Motoring, July 1985

that the Caravelle had no problems at all in dealing with snow, mud or steep inclines – thanks to its amazing traction. The fact that the body rides high on its uprated suspension and all obvious protrusions have been tucked out of harm's way also means that the syncro can approach gradients at a 20 per cent angle and can climb 54 per cent inclines …

Autocar, 'Mass Mover', 6 August 1986

Leaving the 'A' road and heading up into the hills, we found the Caravelle surprisingly sure-footed on bends covered with slush and hard-packed snow; adopting the correct technique of slowing before the corner and then driving through under power produced no noticeable loss of grip, even when deliberately overdone. Climbing still higher, where we found ourselves driving through several inches of snow cover, we were still unable to cause the syncro any embarrassment, despite attempting a narrow mountain road that had been pronounced 'blocked by snow'. Here there were deep wheel ruts left by a farm tractor, in which the Caravelle's wheels insisted on 'tramlining'; and even though the underside was clearly bottoming on occasions, it never so much as spun a wheel …

VW Motoring, 'They'll take the high road', March 1986

Richard Holdworth's Villa Mk3 conversion.

6 *third-generation Campers*

The idiosyncrasies of the relationship between Transporter manufacturer Volkswagen and the numerous companies offering camping conversions on such models is worth exploring before launching into a kaleidoscope of what was on offer between the last months of 1979 and the early 1990s. To clarify the muddied waters, particularly in Vanagon territory, where brochures would illustrate vehicles without a camping interior on one page and with such fittings on the next, no vehicle left any of Volkswagen's factories kitted out as a Camper in this era, just as they had not done in the days of the first two generations of Transporter and would not do during the lifespan of the T3's successor, a vehicle which took the story into the first years of the current millennium.

Instead, once the concept of adding sleeping and dining arrangements to the vehicle had become established, Volkswagen partnered with or licensed independent companies to produce Campers from vehicles supplied by the Hanover factory. In Germany, the relationship with the long-established coach building firm of Westfalia blossomed and bore plentiful fruit for both companies, but this didn't preclude other operations successfully marketing their own unofficial conversions.

The scenario in America was essentially the simplest and yet the most complex of all. Even before the Camping phenomenon took off in the early 1960s in the USA, Volkswagen of America had decided to promote a Camper as an integral part of the range, alongside Station Wagons, Beetles, the Karmann Ghia, *et al*. Relevant publicity material included a Camper amongst the options, while 'model-specific' literature, if that is the correct terminology, was on offer at the dealerships. Such was the demand for Campers that VW of America had to supplement the supply of vehicles finding their way across the Atlantic with home-bred camping kits that could either be fitted by a competent DIY enthusiast or supplied by the dealer ready installed at higher cost.

From what appeared to be an incredible peak in 1968, when 75 per cent of Westfalia Campers were exported, by 1971 this figure had reached 84 per cent and, while the successive oil crises of 1973 and thereafter left permanent damage as far as the Camper market was concerned, by that time the importance of the American market was so firmly established that irreversible steps had been taken to cater for its needs. Models specific to the US market had been introduced, while the US branding of Campmobile had relegated the Westfalia name to little more than decals noticeable on publicity images in brochures and press packs. Hence, at the time of the arrival of the third-generation and the decision to brand this model as the Vanagon in the USA and Canada, the complete integration of the Westfalia model as the all-new Vanagon Camper was readily accepted.

In the UK, as the most pertinent example of a country importing Transporters for sale across the network of distributors and dealers, names such as Canterbury Pitt, Danbury, Devon and Dormobile emerged in the formative years as amongst the most prolific, popular and best engineered

Richard Holdsworth's Villa Mk3 conversion was based on the T3 Delivery Van, a fact most clearly indicated by the lack of a window towards the rear of the vehicle on the driver's side. It could be specified without an elevating roof, with a solid-sided elevating roof as illustrated, or as a conversion on the High Roof Delivery Van. All conversions were based on the 1.9-litre 78PS petrol engine, but it was possible to specify the 2.1-litre engine in fully fledged form and with a catalytic converter, which reduced power to 92PS. Both the standard and turbo-diesel were offered, as was a syncro version of the latter. For the laid-back camper, an automatic box could be specified on both the 78PS and 112PS engines. With the elevating roof fitted, Caravan magazine described the conversion as a 'neat and practical motorhome for people with height problems.' The publication was equally complimentary about Volkswagen, noting that it had carved out 'its reputation as a multi-national vehicle maker with an attention to detail and fine engineering, which is always associated with West Germany.'

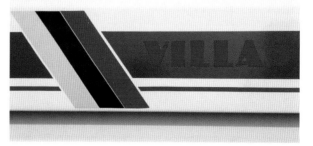

conversions. Some, but certainly not all, sought and maintained a relationship with Volkswagen in the UK. Of these Devon, established in the late 1950s by Sidmouth-based builder Jack White, enjoyed the longest working relationship with Volkswagen. For a time during the era of the second-generation Transporter they were licensed as the only official conversion operation, with the result that their products were marketed as if they were Volkswagen's own. Meanwhile the ties in Germany with Westfalia ventured across the English channel, as Devon sold a right-hand-drive conversion known as the Continental, which was assembled by the German operation alongside its home-built models.

By the time the T3 made its debut, Canterbury Pitt was but a distant memory, the company's association with camper conversions having come to an end with the death of Peter Pitt, who as the initiator of this division of the business had been wily enough to retain design rights when it became absorbed into the Canterbury enterprise. Similarly, Dormobile, a name that for many years had been synonymous with camping, had fallen on hard times as the 1970s came to an end. While the company managed to eke an existence out of other products until 1984, circumstances were such that no conversions based on the T3 were offered.

While Danbury and Devon appeared to prosper as the 1980s dawned, with both companies eager to develop conversions based on a combination of experience gained over the last two decades and the increase in available space offered by the new model, other names had entered, or were attempting to enter, the fray, only too eager to fill the gaps left vacant for various reasons, including financial misfortune. Of these Auto-Sleeper, CI Autohomes, Holdsworth, and Motorhomes International were amongst the most prominent. However, the 1980s were not the easiest of decades for Camper companies, with two of the above either disappearing from the market or undergoing receivership and rebirth, while old-timers Devon and Danbury similarly were either bought out or had ceased trading by the end of the decade.

A further note is needed to clarify which model of T3 would most likely form the basis of a conversion. In the early days of Camper activity there was a distinct probability that a Microbus would have been used as the source for work, with the possibility that if a cheaper conversion was available it might be Kombi-based. As the years went by, the latter vehicle increasingly became dominant, with a number of conversions being offered on the Delivery Van at the lower end of the market. Despite the changes in model designations during the lifespan of the third-generation Transporter, the basis of all Camper conversions remains easy to detect, with a large percentage either being offered on the most basic of Buses or later Caravelles, while some were prepared on the Transporter in Delivery Van guise.

The proliferation of engine options, from the days when there was only one power unit to two at the start to the T3 era in 1979, to many once water replaced air as a means of cooling, only has a bearing on the Camper story in that manufacturers could select to include all, some, or just a couple of choices. Devon, for example had the following to say when introducing their 1986 range:

> The Transporter has a number of engine and transmission options to suit a wide variety of driving conditions. Petrol engines include the 78bhp carburettor model and the 112bhp fuel injected power-plant. Diesel and turbo diesel engines are available where fuel economy is paramount. 5 speed and automatic gearbox options promote more restful progress, and to complete the package, the Syncro [sic] 4 wheel drive system can be specified for superior driving performance even under the most adverse conditions, something few rivals can match.

A final preliminary word relating to the dates when a T3 Camper might be built is useful. Whereas Westfalia had enjoyed the advantage of being offered prototypes in order that they might adapt their conversions to suit the new model in advance of its launch, other Camper manufacturers did not have this privilege. They had little option therefore but to start their necessary design revisions once the latest Transporter was available to the buying public. In the interim, many were likely to have snapped up remaining stocks of the outgoing model so that they had something to offer, while fortunately numerous conservatively minded Camper aficionados seemed eager to acquire a tried and trusted design in preference to new, untested and unproven models. This was the case when the T2 made way for the T3 – for at least two years after the older model's demise some camper companies were offering either new old stock, or carefully refurbishing second-hand examples with new camping equipment. Ten years later when the T3 bowed out, the same thing happened, and it isn't unusual to see camper conversions based on the third-generation model bearing licence plates indicating a first road registration two years after the T4 had made its debut.

THE CAMPER COMPANIES

As this is not intended to be a Camper book, there is no need to attempt a comprehensive review of all the companies offering conversions based on Volkswagen's third-generation Transporter. Rather, the objective is to focus on a few prominent names, most of which have been referred to above, plus a couple of then recent innovations in camping design, with the aim of showing how the availability of the extra 14 per cent interior space in the third-generation Transporter coupled with the demands of an increasingly sophisticated camping fraternity signalled progressively more luxurious layouts and arrangements that remain compatible with the needs of weekenders and holidaymakers today.

Westfalia

Concurrent with the launch of the third-generation Transporter, Westfalia debuted the Joker, instantly identifiable by prominent decals on both the driver's and front seat passenger's doors – except in America, where it was the Vanagon Camper and these were absent. Two versions were offered initially, the Joker 1, which accommodated two people on the rear seat and the Joker 2, which had a full-width bench seat at the expense of comprehensive furniture units. Key to both variations

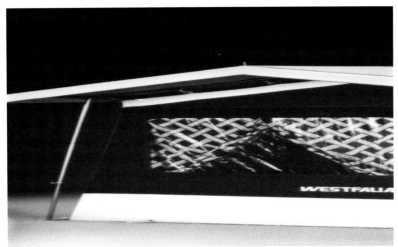

As Volkswagen's official partner in all matters camping, Westfalia's Joker was promoted with a multitude of press images showing it in a variety of guises.

was continuity in essential features from the later second-generation models, combined with the use of state-of-the-art materials to offer the increasing refinement demanded by an allegedly more affluent buying public. Cabinet work was in light teak laminate secured from damage by brown plastic bonding trim on all edges, the days of solid wood being long since gone. The seats were upholstered in material of a contemporary design incorporating colourful banded stripes on either a dark or light brown background. An early US brochure described the lighter option as having a 'Gazelle background'

on the delightfully named 'Boogie Woogie' cloth. (The darker option was known as Van Dyck and both were part of Volkswagen's range of upholsteries, as discussed in Chapter 5.)

What made the Joker layout stand out was the abundance of storage space in neatly compartmentalized units, which included a wardrobe on Joker 1 and a roof locker on both models, more than adequate provision of tables on which to dine or snack, and both a modern twin-burner cooker and generous 45ltr absorber fridge incorporated into the elaborate kitchen unit, which also included a washing-up sink

and drawer for utensils, all of which was positioned behind the driver's seat. Whereas once upon a time an elevating roof was considered to be very much an extra cost option, all Jokers came with a rear-hinged one complete with double bed as standard, although a fixed high roof could be specified as an option.

By 1983, just as the passion for teak and similar laminates was waning, the Joker had moved forward as a concept. Models of this vintage and beyond are recognizable by the use of a light grey laminate with dark grey plastic trim, which not only made the vehicles appear roomier and lighter, but have also stood the test of time remarkably well. From the amazing variety of six Joker options that had emerged in the intervening years, the range was rationalized, with both 1 and 3 becoming available in two formats, the latest being the Club Joker – allegedly a more sporty offering, according to Westfalia's releases of the day, but in reality demonstrating luxury at its finest. (To make life more complicated, for a time there had also been the option of the Sport Joker, which despite its appealing name was actually a basic weekender with double bed and table.) The Club Jokers, recognizable once again by prominent decals on both front doors, included such opulence as double glazing and better seating, although a downside of the latter was that storage was more limited, making the Club models more suited to two or, at the most, three people.

For 1988, the Joker name was replaced with two new ones, the first of which was the California, a title destined for a long and interesting future. Shortly afterwards, this model was joined by the even more luxurious

The California made its debut in 1988 and in essence was the same as the Joker 1.

The Atlantic was a particularly luxurious conversion angled towards the American market. Its decals were full of fun and looked particularly striking against red paintwork.

Westfalia's top of the range T3 conversion – the Atlantic.

The house that Westfalia built. Vanagon GL Camper's famous cabin is the product of superb craftsmanship and the cabinet-making tradition of Germany's Westfalia region. But the space-efficient Westfalia package also relies on a thoroughly space-efficient design below: the engine is mounted in the rear and coupled with rear wheel drive, thus eliminating normal drive-shaft obstruction and increasing available floor space. Partly as a result, the Camper boasts a full 1.47 metre interior vertical height from floor to ceiling, the highest in its class. And with the roof up, much more. The cabin is a model of simplicity, quality and intelligent design. Rich velour, reclining body-contoured swivel seats are forward and backward adjustable. Fold-away tables, rear bench and rear door storage provide space-saving convenience. Carpeting is easily removable for convenient cleaning. And every cabinet and locker door is fully removable, laminated on both sides, counter sunk and rubber mounted for extra durability and a simply perfect fit. Vanagon GL Camper: a place for everything, and everything in its place.

Dehler

Atlantic. Essentially, there was little change, with most agreeing that the former was a slightly slimmed down version of Joker 1 and the latter a take on the particularly upmarket Joker 3. Both models took account of the most recent trends and had been updated to the latest in contemporary fashion. Westfalia, backed by Volkswagen, clearly intended to stay ahead of the game, despite the challenges presented by the Far Eastern market and increasingly sophisticated conversions produced either in Germany or abroad.

At a time when the T3, or perhaps more appropriately in this case, the Vanagon, was rapidly approaching the end of its production run, Volkswagen of Canada had become much more open in promoting the Westfalia name in their literature: although simply entitled 'Vanagon', it featured a Camper on the cover as the sole representative of the family of vehicles on offer. Equally interesting is use of the same internal images for the 1987 model year and the '91 edition; more than ever a demonstration that despite any variations for the North American market, the Joker and the California/Atlantic were essentially the same animals. This is from June 1990:

The exterior of yacht-builder Dehler's campers, though clearly customized, didn't shout luxury and high-tech craftsmanship. However, the top image opposite illustrates what the company was capable of.

Although with such a lengthy pedigree of excellence it seems unlikely that Westfalia were forced to review and upgrade their offer during the 1980s, the possibility remains that the leading West German converters glanced over their shoulders only to find potential rivals, both old and new, producing increasingly sophisticated campers more than ever capable of challenging the old master. Of all such companies, the yacht-builders Dehler stood out from the crowd, when they launched an ultra-luxurious Camper, named the Profi, in the 1980s. Apart from its specially designed, contemporary, striking and aesthetically balanced, aerodynamic fixed high roof, which came with its own built-in cab sunroof, skylights and moderately sophisticated system of roof air vents, the Profi offered a mass of modern wizardry and catered for a community no longer satisfied with the basin and sponge approach of old. From the addition of a carefully moulded dashboard fitment to house drink containers, cassettes and a fold down map-tray, via carefully inserted luxury wood trim, to the innovation of a sensibly sited TV in the roof space and a convenient and well-appointed bathroom or shower compartment behind the driver, the emphasis was on luxury, while the years of experience gained in yacht building were easy to recognize. Beautifully padded upholstery, bolsters of generous proportions, and the careful selection of light laminates and matching cloth were completely right

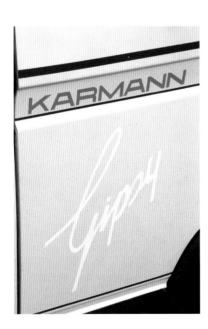

LEFT, ABOVE AND OVERLEAF TOP: From Karmann Mobil to the Karmann Gipsy, the products were essentially motorhomes rather than simple campervans.

A camper with a difference, the Pick-A-Back was designed for owners to be able to drive away leaving their overnight accommodation behind.

for the time and for a market increasingly dominated by affluent couples approaching midlife who had a yearning to join the world of the great outdoors (providing this did not require too many sacrifices).

Karmann

Neither an invention of the Osnabrück Karmann factory, nor an innovation created by German technology, the T3-based Karmann Gipsy still epitomized a further development in camping with the Transporter: a coach-built caravan conversion on a Volkswagen base. On holiday in South Africa in the mid-1970s, Karmann Karosserie director, Wilhelm, came across the recently launched Jurgens Caravans 'Auto Villa'. So impressed was Herr Karmann with this aluminium-clad camper of epic proportions and untold luxuries that he negotiated with Jurgens and successfully won the rights to build his own version under due licence. The result was the second-generation Transporter-based Karmann Mobil, a vehicle that was reborn as the Gipsy following the debut of the T3 platform.

With an aluminium frame for reasons of weight and clad with insulated aluminium panels, the slightly less than graceful Gipsy also encompassed a Luton top over the cab, all of which resulted in the provision of unprecedented space and the consequent ability to offer facilities and accommodation previously only associated with RVs. The walk-through cab led past an enclosed bathroom offering complete privacy and providing a shower unit, wash basin and portable toilet, as well

as a built-in mirrored wall cupboard and shower curtain. Opposite was a generous kitchen unit, encompassing both an electric fridge and storage cupboards, plus a two-burner hob and a stainless steel sink. The rear area of the Gipsy was set out in traditional caravan style with U-shaped seating and a manoeuvrable table, which also helped to form the base of a double bed. The rear seats were suitably raised to generate extra storage, all of which could be easily accessed. A typical caravan door on the passenger side of the vehicle provided easy access in and out of the vehicle, while additional sleeping space to the already generous home-sized double bed was offered through the use of the Luton top. Gas-blown central heating, a 10ltr (2.2-gallon) hot water cylinder, plus onboard fresh water and even waste water tanks, plus double glazing throughout, all illustrate that here was a Camper intended for all-year-round usage. Once syncro was an option, the ability to choose the remotest of locations for the finest of breaks were greatly enhanced.

Campers in the 21st century are still enjoying 'Instant Holidays', the marketing slogan of the company in the early 1980s.

Tischer

The German firm Tischer adapted the popular American concept of mounting a camping unit on a pick-up truck to European usage with the *Huckepacksystem*, marketed in Britain as the 'Pick-A-Back' system. Once again, this was not a development concurrent with the launch of the third-generation Transporter, but it was during the lifespan of that vehicle that the momentum of interest in such an option gathered pace, leading Tischer to progress the concept through the years of the T4 to the current model, the T5.

The versatility of the Pick-A-Back system was marketed by Tischer as its biggest plus point. Against a sequence of explanatory pictures, the company revealed how the 'cabin', as the living accommodation was referred to, was 'quickly removable from the base vehicle so both could be used independently', with the result that the load-carrying Pick-up could be used 'for excursions or as your everyday vehicle when at home (the Pick-up sides are easily replaced and we also offer a polyester hardtop)'. To emphasize the practicality of the arrangement, the text

stressed that it only took 'a few minutes to remove the cabin – much easier than packing everything away every time.'

Not necessarily the easiest of camping areas in which to manoeuvre, the optional cab/cabin access door required a degree in contortionism to negotiate successfully, and the split level between the hob and washing arrangements at the rear of the cabin and the dining/seating area above the Pick-up's platform demanded compromise on the part of holidaymakers, the fittings included as standard demonstrated an opulence compatible with the age. From the well-appointed 'bathroom', with full-size shower, to interior panelling in 'hi-class' plywood, with what Tischer described somewhat unfortunately as 'synthetic' surfaces and the suitably bolstered and bespoke upholstered seats, the product exuded at least moderate affluence. Four opening and three fixed double-glazed windows, a stainless steel two-burner cooker and sink unit, water storage and waste systems, Truma's 3002 heating system (whatever that might be) and a 60ltr (2cu ft) fridge were all standard, although an extra cost 'L' package added such luxuries as fly-screens/solar blinds to all opening windows and blown air and convector heating.

British Manufacturers

Having outlined official conversion partner Westfalia's products and devoted space to examples of German latent luxury and emerging trends, which in theory complemented the long established businesses but nevertheless might detract from their overwhelming predominance in Germany, this brief spin through the gamut of T3 campers now turns the spotlight on British brands.

Devon
For a time in the 1970s the only camper conversion firm officially recognized by Volkswagen in the UK, and with well-known brand Dormobile out of the running, Devon were undoubtedly the best recognized of the British players when the third-generation Transporter appeared on the scene.

Over the decades Devon's offer had evolved from a luxury conversion supported by a more basic model with three possible levels of equipment, to one model that might best be described as being designed with camping and little else in mind and another that was intended to play a multifarious role – people-carrier, weekend adventurer, or conceivably, glorified dining room and beach hut! Similarly, from the distant days of solid oak and a joiner's workshop full of master craftsmen the business had followed the trend and the practicalities of cost, eventually resorting to the use of melamine-covered chipboard and plastic trim. In 1978 two new conversions were introduced – a revival of the Moonraker name for the Camper and the birth of a new name, Sundowner, for the all-purpose vehicle. When the T3 debuted, Devon saw no reason to throw away the experience gained over the years of the second-generation Transporter and simply carried their latest layouts over to the new Volkswagen, while making the recently introduced optional Devon 'Double Top' elevating roof standard on both models.

Virtually contemporaneous with the move to the T3 in 1980, Devon adopted a decidedly quirky marketing approach, producing sales material in the style of spoof recipe books. Limited by

Journalists would have found that the text accompanying this press image required a little elaboration – 'The new Devon Moonraker Hi-Top'!

their self-imposed boundaries, the selling points of the latest models weren't perhaps as clear as they should have been. The following extracts from the glossiest of early publicity material not only covers the specific aspects of the Moonraker but also amply illustrates the built-in absurdity of relying on such an off-beat marketing device.

The perfect recipe from Devon. Devon Conversions present their 1980 Moonraker and Sundowner models, based on the new Volkswagen Transporter. Instant minibus shopper, delivery van, saloon car, and spare room too …

Method. Take one Devon Moonraker and add to it the following ingredients.

First, make the seating deliciously comfortable and adaptable. … The rear-facing single seat extends to become a 2 seater for dining … the rear seat and engine deck cushions together forming a deep foam mattress.

Add a tastefully designed kitchen and storage unit. …A complete kitchen and storage unit is fitted along the offside of the vehicle … the first section lifts to reveal a stainless steel sink unit … an optional refrigerator can be fitted beneath the sink. … concealed beneath the lid of the middle section is a two-burner gas cooker with a grill and heat shield. … The end section is a deep storage locker … the portable cool box (when an optional refrigerator is not fitted) is stored in this locker.

Blend with a generous helping of luxury. Rich carpet-style trim covers all interior panels, in dark brown up to window level and above in beige. The buttoned deep foam cushions are upholstered in a patterned fabric with a luxurious soft-as-velvet pile … Flotex covers the floor – a unique carpet which combines wear- and stain-resistant qualities with luxury and warmth … Brushed nylon seats with head restraints add a touch of luxury for the driver and passenger. At the offside rear there's a wardrobe with a hanging rail, and a small shelf.

Scrutiny of the equivalent Sundowner specification soon revealed where costs had been cut, or how the design had been amended to create a people-carrier, although to be fair to Devon the vehicle's purpose was never disguised.

Deemed to be a people-carrier for up to eight people in comfort, whether a short trip or a long journey was envisaged, the Sundowner's versatility came in the form of a reversible front seat back rest, so that passengers could face front or rear; it also included a table top below the offside window (with single screw-in leg), and carried a portable gas range with two burners. The gas bottle was stored behind the backrest of the front seat when not in use. Two 11.5ltr, (2.5-gallon) freshwater tanks were at the rear of the vehicle. That the Sundowner was not seriously intended as a Camper was amply illustrated by the provision of a simple washing-up bowl rather than a built-in sink.

The variances established, a word or two about the Devon 'Double Top' completes the picture. As the name might imply, and the image on page 115 confirms the latest elevating roof ran the full length of the vehicle and was a side-hinged affair, lifting concertina style on the nearside and hinged on the offside, very much in the style of the old Martin Walter version Devon had bought in for many a year. With gas-filled struts, all owners had to do was 'give an initial push' and as Devon noted 'it will open of its own accord'. Aesthetically attractive, whether up or more particularly down, the 'Double Top' fibre-glass roof afforded substantially increased sleeping space, and in T3 terms no wonder it was fitted to both models.

Indicative of the trends of the affluent eighties, the Moonraker outsold the Sundowner by a margin of ten to one and, as a result, a new model, the Sunrise, joined the range at the expense of the people-carrier. Subtitling the newcomer as 'a truly luxurious motor caravan', Devon were eager to compare it with 'Britain's best selling motor caravan ever', the Moonraker, by noting the similarity of its layout but 'with an upgraded level of luxury fittings'. Self-indulgent accolades dripped from the copywriter's pen. 'Top quality' related to the plywood cabinets; 'attractive' and 'matching' were used with reference to the 'vitreous enamel' hob and sink; 'spacious' described the as standard Electrolux fridge; 'sumptuous', 'hard-wearing', 'tasteful' and 'stylish' catalogued the Draylon upholstery, wool-mix carpet, and curtains, leading the text to

conclude that 'the Sunrise is a vehicle of rare distinction. It will keep you in the lap of luxury at all times. Wherever you go, whatever you do'.

Later in the 1980s Devon succumbed to the wishes of the public for conversions on Ford models, Bedfords and even Toyotas, but they did make one final attempt to boost interest in the T3 through the reintroduction of old favourite names from years gone. At the top of the somewhat shaky tree stood the 'ultimate' in design, the Eurovette, with a fixed high-top roof and attributes such as doors framed in solid wood, while the Moonraker's progress continued unabated. This model could now be specified with either a Hi-Top or a Double Top, while the third member of the latest trio, the versatile Caravette, came with a Space Top as standard.

Despite a change of ownership in 1989, at least as far as the conversion side of the business went, Devon persevered with Volkswagen Campers for the remaining years of T3 production. However, the T4 didn't impress and work concentrated on Toyotas. Probably the most interesting aspect of the Devon third-generation Transporter evolution was the proliferation of roof options. Detailed reference has already been made to the Double Top, while the nature of the fixed Hi-Top is obvious. However, following a period of championing the 'new Aerospace roof', an option which rose from all points 'easily' on four gas struts, and which could be both opened and closed without getting out of the vehicle, Devon turned to the Space Top, which also lifted at all corners, but benefited from solid sides and full insulation. Never had there been such variety; like Westfalia in Germany, Devon – the cream of motor caravan manufacturers – saw the need for luxury, comfort and versatility.

Danbury

If one other British operator deserves a dedicated section, it has to be Danbury, whose origins in the camping business stemmed back to the mid-1960s, and who had enjoyed official conversion status for a time before Devon entered into an exclusive deal in 1972 and regained it once more when that expired.

The Danbury Volkswagen series 11 with fully automatic elevating roof.

Danbury models had consistently sold well, but this was not necessarily due to their increasingly sophisticated specifications, but rather to the simplicity and consequent economy of their work. During the early years of the third-generation Transporter Danbury produced the Volkswagen Danbury Series 11, the newsworthy feature of which was that it was the 'first ever motorised caravan to have an electrically operated fully automatic elevating roof. … It's so simple. Just press UP for up and DOWN for down. Even a child could operate it – which is why we have housed the switch in a lockable cupboard!'

Mention was also made of another Danbury innovation of earlier times:

We were the first company to introduce forward facing seats in motorised caravans … which is why the new DANBURY SERIES 11 gives full comfortable forward-facing seats for a minimum of six people. Upholstered in the latest fabric from America – easy to

wipe clean, and extremely durable. So use your Danbury all the year round – it's a luxurious estate car.

This was undoubtedly the essence of Danbury conversions: carrying people was considered the top priority, which resulted in less comprehensive camping attributes and simple appliances. With the Danbury Series 11, a pine-framed kitchen unit came with hessian door inserts and Warrite laminated tops. While the cupboards were cleverly crank-hinged to allow them to fold flush against the units, the appliances were comparatively basic. The two-burner and grill Camping Gaz cooker was surrounded by an aluminium shield in true picnic style, while the admittedly attractive stainless steel sink was simply accessed by lifting a section of the unit's laminated top. The freezer box-style fridge, though practical, was basic and could only be opened by similar means.

For a time Danbury also offered the more upmarket Danbury Showman –

'everything you expect from a Danbury Volkswagen Series 11 and much more', a vehicle which came closer to a Devon specification in terms of such assets as a front opening Electrolux fridge and carefully crafted teak finish fitments. At the other end of the scale they presented the Danbury Volkswagen Travelette, a base model, that had evolved from the simplest of offerings of a decade earlier.

Later, when water-cooled engines were firmly established, Danbury were still offering the most basic of conversions. Although at last possessed of storage units either side of the rear seats, and a practical wardrobe near the vehicle's tailgate, they still lacked a full kitchen unit, and the primitive method of housing a portable cooker and a stainless steel bowl, admittedly with pumped water supply, under the front rear-facing seats, must have left many potential purchasers cold.

Another model, the 'Luxury Lounger', didn't really live up to its name, as the extent of the extravagances appeared limited to 'lush' velvet curtains, garish

Autosleeper conversions became increasingly significant in the era of both the T4 and the current T5.

Weinsberg Terra.

striped upholstery and a cocktail cabinet. At least a bought-in Hi-top was offered, but Danbury's days in business were by now strictly numbered.

Other Companies

Without wishing to denigrate names that were either emerging as major players during the era of the third-generation Transporter and are still with us today, or, who were significant at the time but would later be absorbed by others or simply go out of business, space precludes detailed descriptions of all the models produced. The accompanying images, however, do include the work of Cotswold-based Auto-Sleeper, influential CI Autohomes, and the controversially marketed products of Motorhomes International.

At the time the Autohomes Kameo was on the market the company also produced the Kamper and the Karisma. The Kameo was the budget version of the Karisma, while the Kamper had an elevating roof.

Holdsworth's Vision was marketed as the camper with a rear-end kitchen.

The Motorhomes International Xplorer was instantly recognizable by its Spacemaker overhanging elevating roof.

epilogue

This modern picture supplied by Volkswagen of a syncro model T3, with a later and larger-engined T4, (as evidenced by its longer bonnet) in hot pursuit, is an image befitting the conclusion of the T3 story.

When the all-new T4 front-wheel drive Transporter was presented to the world's press in May 1990 against a backdrop of announcements such as that made by Karl Nachbar, head of Volkswagen's commercial vehicle development division, where he suggested that the new vehicle represented 'as radical a change as that from the Beetle to the Golf was at the time', and that 'although the one model was already good, the other became considerably better', all assumed that the third-generation Transporter would be swept under Hanover's proverbial plush carpet as quickly as possible. After all, the factory was only a couple of weeks away from opening a completely restructured production facility, which included the automated installation of axles, engines and gears, all designed to make T4 assembly less onerous and T3 production obsolete.

Likewise, when it emerged that the T4 had been under development since

as long ago as 1982, with the first pre-prototype having being built in 1983, and with second-phase prototypes that passed all scrutiny with flying colours following in 1987, there was no reason to procrastinate. As far as the buying public went, all the necessary steps had been taken too. In 1989, Volkswagen had produced two special versions of the Multivan, known as the Bluestar and the Whitestar, and in typical run-out style, both were suitably laden with upgrades, such as velour upholstery and desirable accessories at little extra cost. Decals announced their status and all who feared what Volkswagen would do next dipped into their savings to buy the best of the last. The time had surely come.

Most write that production of the T3 did indeed come to an end when the Hanover factory closed for its annual summer holidays at the end of July, but it appears that just like the second-generation before it, the odd cobweb-encrusted panel and no doubt

accompanying grizzled employee came to light after the break to continue to assemble a trickle of third-generation models into September. Bearing in mind that the American market wouldn't receive the appallingly named Eurovan until 1993 (the T4 was debuted at the Boston Auto Show in late 1991, but did not go on sale in the dealerships until a full twelve months later), and at the time was undergoing such a fall-off in sales of all Volkswagens that serious consideration was being given to withdrawing from the USA altogether, no doubt a drip feed of Vanagons had its uses.

In fact, the T3's production life was far from over. Rumour has it that both the German armed forces and the Deutsche Bundespost (German post office) complained about the third-generation Transporter's demise and, with nearly indecent haste, the remaining body shells and parts were transported to the Steyr-Puch works in Austria, where syncro models had always

The last of the T3 models were appropriately marked with decals to promote their status. Each was individually numbered as illustrated. The paintwork colour is Orly Blue metallic.

The very last T3 to be produced was finished in Tornado Red and is resident in Wolfsburg's Stiftung Museum.

been built. Echoing the story of the Karmann-built Beetle Cabriolet, a vehicle which continued in production for nearly five years after the demise of the MacPherson strut 1303 Beetle on which it was based, primarily thanks to panels and parts being posted to the Osnabrück factory, T3 syncro production carried on unabated for a further two years until September 1992. The figures weren't massive, but then they never had been for this somewhat expensive niche market vehicle.

Once again, when the axe had finally been raised, the decision was made that a run-out model, the terminal-sounding Limited Last Edition, should be marketed and 2,500 examples were duly produced. The majority of these special T3s were finished in Orly Blue metallic, but a percentage, including the very last example, which is resident in a shady and easily forgotten corner of Wolfsburg's Stiftung Museum, appeared resplendent in Tornado Red paint. Two engines were offered, although it has since transpired that one was available in far greater numbers than the other. Few will require a second attempt to guess that the 70PS turbo-diesel was produced in greater numbers than the strangulated 2110cc fuel-injected petrol engine, which, with a surfeit of catalyzers, had been reduced to 92PS. The specification of these Limited Last Edition models was nothing short of spectacular and not surprisingly the edition sold out very quickly, leading to another T3 anomaly, more of which shortly.

The exterior specification, excluding obvious items, was as follows:

◆ Heat-insulating tinted glass
◆ Sliding glass on passenger area sliding door and window on panel directly opposite
◆ Electrically heated and adjustable colour-coded door-mounted mirrors
◆ Central locking
◆ Rear window wiper
◆ Plastic aero-style colour-coded bumpers and side skirt panels
◆ Suspension lowered by 30mm
◆ 6J × 14 five-spoke alloy wheels
◆ 205/70R 14 C steel belted radial tyres

◆ Decal below windscreen at left 'Limited Last Edition'
◆ Decal on both cab doors reading '[number] von 2500'
◆ Decal bottom left of tailgate 'Limited Last Edition'

The interior specification, again excluding the obvious, included the following:

◆ Platinum/Blizzard velour upholstery
◆ Illuminated vanity mirror
◆ Trip meter
◆ Tachometer
◆ Digital LCD clock
◆ Intermittent front wiper control
◆ Dual circuit brake warning light
◆ Power steering
◆ Four-speaker radio/cassette 'Gamma' with window antenna
◆ Cigar lighter
◆ Illuminated and lockable glovebox
◆ Driver's door storage pocket
◆ Contoured cab seats with fold down adjustable arm rests
◆ Two rear-facing rear seats
◆ Sliding door child lock
◆ Auxiliary rear heater
◆ Fluorescent light above fold out table integrated with panel-work of interior
◆ Side panel with integrated arm rest, folding table, cup holders and ashtrays
◆ Removable window curtains
◆ Contoured rear bench seat to hold three people with facility to fold down to make bed
◆ Large cushion over luggage compartment (part of bed)
◆ Open-style head rests on all seats
◆ Storage area under rear seat
◆ Velour upholstery – all seats
◆ Velour carpet covering cab and passenger area floors
◆ Numbered certificate declaring position in run of 2,500

Such had been the demand for the Limited Last Edition Models that there was a danger that Volkswagen employees eager to acquire one would be disappointed. The company therefore reserved a quantity and, while the specification was more or less the same as that of the LLE, branded these models as Redstar or Bluestar editions. Some enthusiasts argue that they were built

after the LLE model, but chassis numbers appear to suggest otherwise, although the order of individual LLE numbers does not tally with incremental chassis digits. What is clear, though, is that the final Limited Last Edition model residing at Wolfsburg bears a chassis number after those of all surviving Redstars or Bluestars.

With no prospect of a revival in production in Europe, the age of the third-generation Transporter was surely over once and for all; but no – one satellite operation kept the T3 cause going for more than a decade to come. Just as Brazil and Mexico had first been reluctant to abandon the first-generation Transporter when it gave way to the second, and had since continued to produce their own versions of the Bay throughout the production run of the T3 in Europe, now South Africa determined that it would avoid manufacturing the new T4 by continuing with the third-generation model. Of all Volkswagen's manufacturing satellites, previously the Uitenhage had been the most conformist. Fortunately, having once broken the rules by deciding to perpetuate the third-generation Transporter, they proceeded to conform once more and followed in Wolfsburg's and Hanover's deeply imprinted footsteps and set about continually updating the product.

In the final days of 1991 all passenger-carrying versions of the South African T3 benefited from larger side windows, a change achieved by lowering the window line and instantly identifiable by comparing the size of the cab door glass, which remained unaltered, with the remaining windows. At the same time, but with the exception of the syncro models (which remained unaltered while Steyr-Puch continued to produce such models), two new engines were introduced. The first, a 1.8-litre in-line carburettor offering was taken from the VW Golf, while the other, altogether more appealing, unit was a 2.5-litre, five-cylinder, in-line, fuel-injected Audi-derived petrol engine. In 1996, a less powerful 2.3-litre fuel-injected petrol engine was added to the range, while the 2.5-litre engine gave way to a 2.6-litre unit of very similar power but with a noticeably greater degree of low-down torque. At roughly the same time the cab door quarter-lights were deleted and the air intake vents and rear light clusters were amended, the latter growing in size. Likewise, Uitenhage created its own version of a grille with round headlamps – with twin lamps as befitted a vehicle of this type and size. Pick-up models had been deleted from the range as early as 1991, and in May 1999, the 1.8-litre Delivery Van and a model known as the Volksiebus were also discontinued. Sadly, production of all Transporters based on the design and layout of the third-generation Transporter was axed in 2002, allowing Toyota to grab a good percentage of the hastily evacuated market. Today Volkswagen of South Africa sells virtually all the derivatives of the current-generation T5.

As a fitting epitaph to the third-generation Transporter and its extra years eked out on South African soil, and after noting that for 'those who can afford it, … [the 2.5 litre] luxury seven-seater offers a blend of performance, comfort and low-stress travel', a further but later extract from *Car South Africa*'s occasional reviews of the Transporter summarizes the good, bad and indifferent of the largest engine model of all, the 2.6-litre Microbus.

The increase in capacity from 2,480 to 2,553 cm^3 has been achieved by increasing the stroke from 92.8 to 95.5mm, the bore remaining at 82.5mm. On currently available fuel this has done nothing for the engine's maximum power and torque outputs, which stay at 100kW at 5,000rpm and 200Nm at 3,500rpm respectively. What it has done is improve the torque at 2,000rpm from 175 to 190Nm, an increase of almost nine per cent right where it counts, low down in the lugging range.

Part of this improvement can be attributed to the adoption of the more up-to-date Bosch Motronic M1.5.4 electronic management and fuel injection system in place of the same supplier's mechanical K-Jetronic …

The 'Kombi' has endured and the title has been the accepted generic term for such vehicles for almost as long as they have been in existence. Plus points are a comfortable interior and a smooth, quiet ride. Ready access from the front to the rear seat is a boon too. From the driver's point however, the awkward gear-change seems to be something that can't be fixed. Notwithstanding this criticism, VW's Microbus remains the benchmark for all locally available family carriers and with its new heart, looks set to carry the mantle for some considerable time.

bibliography

Bobbitt, Malcolm, *The Volkswagen Bus Book* (Veloce, 2007)

Clarke, R M (editor), *Volkswagen Bus, Camper, Van – Performance portfolio 1979–1991* (Brooklands Books)

Copping, Richard, *VW Bus – Forty Years of Splitties, Bays and Wedges* (Veloce, 2006)

Copping, Richard, *Volkswagen Camper – 40 Years of Freedom* (Veloce, 2007)

Copping, Richard & Screaton, Brian, *Volkswagen Transporter – the First 60 Years* (Haynes, 2009)

Eccles, David, *VW Camper – The Inside Story* (Crowood, 2005)

Glen, Simon, *Volkswagens of the World* (Veloce, 1999)

Gunnell, John, *Standard Catalog of Volkswagen 1946–2004* (KP Books, 2004)

Harvey, Jonathan, *Volkswagen Transporter* (Haynes, 2008)

Kuch, Joachim, *Volkswagen Model History* (Haynes, 1999)

Meredith, Laurence, *VW Bus* (Sutton Publishing, 1999)

Meredith, Laurence, *Volkswagen Transporter – The Complete Story* (Crowood, 1998)

Volkswagen AG, Corporate History Dept (editor), *Volkswagen Chronicle, Vol 7, Historical Notes* (Volkswagen AG, 2003)

Beetling magazine, various issues, Autometrix Publications

Volkswagen Audi Car, various issues, Autometrix Publications

Safer Volkswagen Motoring, various issues, RFWW Publications

VW Motoring, various issues, Warner Group Publications

index

Related titles from Crowood:

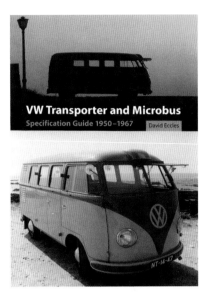

VW Beetle Specification Guide 1949–1967

James Richardson
ISBN 978 1 86126 940 9
128pp, over 300 illustrations

VW Beetle Specification Guide 1968–1980

Richard Copping
ISBN 978 1 84797 167 8
128pp, over 400 illustrations

VW Transporter and Microbus Specification Guide 1950–1967

David Eccles
ISBN 978 1 86126 652 1
96pp, over 400 illustrations

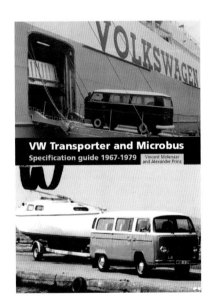

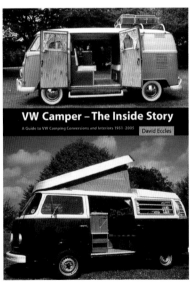

VW Transporter and Microbus Specification Guide 1967–1979

Vincent Molenaar &
Alexander Prinz
ISBN 978 1 86126 765 8
128pp, over 400 illustrations

VW Camper – The Inside Story

David Eccles
ISBN 978 1 86126 763 4
160pp, over 400 illustrations

VW Camper Inspirational Interiors

David Eccles
ISBN 978 1 84797 070 1
224pp, over 700 illustrations